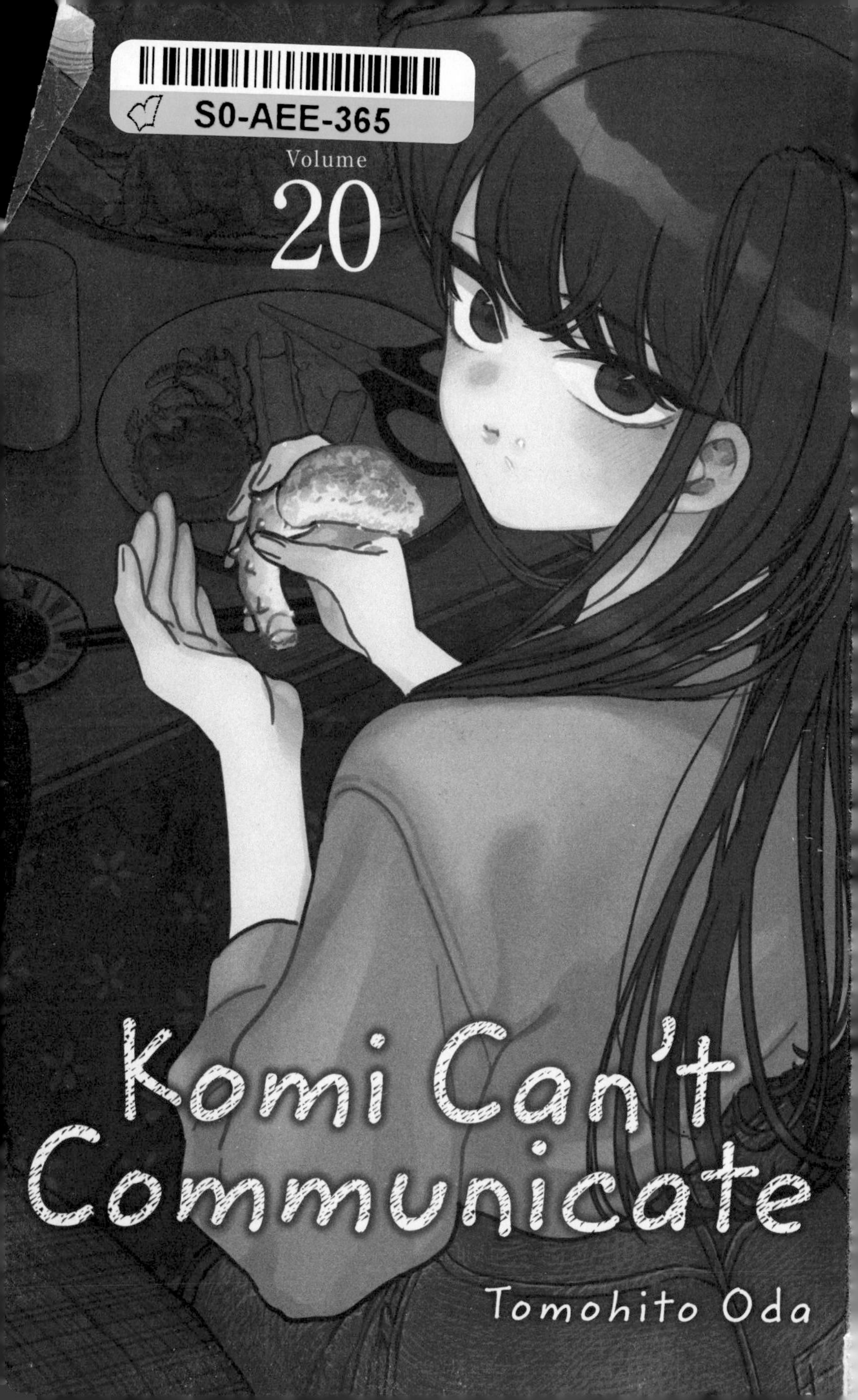
Volume
20
Komi Can't
Communicate
Tomohito Oda

C o n t e n t s

20

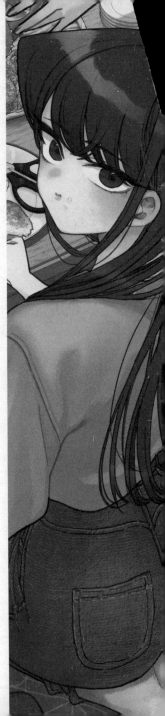

Komi Can't Communicate

One year ago
Decem-
ber
26
The day after ...
...Komi's birthday
YAAAY
AAAAAAND
HAPPY
...the harder it is to pick a seat!!!
WHAT'S THEIR PROBLEM?
So they are living on the edge!!!
I WISH THEY'D HURRY UP...
TAK
TAK
TAK
One symptom of a commu-
nication disorder can be...

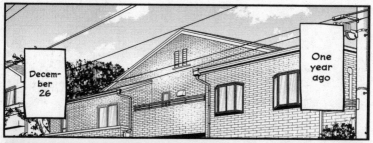

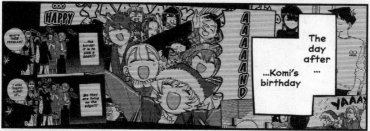

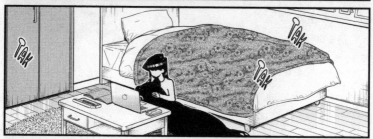

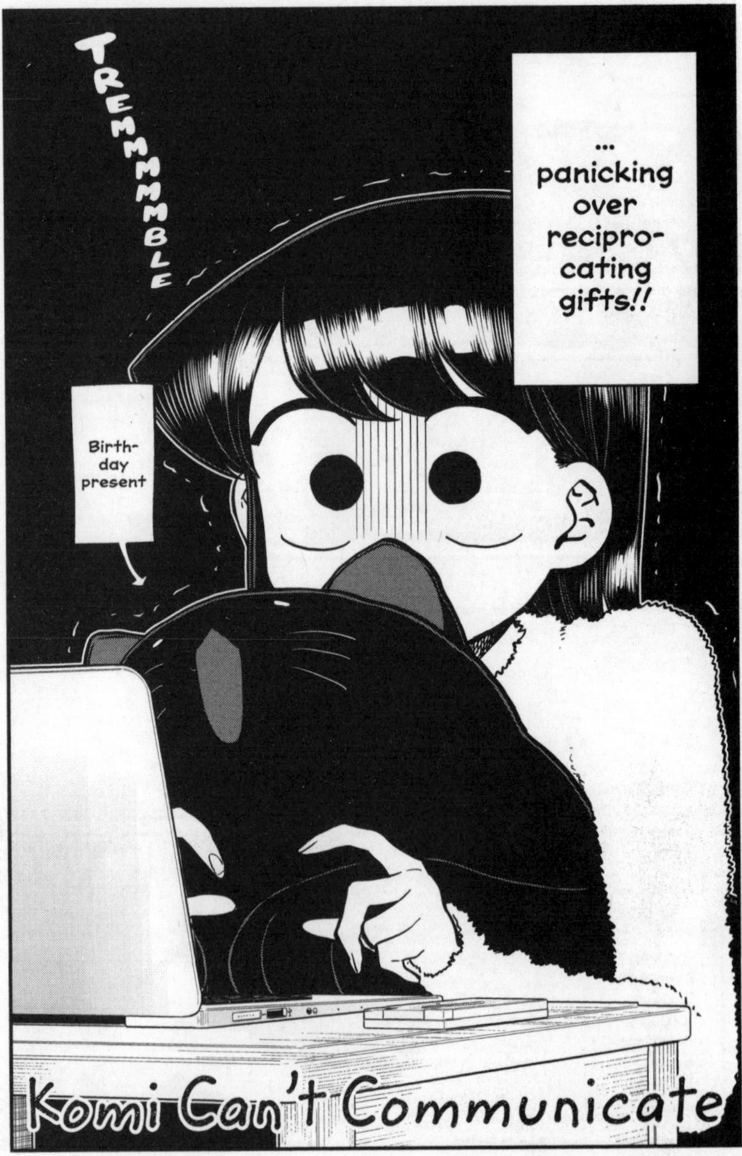
... panicking over reciprocating gifts!!
TREMMMMBLE
Birthday present
Komi Can't Communicate

Communication 259: Reciprocating

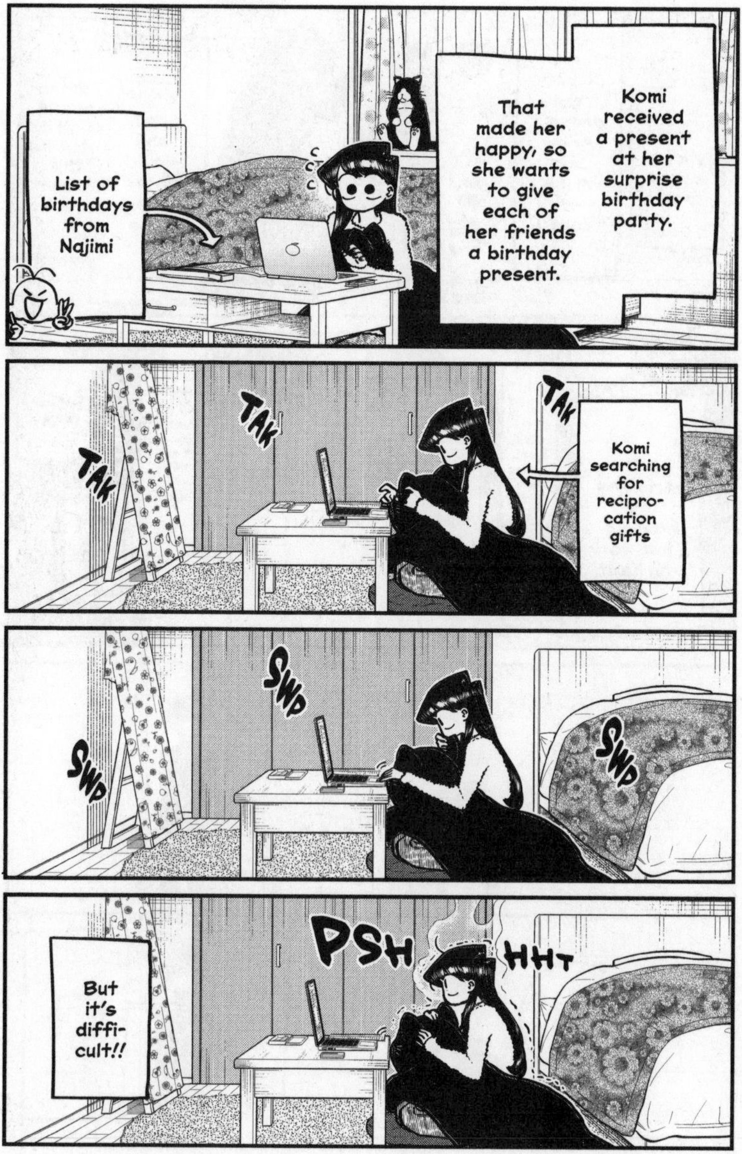

Komi received a present at her surprise birthday party.
That made her happy, so she wants to give each of her friends a birthday present.
List of birthdays from Najimi
TAK
Komi searching for reciprocation gifts
TAK
TAK
SWP
SWP
SWP
PSH HHT
But it's difficult!!

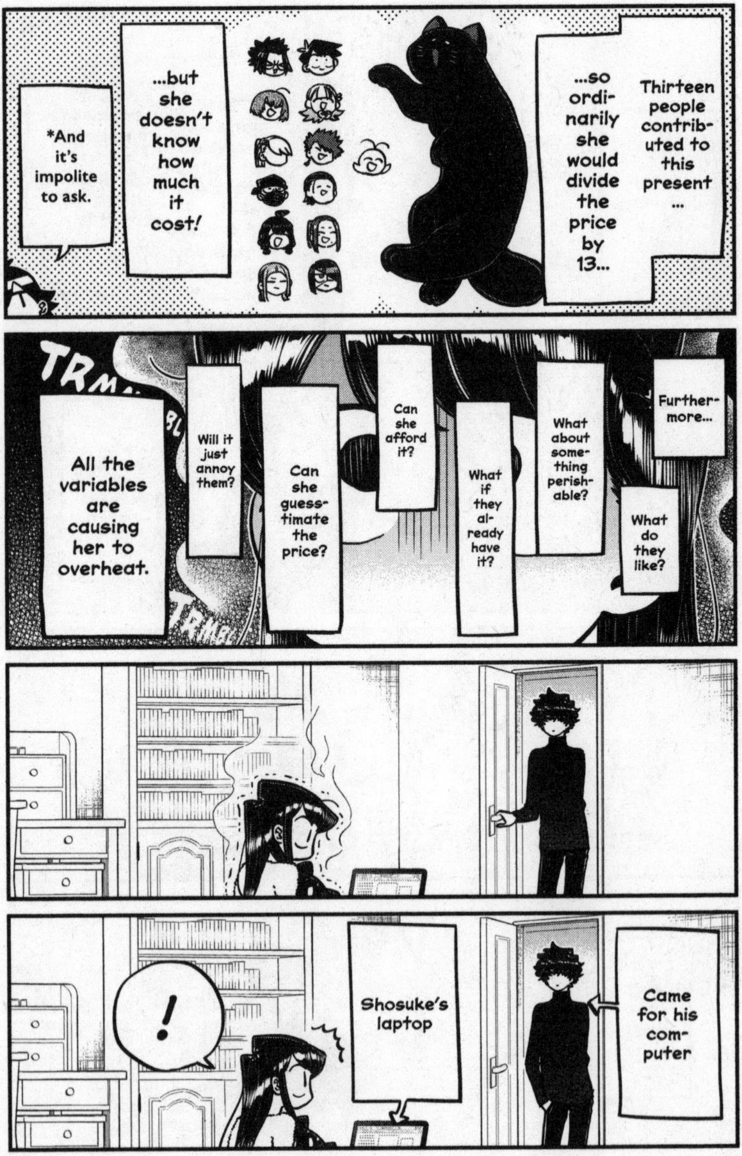
Thirteen people contributed to this present...
...so ordinarily she would divide the price by 13...
...but she doesn't know how much it cost!
*And it's impolite to ask.
Furthermore...
What do they like?
What about something perishable?
What if they already have it?
Can she afford it?
Can she guesstimate the price?
Will it just annoy them?
All the variables are causing her to overheat.
Came for his computer
Shosuke's laptop
!

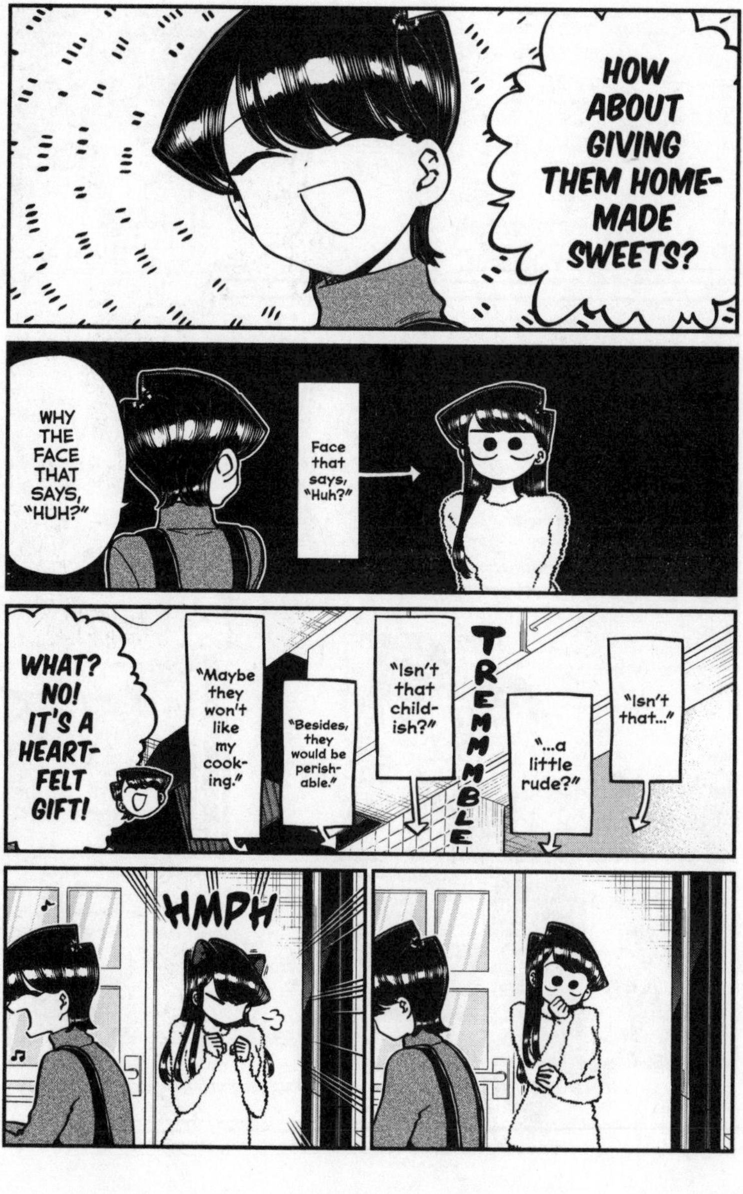
HOW ABOUT GIVING THEM HOME-MADE SWEETS?
Face that says, "Huh?"
WHY THE FACE THAT SAYS, "HUH?"
"Isn't that..."
"...a little rude?"
TREMMMBLE
"Isn't that child-ish?"
"Besides, they would be perish-able."
"Maybe they won't like my cook-ing."
WHAT? NO! IT'S A HEART-FELT GIFT!
HMPH

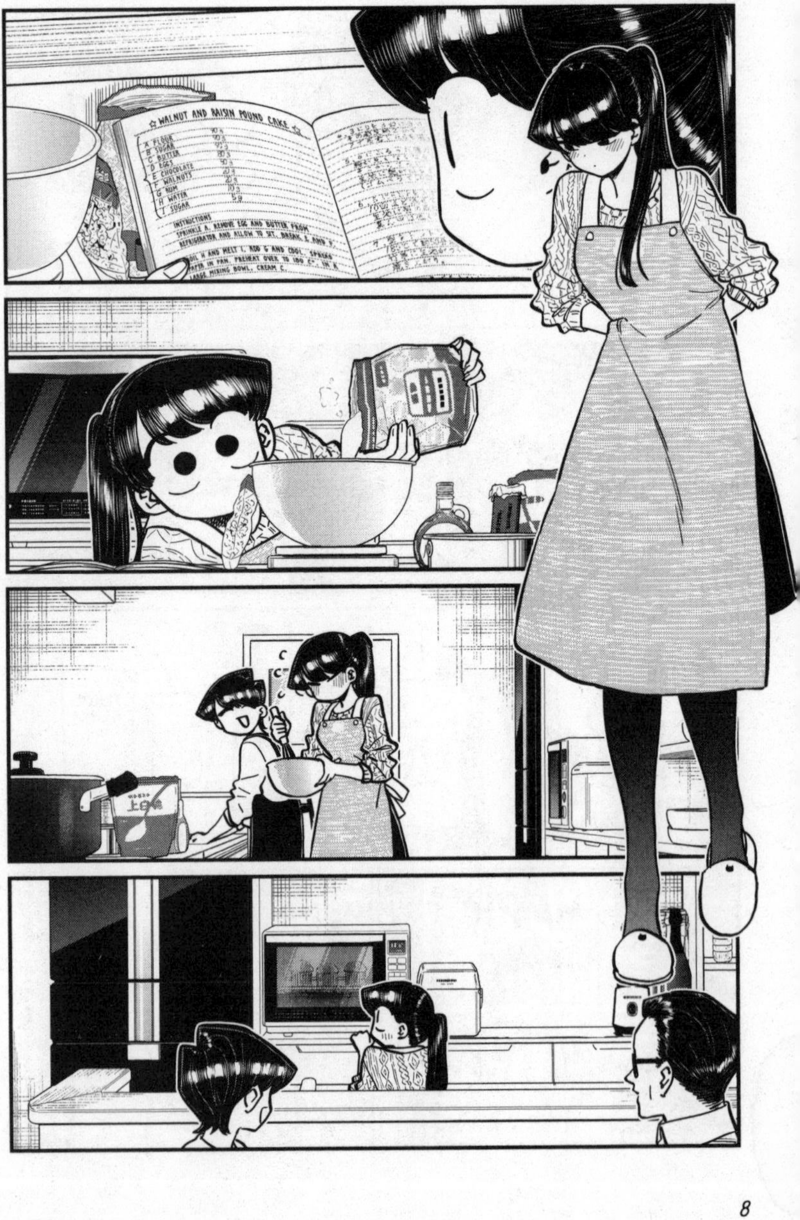
☆ WALNUT AND RAISIN POUND CAKE ☆
A FLOUR
B SUGAR
C BUTTER
D EGGS
E CHOCOLATE
F WALNUTS
G RUM
H WATER
I SUGAR
INSTRUCTIONS
SPRINKLE A. REMOVE EGG AND BUTTER FROM
REFRIGERATOR AND ALLOW TO SIT. BREAK E AND F.
OIL H AND MELT I. ADD G AND COOL. SPREAD
PAPER IN PAN. PREHEAT OVER TO 180 C°. IN A
LARGE MIXING BOWL, CREAM C.

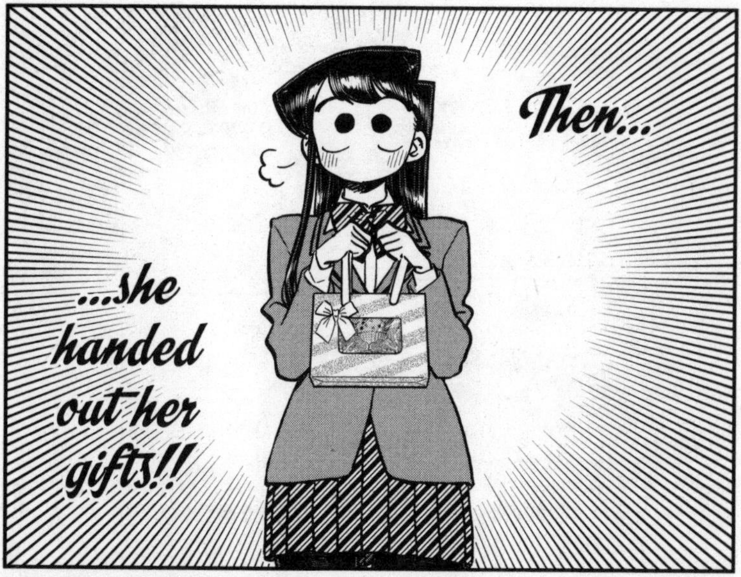
Then...
...she handed out her gifts!!
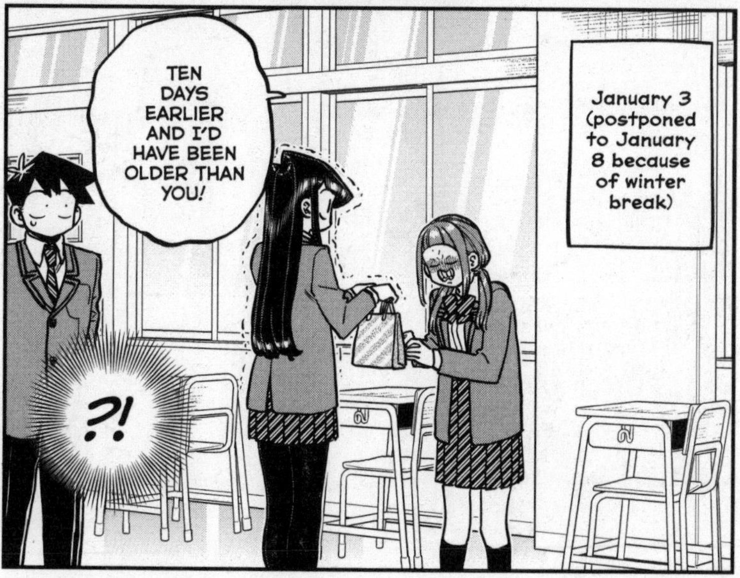
January 3 (postponed to January 8 because of winter break)
TEN DAYS EARLIER AND I'D HAVE BEEN OLDER THAN YOU!
?!

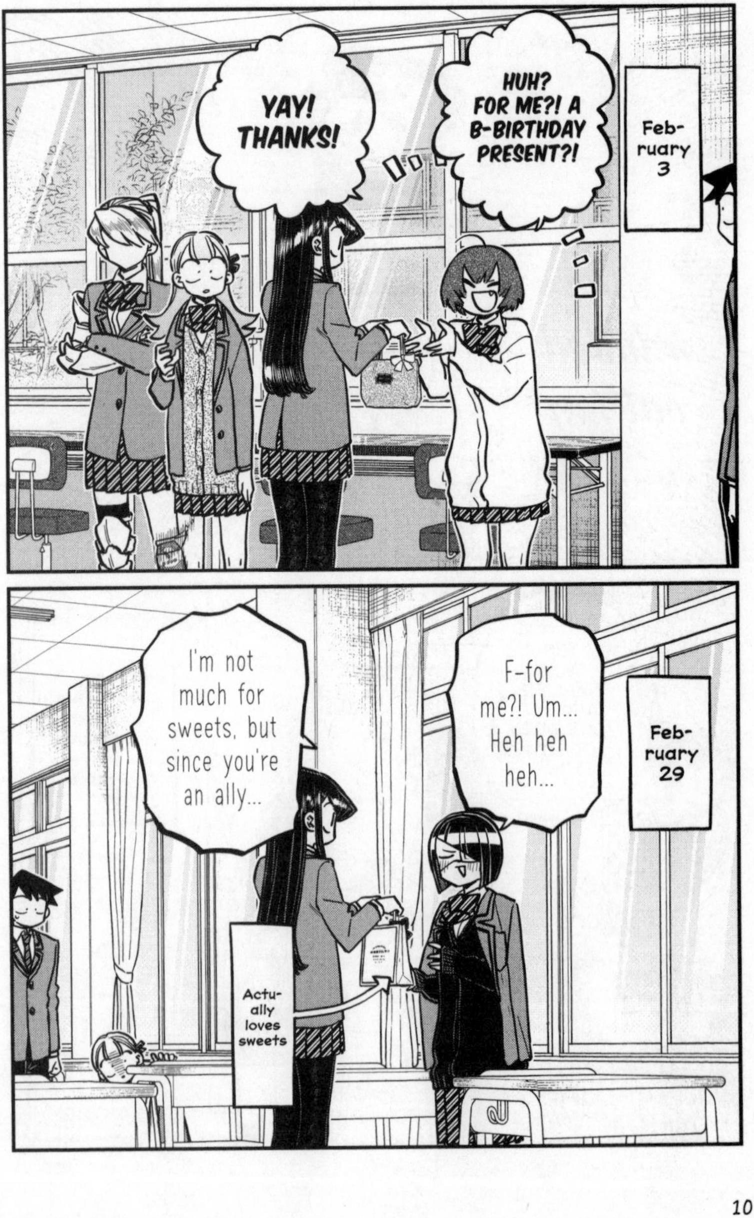
Feb-ruary 3
HUH? FOR ME?! A B-BIRTHDAY PRESENT?!
YAY! THANKS!
Feb-ruary 29
F-for me?! Um... Heh heh heh...
I'm not much for sweets, but since you're an ally...
Actu-ally loves sweets

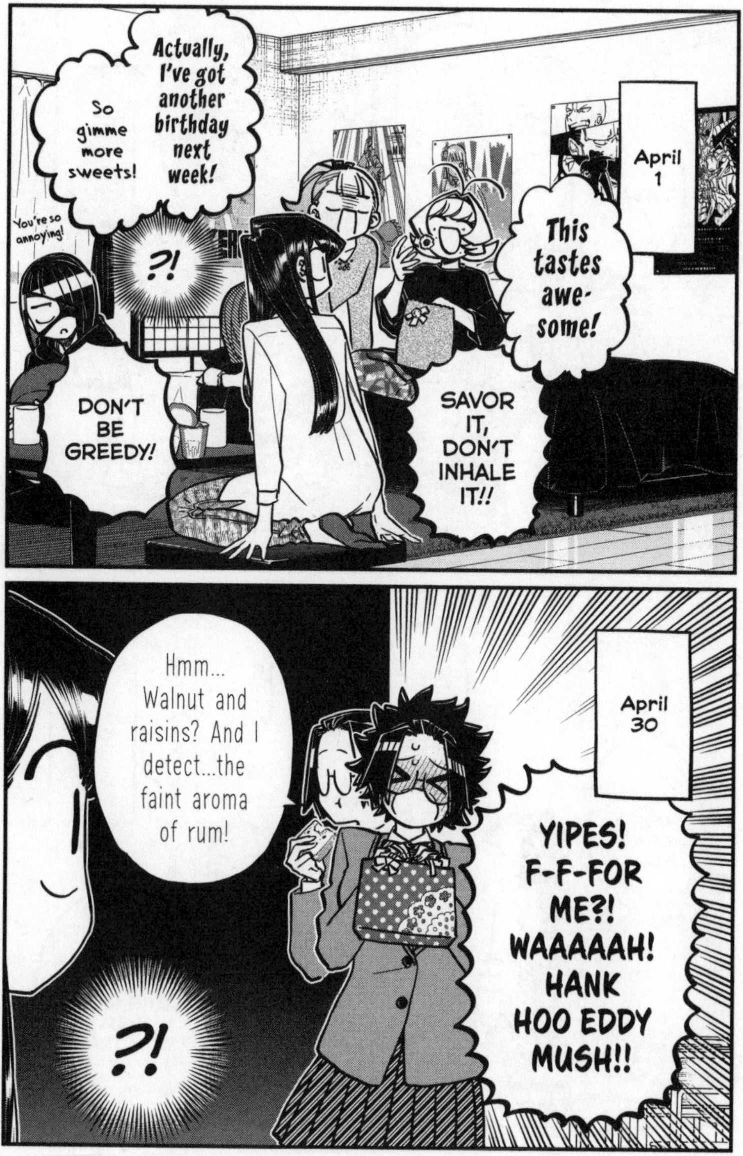
April 1
This tastes awe-some!
Actually, I've got another birthday next week!
So gimme more sweets!
?!
SAVOR IT, DON'T INHALE IT!!
You're so annoying!
DON'T BE GREEDY!
April 30
YIPES! F-F-FOR ME?! WAAAAAH! HANK HOO EDDY MUSH!!
Hmm... Walnut and raisins? And I detect...the faint aroma of rum!
?!

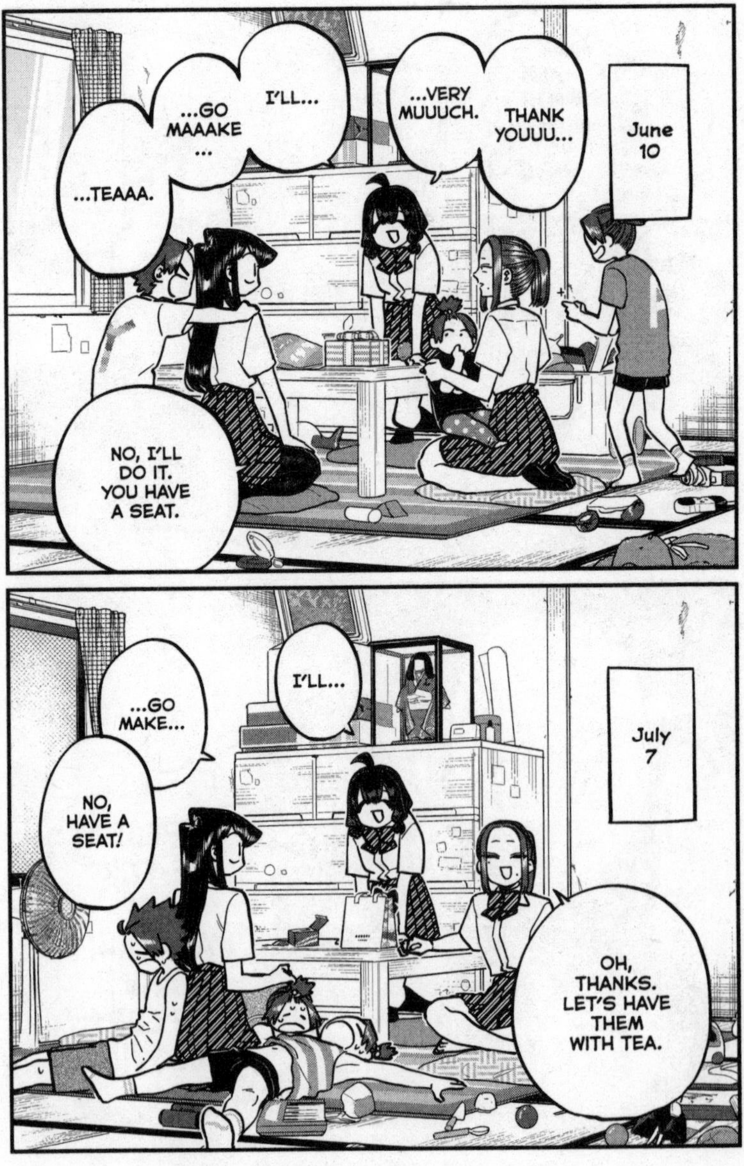
June 10
THANK YOUUU...
...VERY MUUUCH.
I'LL...
...GO MAAAKE ...
...TEAAA.
NO, I'LL DO IT. YOU HAVE A SEAT.
July 7
I'LL...
...GO MAKE...
NO, HAVE A SEAT!
OH, THANKS. LET'S HAVE THEM WITH TEA.

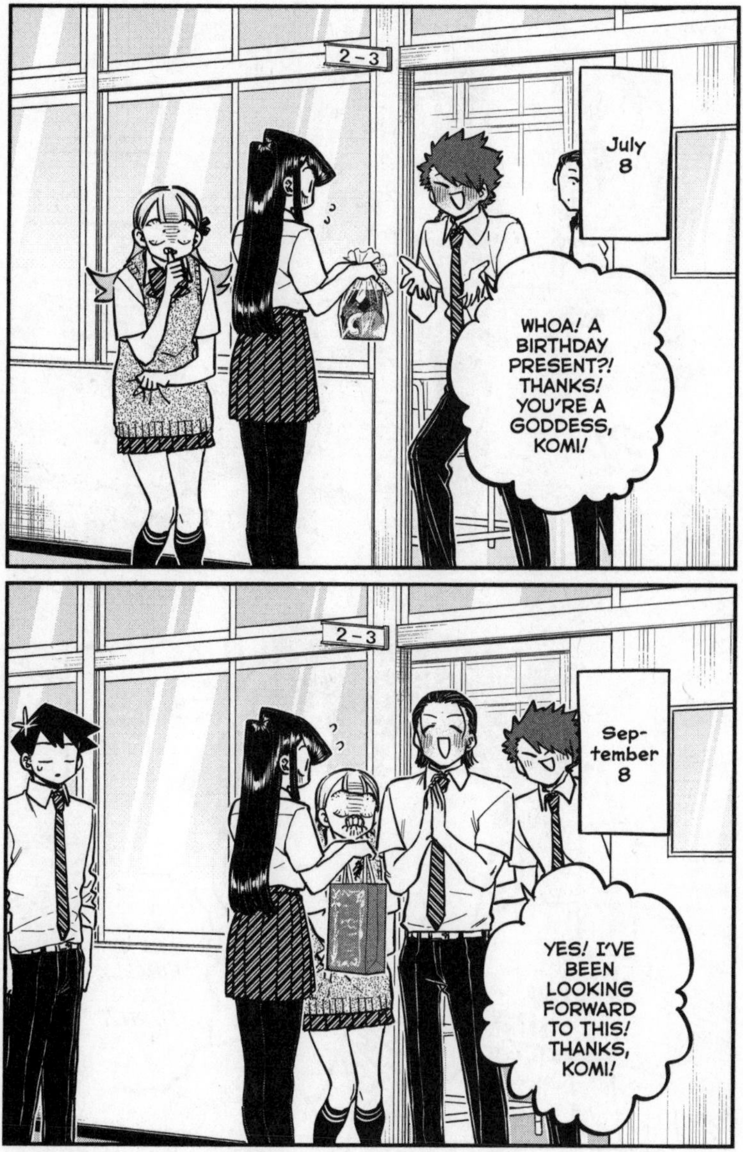
July 8
2-3
WHOA! A BIRTHDAY PRESENT?! THANKS! YOU'RE A GODDESS, KOMI!
Sep-tember 8
2-3
YES! I'VE BEEN LOOKING FORWARD TO THIS! THANKS, KOMI!

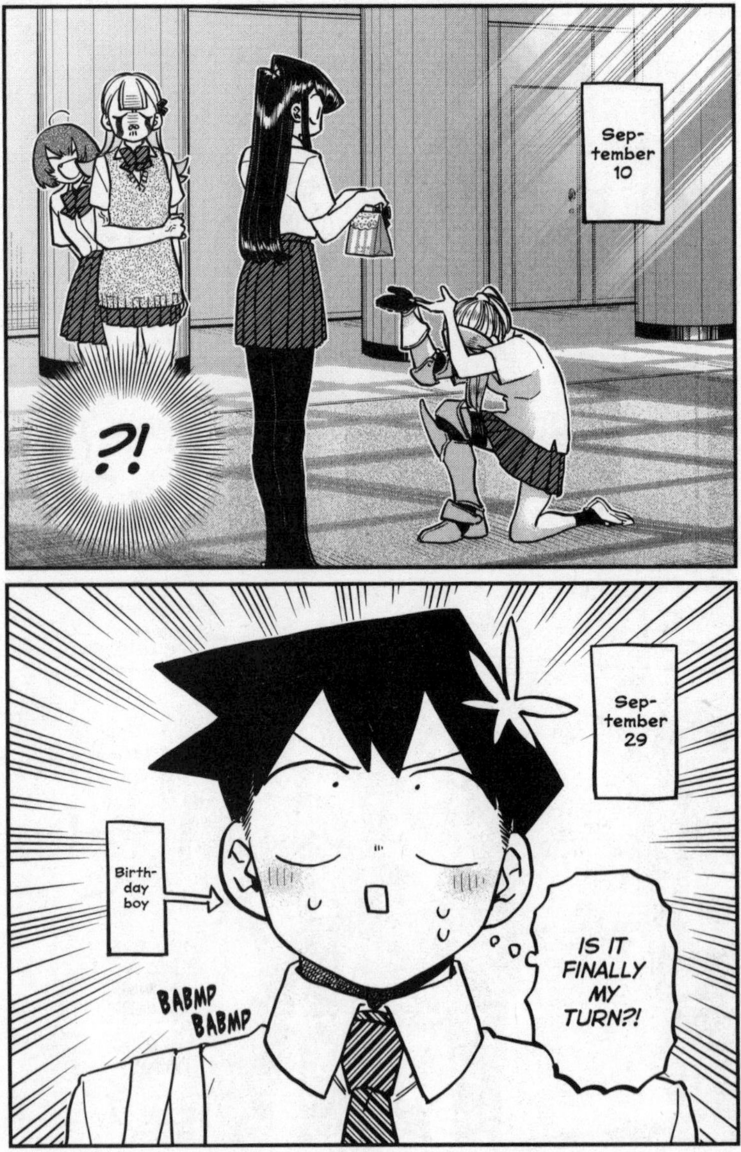
Sep-
tember
10
?!
Sep-
tember
29
IS IT FINALLY MY TURN?!
Birth-
day
boy
BABMP BABMP

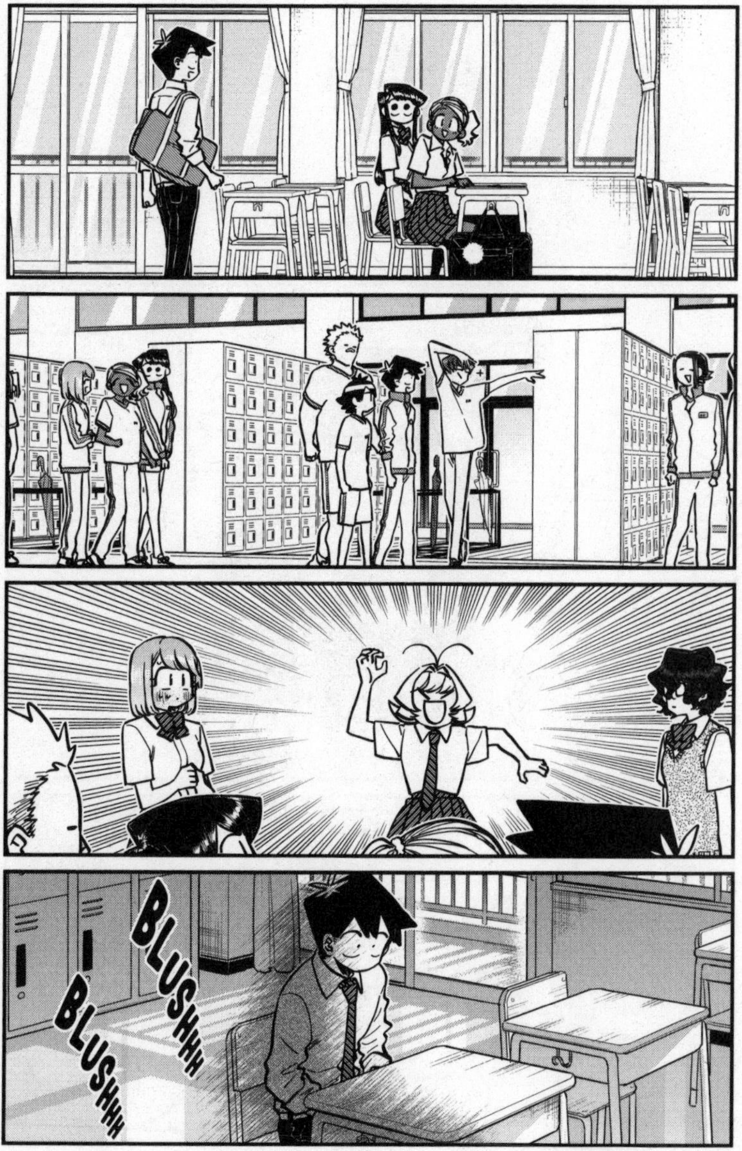
BLUSHHH
BLUSHHH

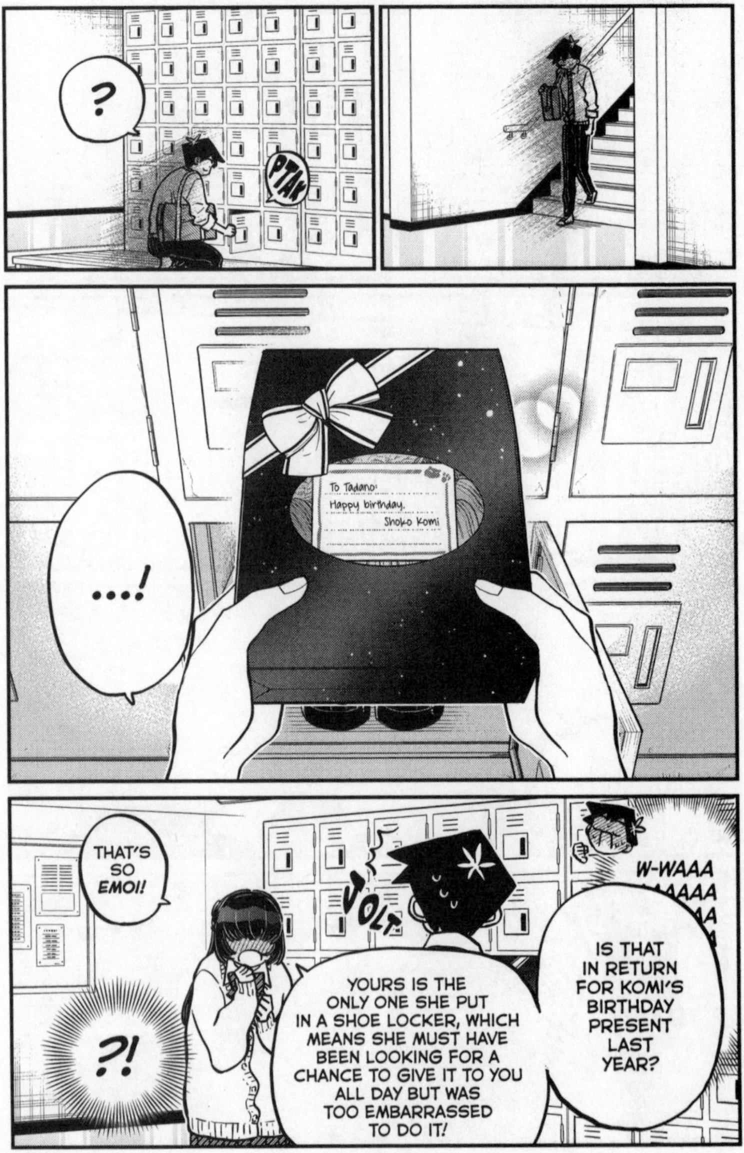
?
PTAK
To Tadano:
Happy birthday.
Shoko Komi
...!
W-WAAA
IS THAT IN RETURN FOR KOMI'S BIRTHDAY PRESENT LAST YEAR?
YOURS IS THE ONLY ONE SHE PUT IN A SHOE LOCKER, WHICH MEANS SHE MUST HAVE BEEN LOOKING FOR A CHANCE TO GIVE IT TO YOU ALL DAY BUT WAS TOO EMBARRASSED TO DO IT!
JOLT
THAT'S SO EMOI!
?!

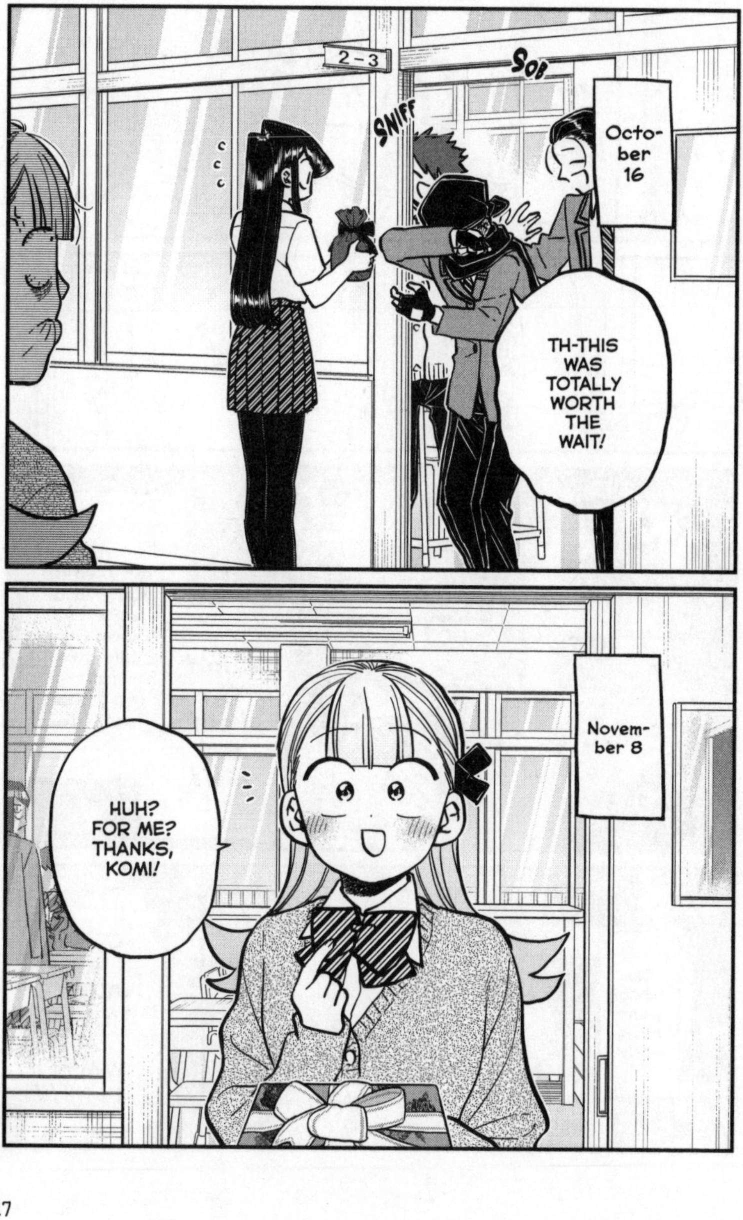
October 16
SOB
2-3
SNIFF
TH-THIS WAS TOTALLY WORTH THE WAIT!
November 8
HUH? FOR ME? THANKS, KOMI!

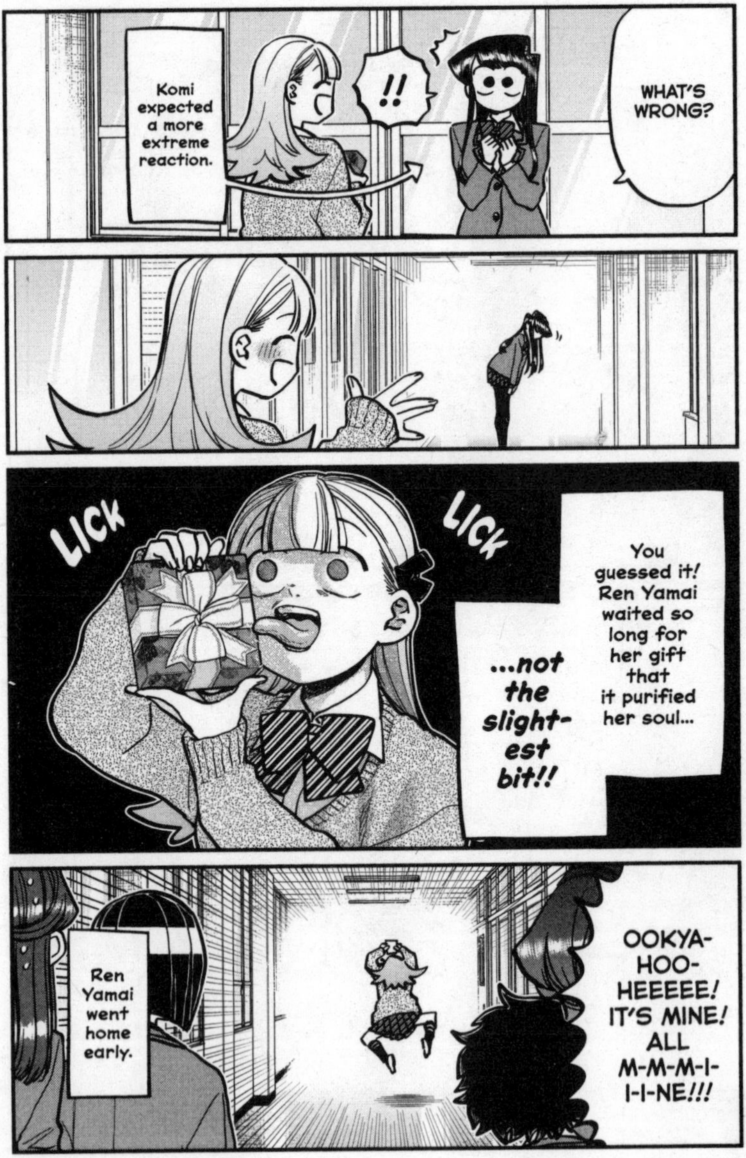
WHAT'S WRONG?
!!
Komi expected a more extreme reaction.
LICK
LICK
You guessed it! Ren Yamai waited so long for her gift that it purified her soul...
...not the slight-est bit!!
OOKYA-HOO-HEEEEEE! IT'S MINE! ALL M-M-M-I-I-I-NE!!!
Ren Yamai went home early.

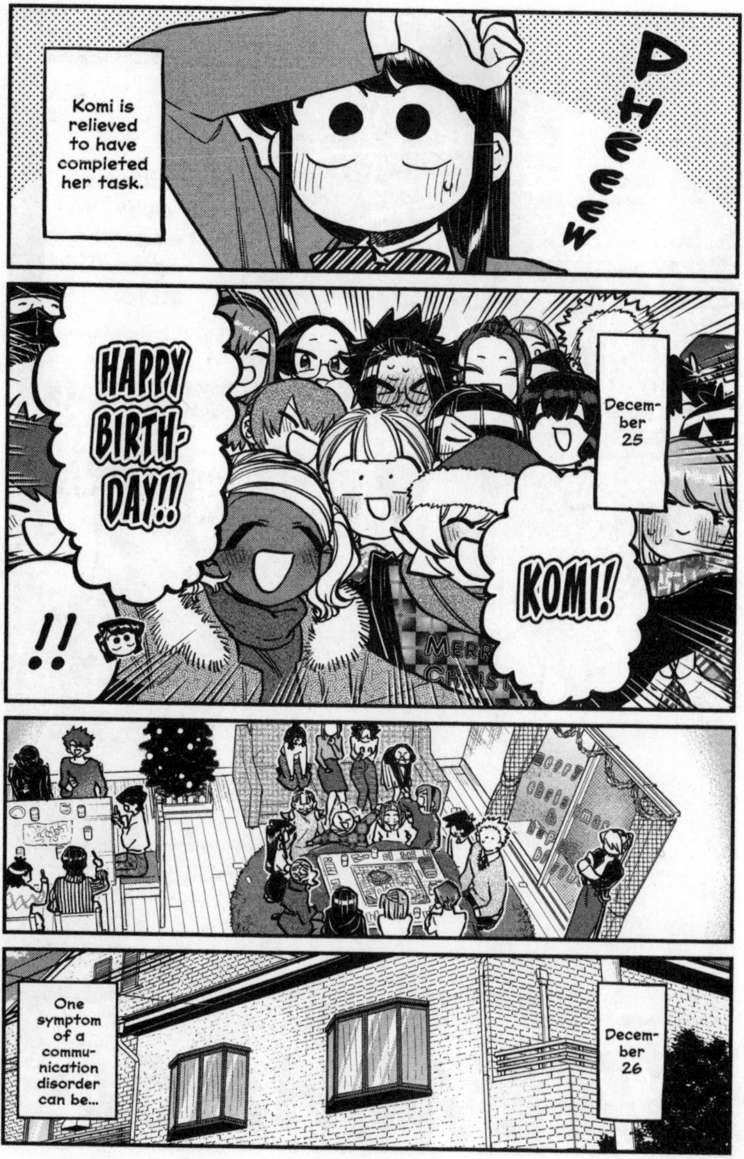
PHEEEW
Komi is relieved to have completed her task.
December 25
HAPPY BIRTHDAY!!
KOMI!
!!
December 26
One symptom of a communication disorder can be...

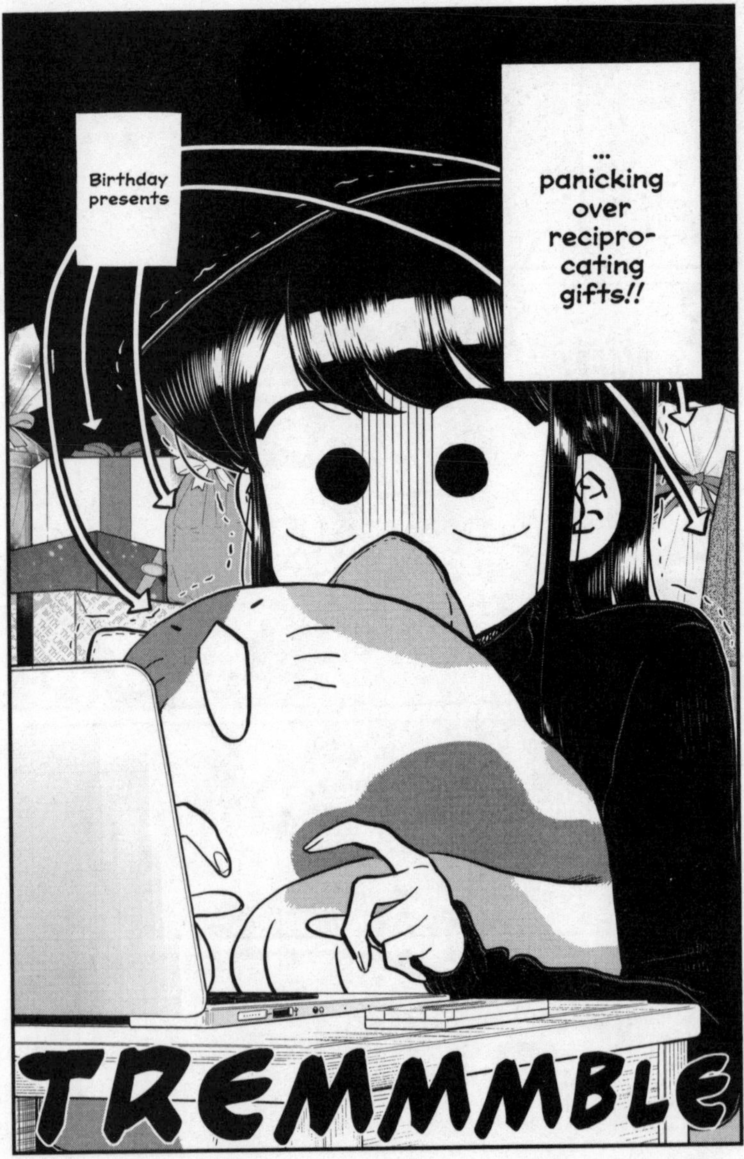
Birthday presents
... panicking over recipro-cating gifts!!
TREMMMBLE

Communication 259 — The End

Komi Can't Communicate

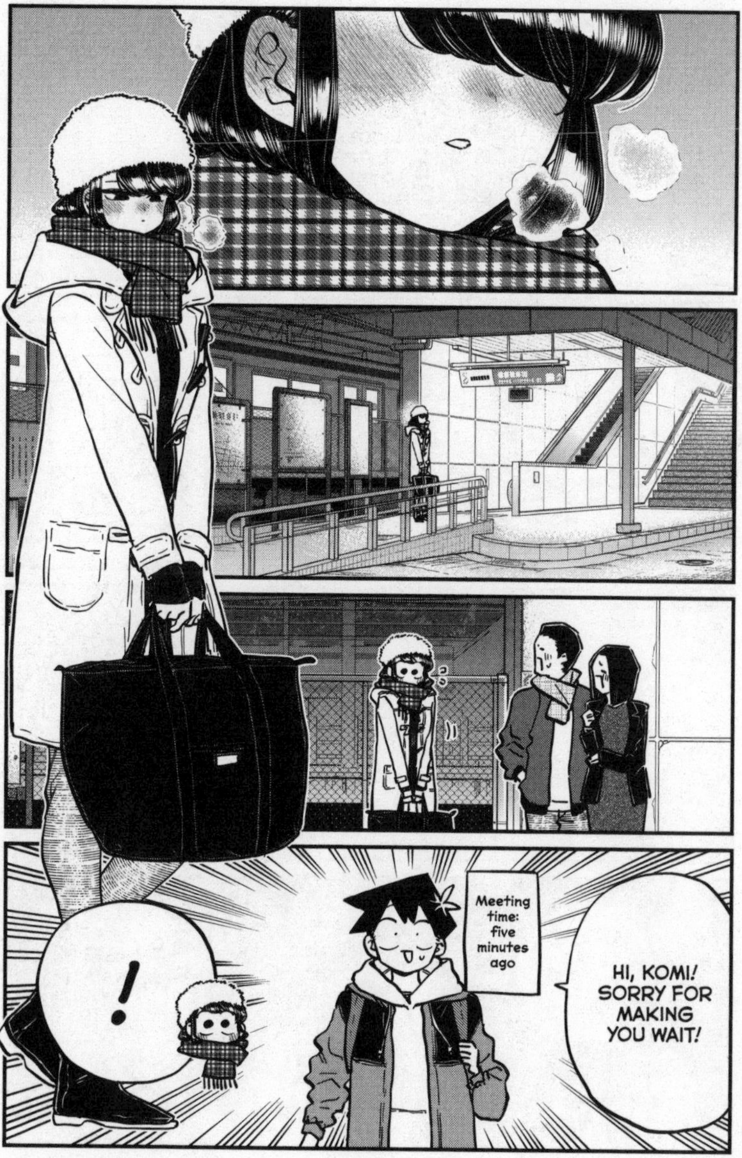
HI, KOMI! SORRY FOR MAKING YOU WAIT!
Meeting time: five minutes ago
!

Communication 260: Can't Sleep

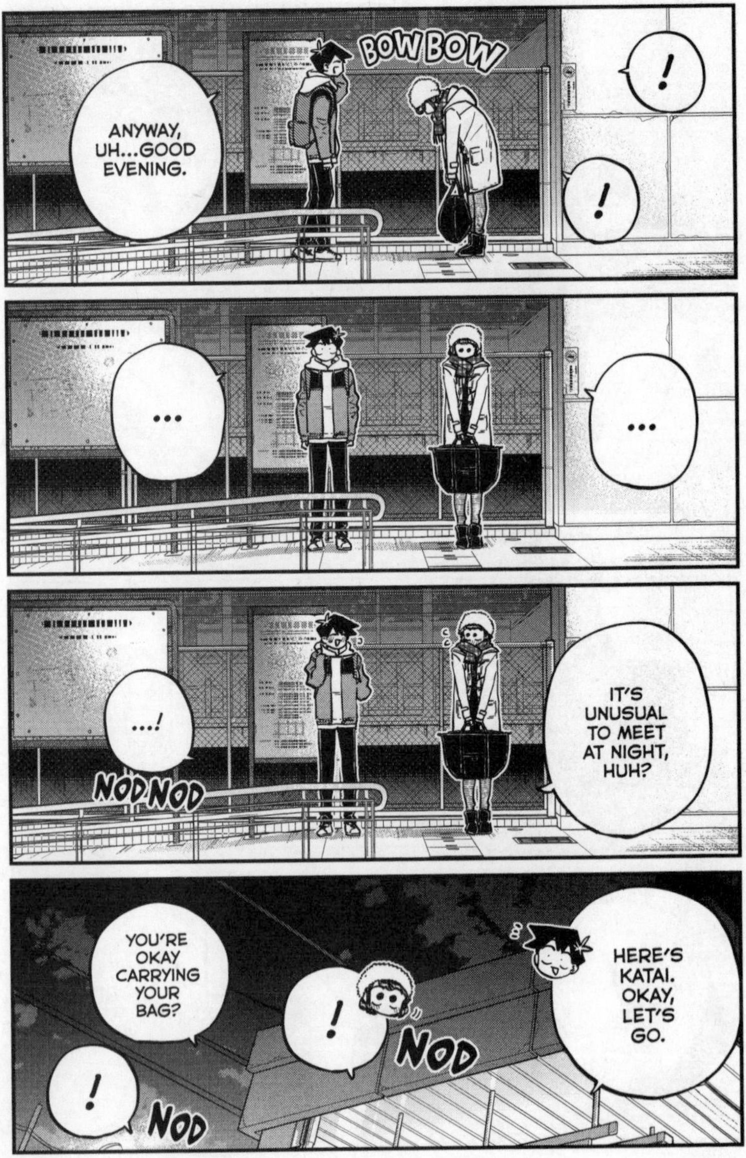
!
!
BOWBOW
ANYWAY, UH...GOOD EVENING.
...
...
IT'S UNUSUAL TO MEET AT NIGHT, HUH?
...!
NODNOD
HERE'S KATAI. OKAY, LET'S GO.
!
NOD
YOU'RE OKAY CARRYING YOUR BAG?
!
NOD

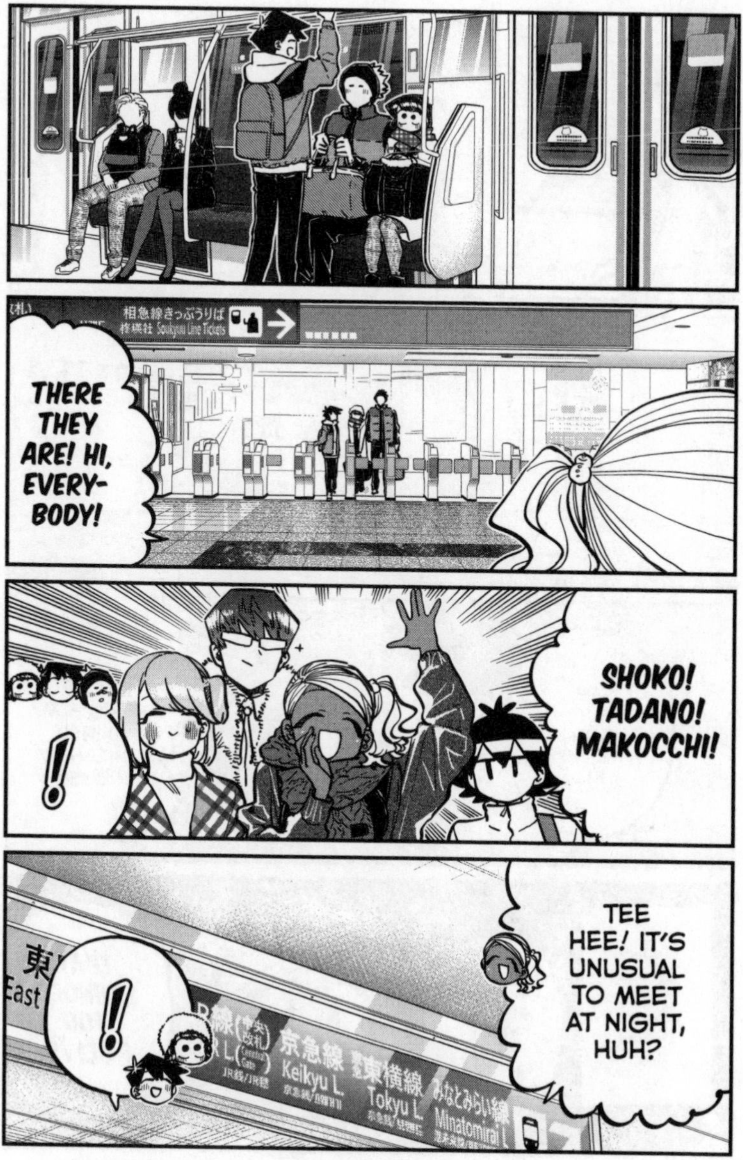

相急線きっぷうりば
Soukyuu Line Tickets
THERE THEY ARE! HI, EVERY-BODY!
SHOKO! TADANO! MAKOCCHI!
!
TEE HEE! IT'S UNUSUAL TO MEET AT NIGHT, HUH?
!
京急線
Keikyu L.
東横線
Tokyu L.

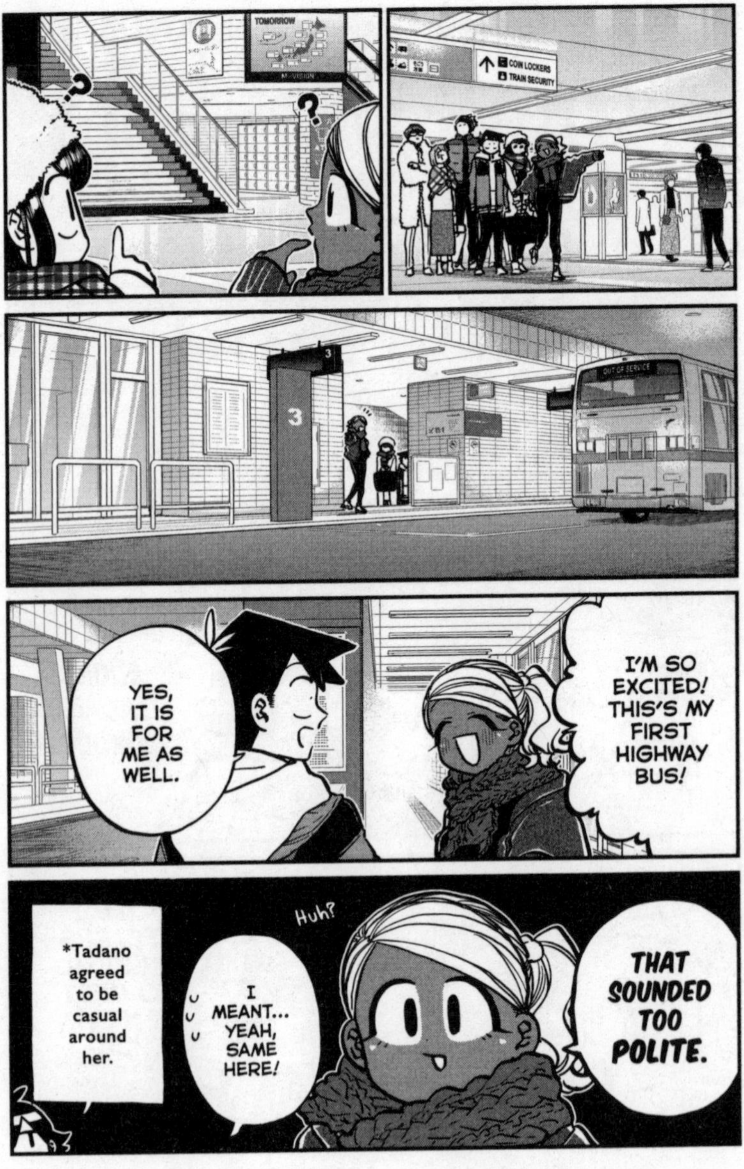
COIN LOCKERS
TRAIN SECURITY
TOMORROW
OUT OF SERVICE
3
I'M SO EXCITED! THIS'S MY FIRST HIGHWAY BUS!
YES, IT IS FOR ME AS WELL.
THAT SOUNDED TOO POLITE.
Huh?
I MEANT... YEAH, SAME HERE!
*Tadano agreed to be casual around her.

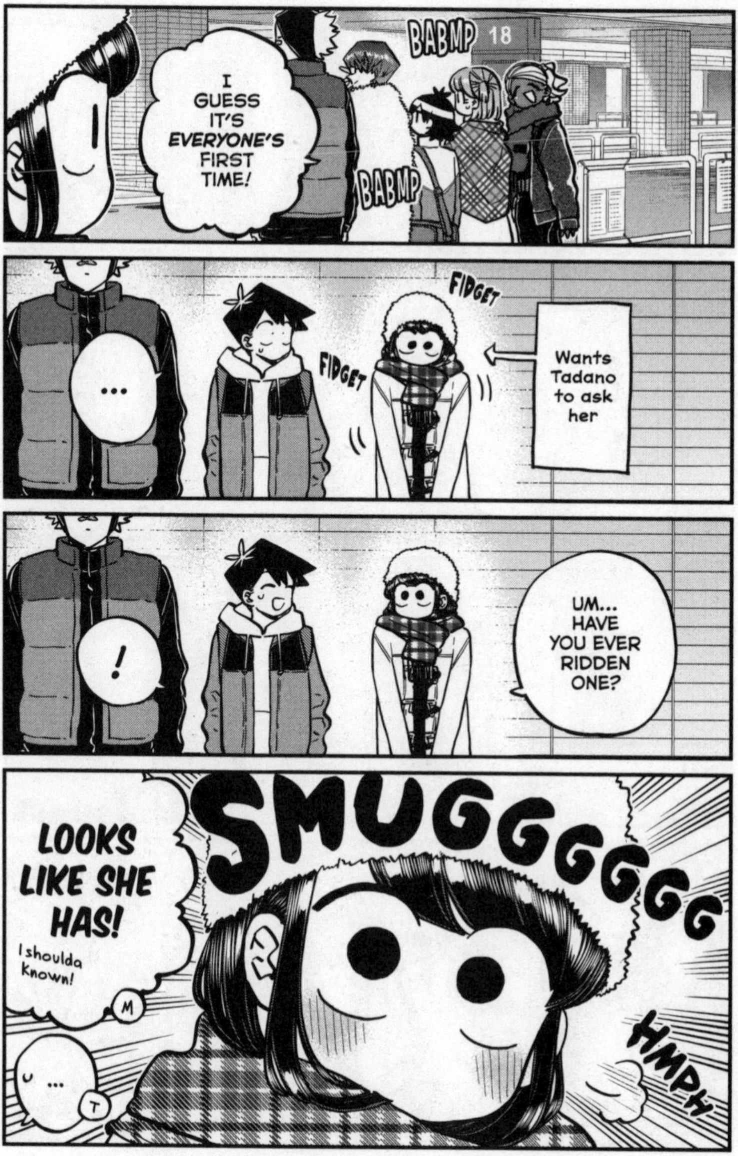
BABMP
I GUESS IT'S EVERYONE'S FIRST TIME!
BABMP
Wants Tadano to ask her
FIDGET
FIDGET
...
UM... HAVE YOU EVER RIDDEN ONE?
!
SMUGGGGGG
HMPH
LOOKS LIKE SHE HAS!
I shoulda known!
M
U ...
T

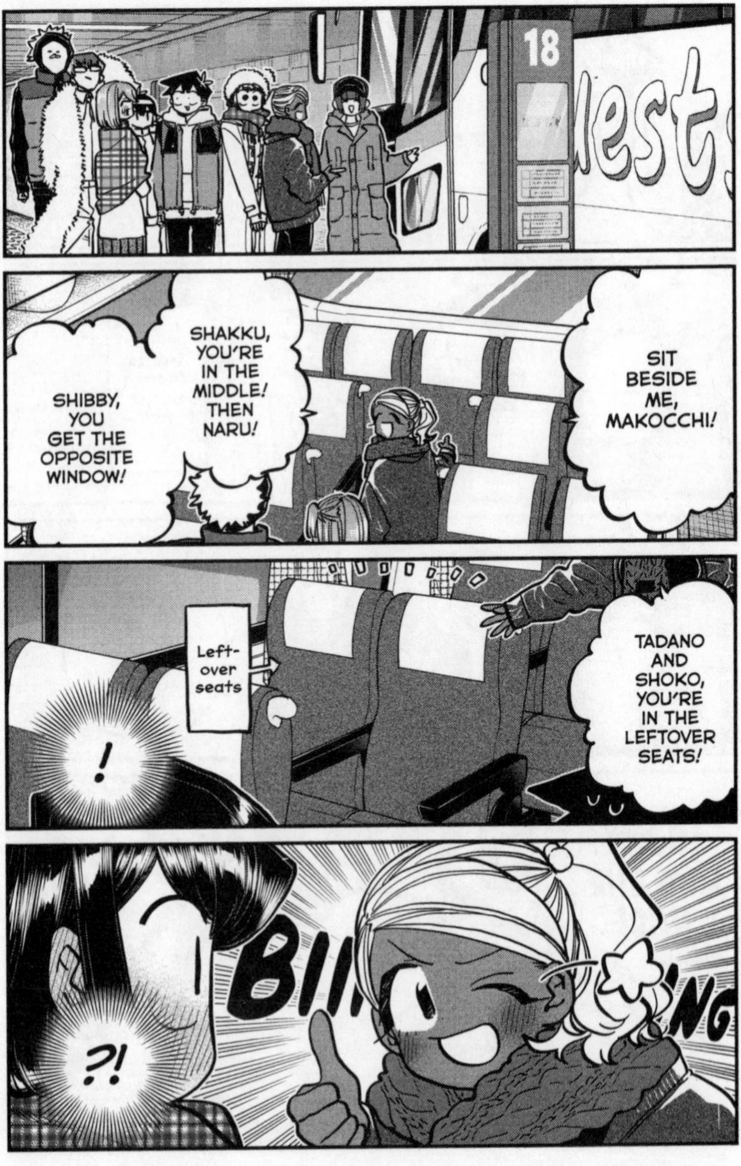
18
SIT BESIDE ME, MAKOCCHI!
SHAKKU, YOU'RE IN THE MIDDLE! THEN NARU!
SHIBBY, YOU GET THE OPPOSITE WINDOW!
TADANO AND SHOKO, YOU'RE IN THE LEFTOVER SEATS!
Left-over seats
!
?!

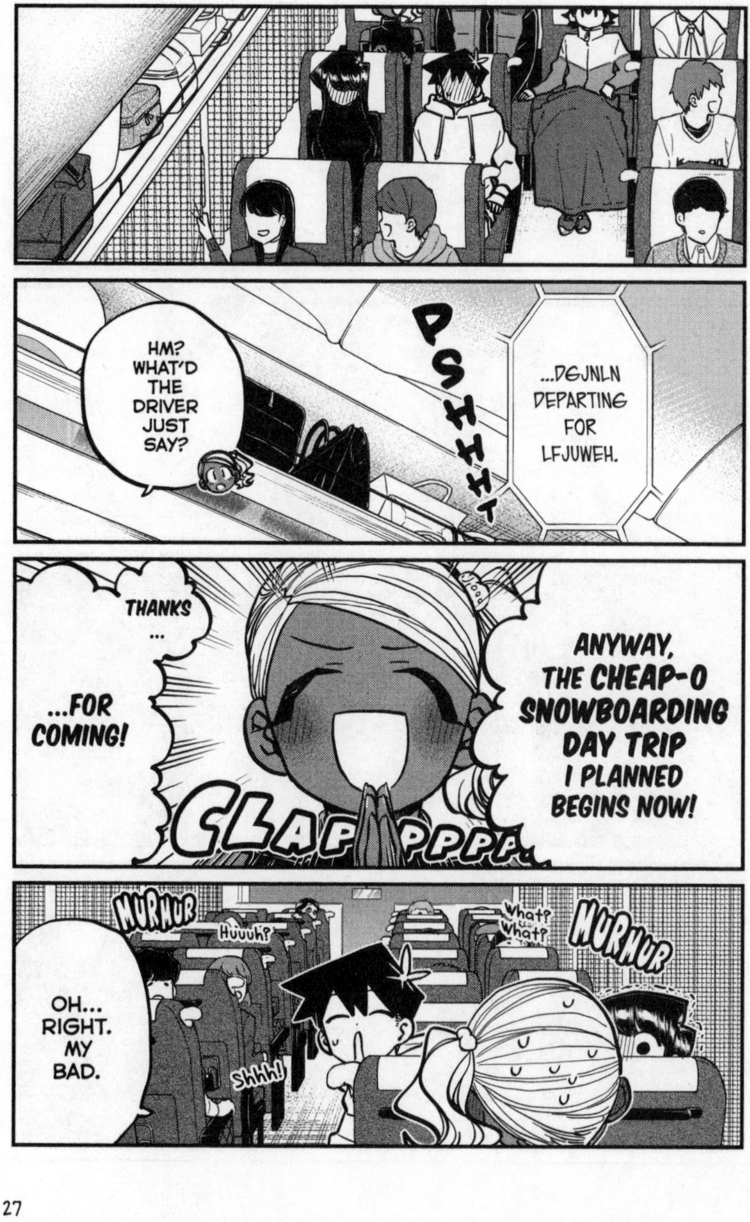
...DGJNLN DEPARTING FOR LFJUWEH.
PSHHHHT
HM? WHAT'D THE DRIVER JUST SAY?
ANYWAY, THE CHEAP-O SNOWBOARDING DAY TRIP I PLANNED BEGINS NOW!
CLAPPPPP
THANKS ...
...FOR COMING!
MURMUR
What? What?
Huuuh?
MURMUR
Shhh!
OH... RIGHT. MY BAD.

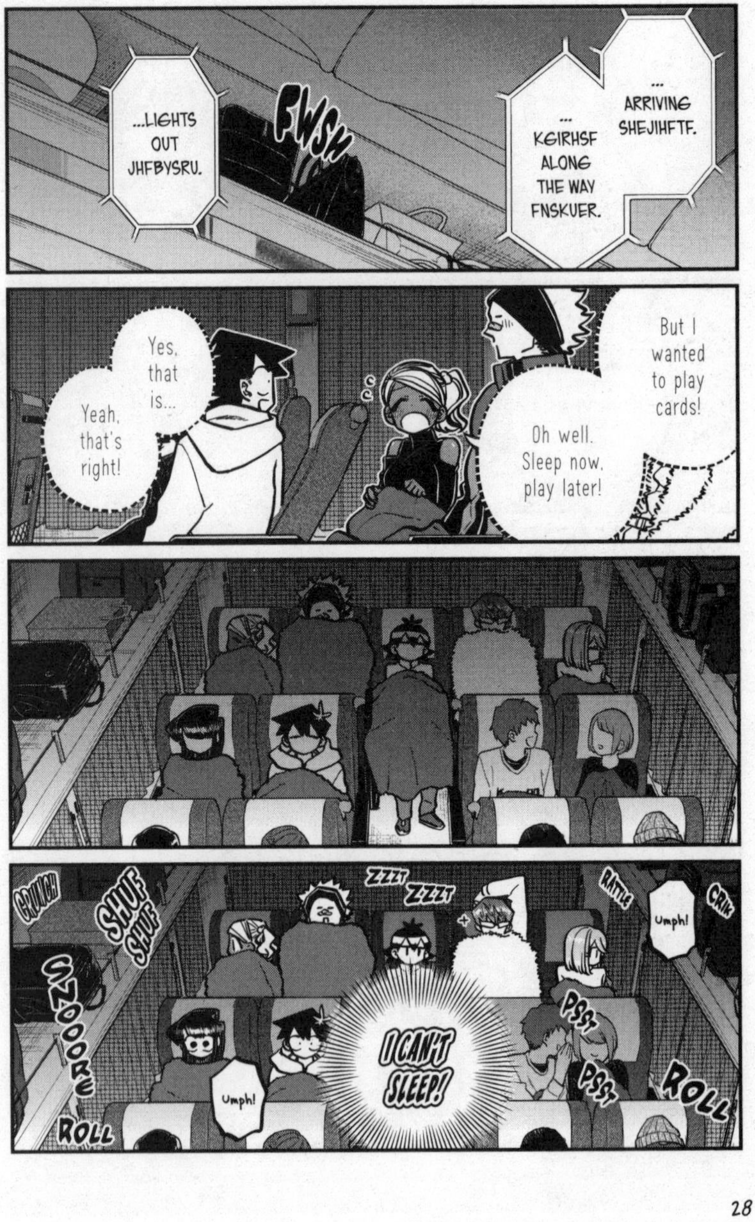
... ARRIVING SHEJIHFTF.
... KGIRHSF ALONG THE WAY FNSKUER.
FWSH
...LIGHTS OUT JHFBYSRU.
But I wanted to play cards!
Oh well. Sleep now, play later!
Yes, that is...
Yeah, that's right!
CRIK
RATTLE
Umph!
ZZZT ZZZT
SHUF SHUF
CRUNCH
ROLL
PSST PSST
I CAN'T SLEEP!
Umph!
SNOOORE
ROLL

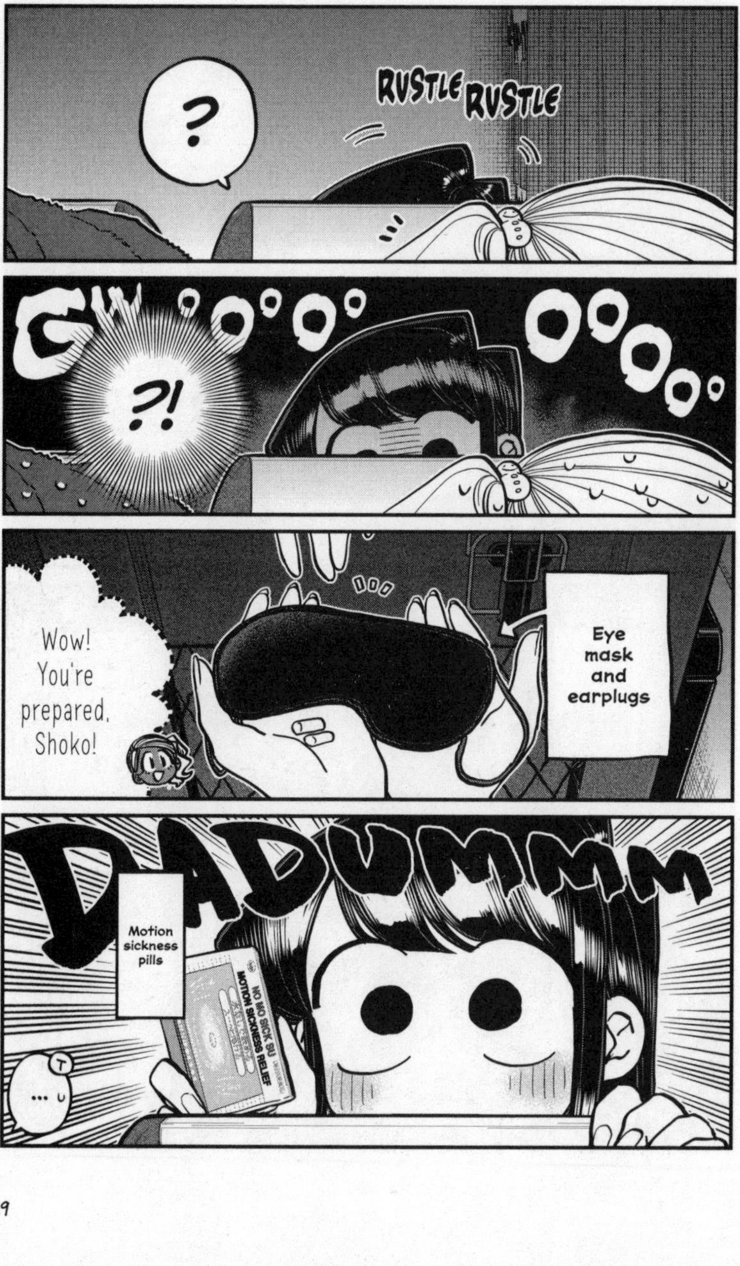
RUSTLE RUSTLE
?
GWOOOOOOOOO
?!
Eye mask and earplugs
Wow! You're prepared, Shoko!
DADUMMM
Motion sickness pills
NO MO SICK SU
MOTION SICKNESS RELIEF
...

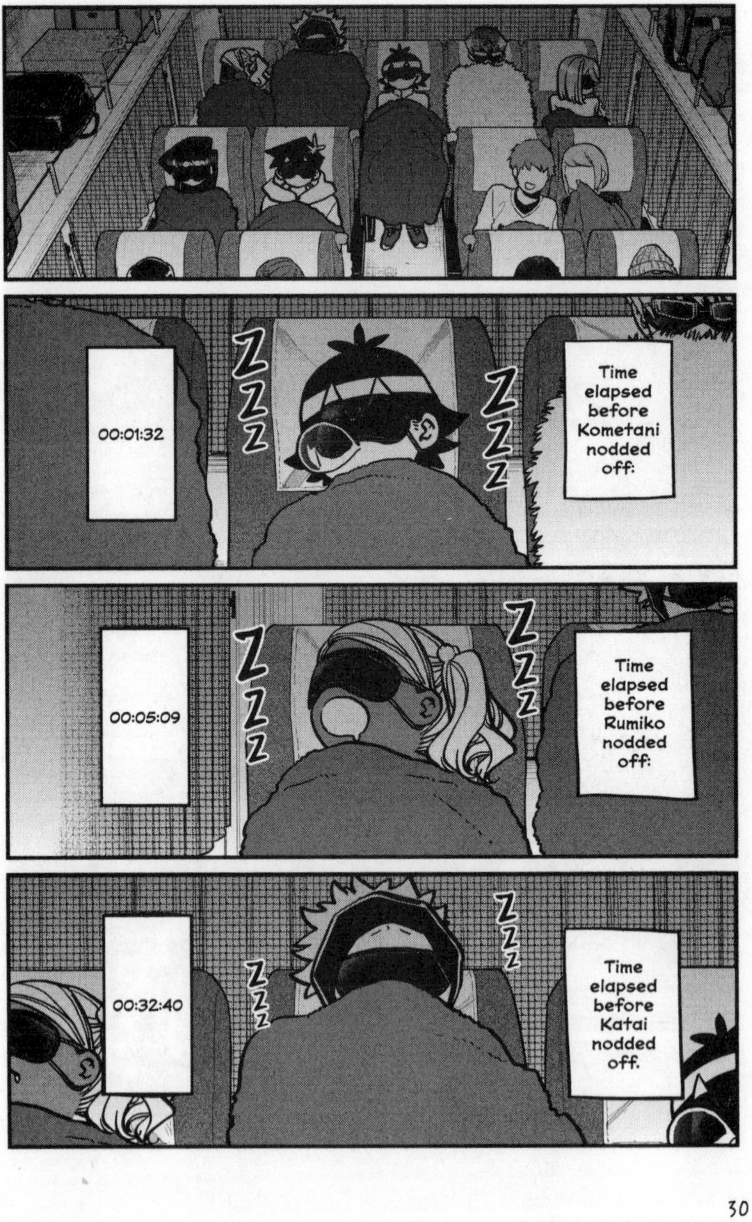
Time elapsed before Kometani nodded off:
ZZZ
ZZZ
00:01:32
ZZZ
Time elapsed before Rumiko nodded off:
ZZZ
00:05:09
ZZZ
Time elapsed before Katai nodded off.
ZZZ
00:32:40

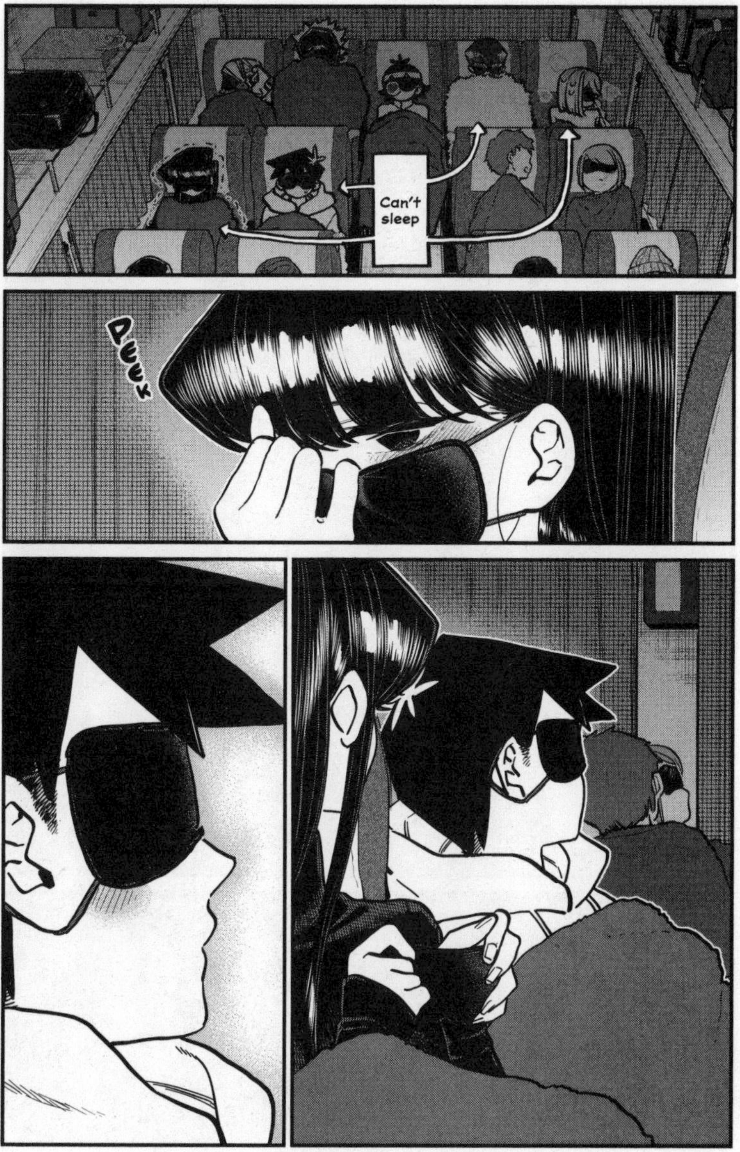
Can't sleep
PEEK

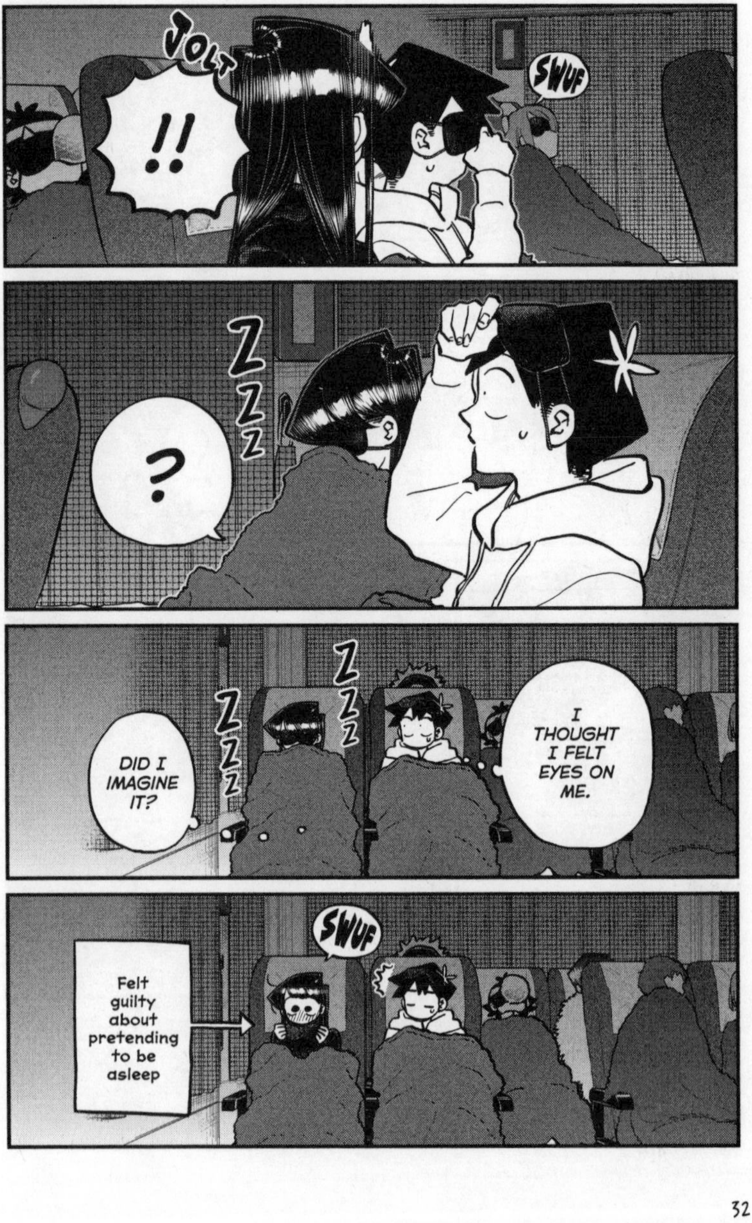
SWUF
JOLT
!!
ZZZ
?
I THOUGHT I FELT EYES ON ME.
ZZZ
ZZZ
DID I IMAGINE IT?
SWUF
Felt guilty about pretending to be asleep

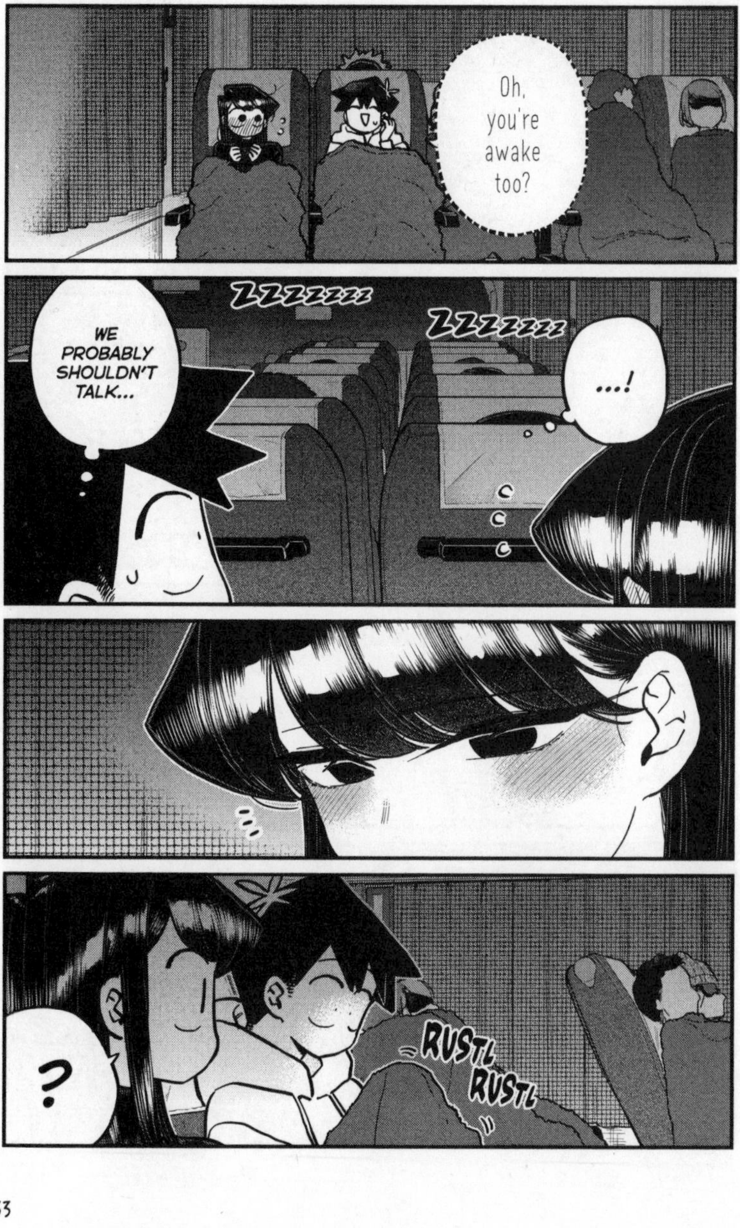
Oh, you're awake too?
ZZZZZZZ
...!
ZZZZZZZ
WE PROBABLY SHOULDN'T TALK...
RUSTL
RUSTL
?

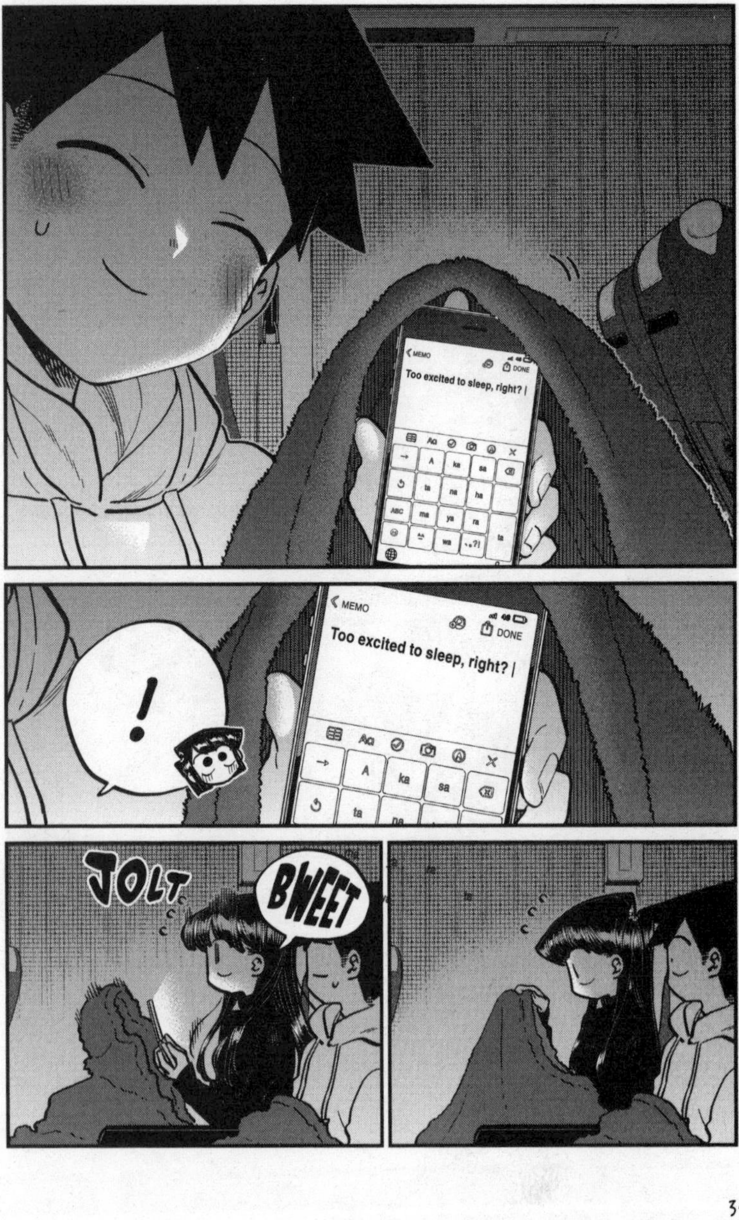
MEMO
DONE
Too excited to sleep, right?
MEMO
DONE
Too excited to sleep, right?
!
JOLT
BWEET

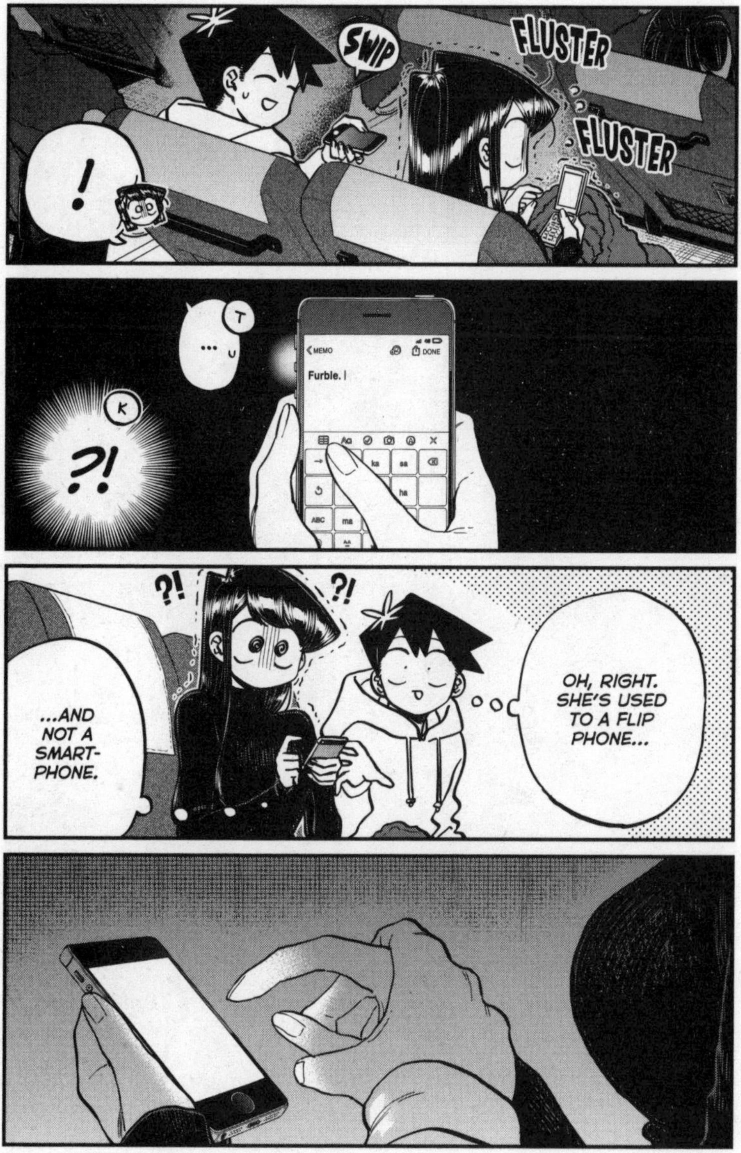
FLUSTER
FLUSTER
SWIP
!
...
MEMO
DONE
Furble.
?!
?!
?!
OH, RIGHT. SHE'S USED TO A FLIP PHONE...
...AND NOT A SMART-PHONE.

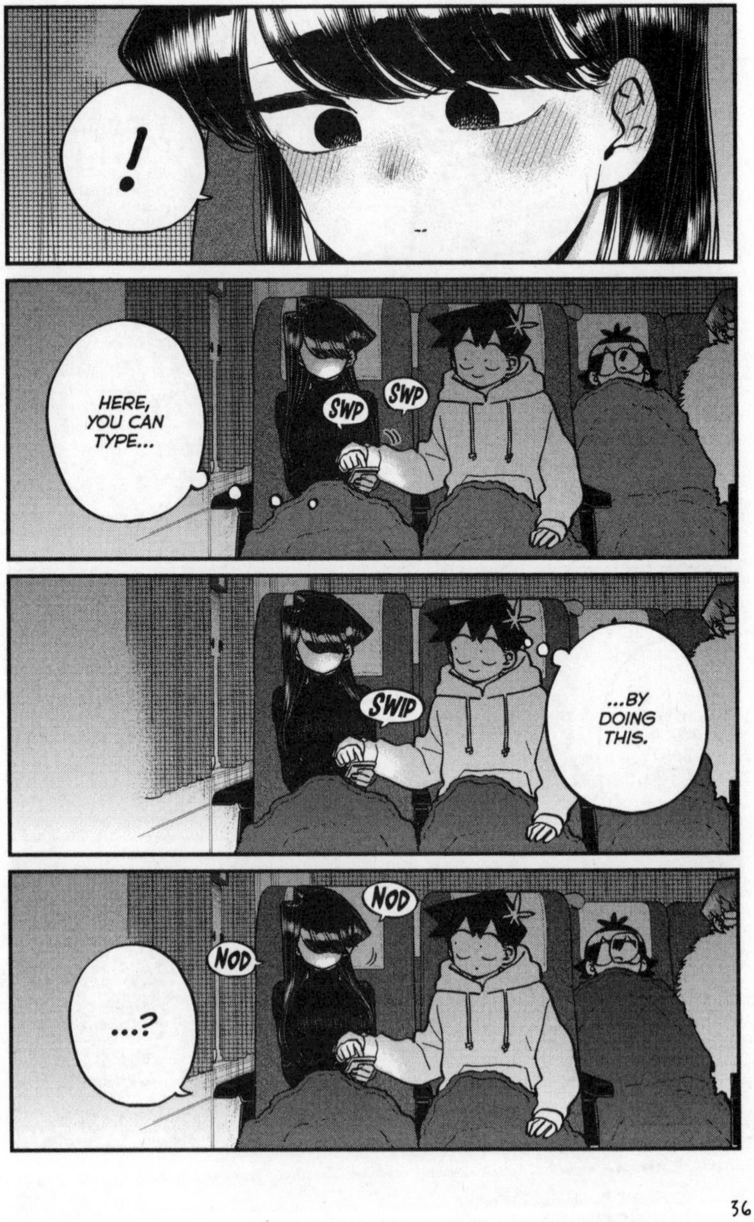
!
SWP
SWP
HERE, YOU CAN TYPE...
...BY DOING THIS.
SWIP
NOD
NOD
...?

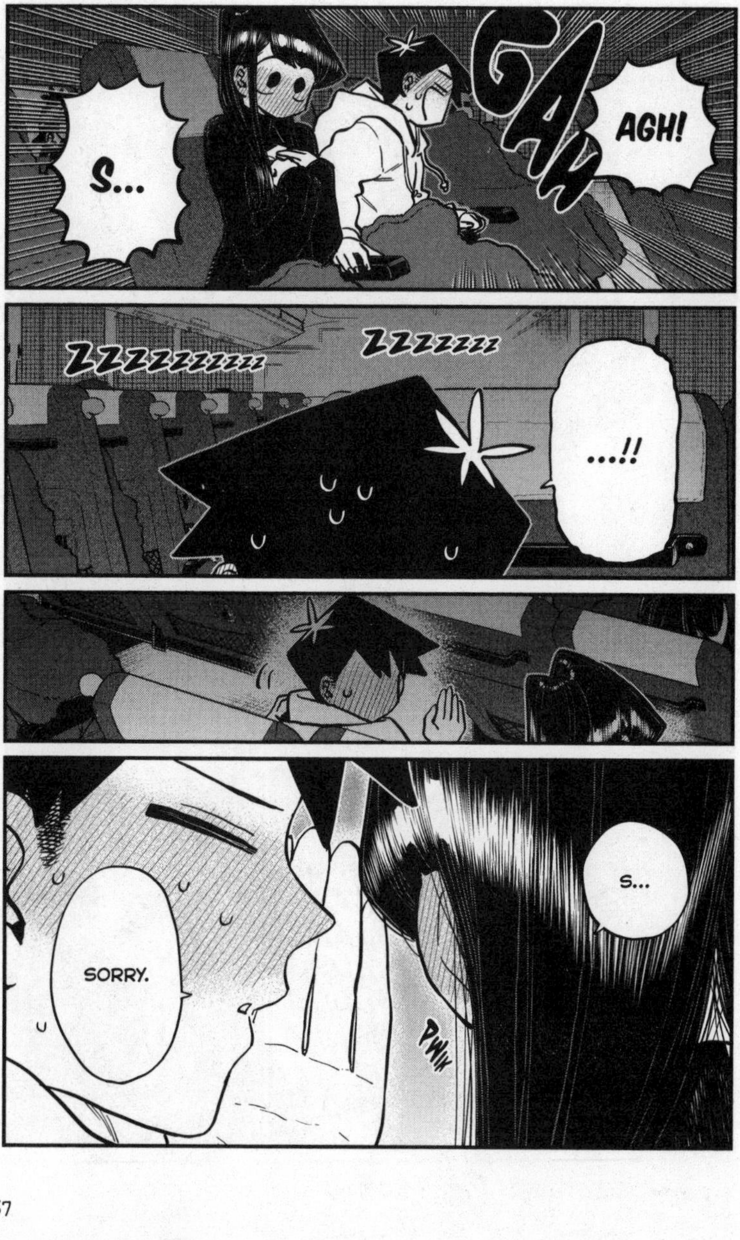
AGH!
GAW
S...
...!!
ZZZZZZZ
ZZZZZZZZZZZ
S...
PWIK
SORRY.

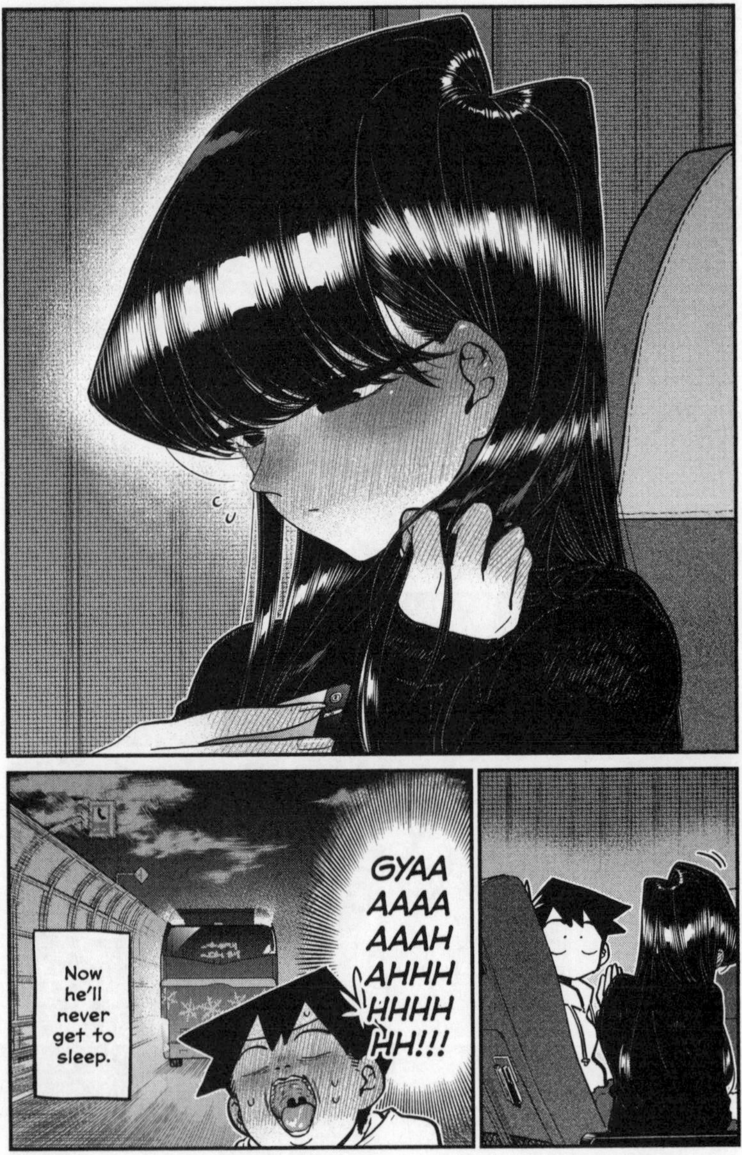
GYAA
AAAA
AAAH
AHHH
HHHH
HH!!!
Now he'll never get to sleep.

Communication 260 — The End

Komi Can't Communicate

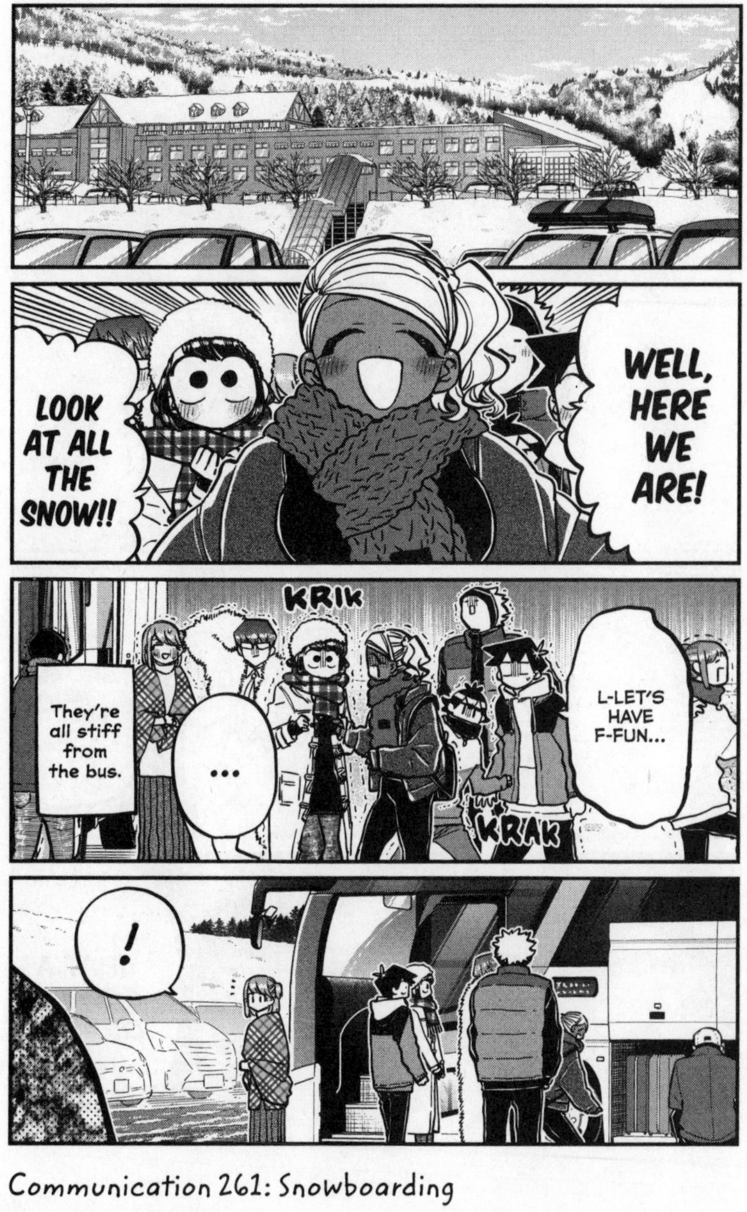
WELL, HERE WE ARE!
LOOK AT ALL THE SNOW!!
L-LET'S HAVE F-FUN...
KRIK
KRAK
...
They're all stiff from the bus.
!

Communication 261: Snowboarding

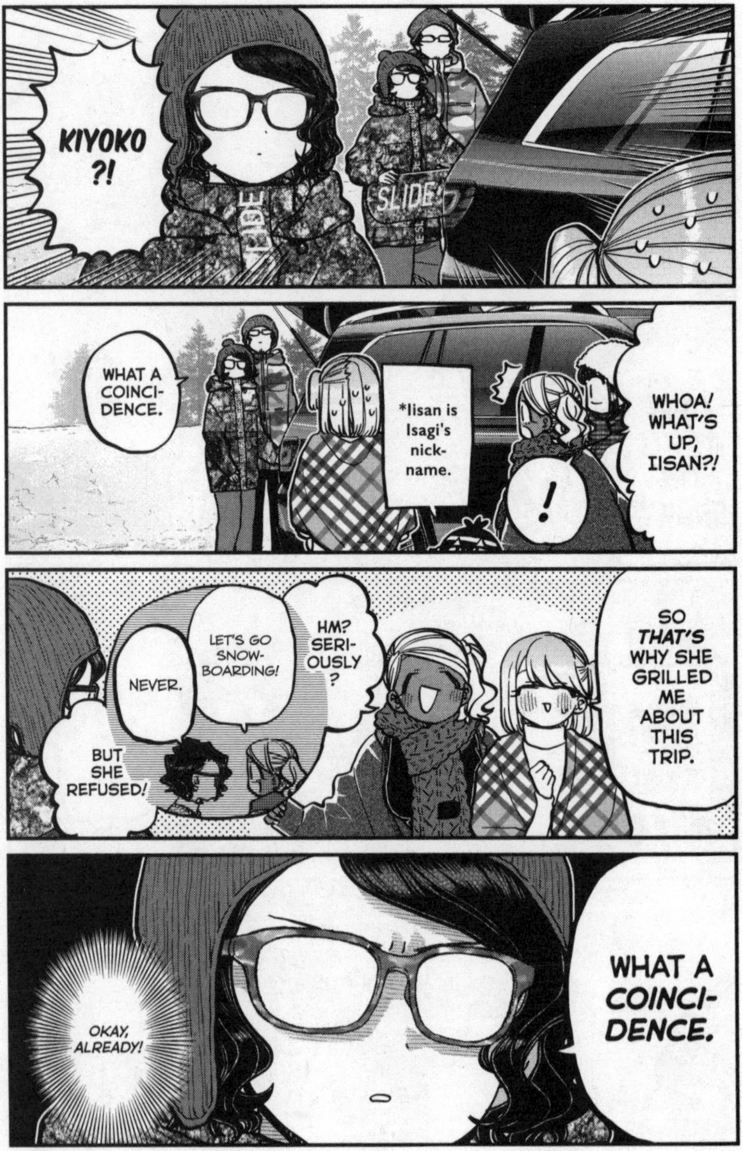
KIYOKO ?!
WHOA! WHAT'S UP, IISAN?!
!
*Iisan is Isagi's nick-name.
WHAT A COINCI-DENCE.
SO *THAT'S* WHY SHE GRILLED ME ABOUT THIS TRIP.
HM? SERI-OUSLY?
LET'S GO SNOW-BOARDING!
NEVER.
BUT SHE REFUSED!
WHAT A *COINCI-DENCE.*
OKAY, ALREADY!

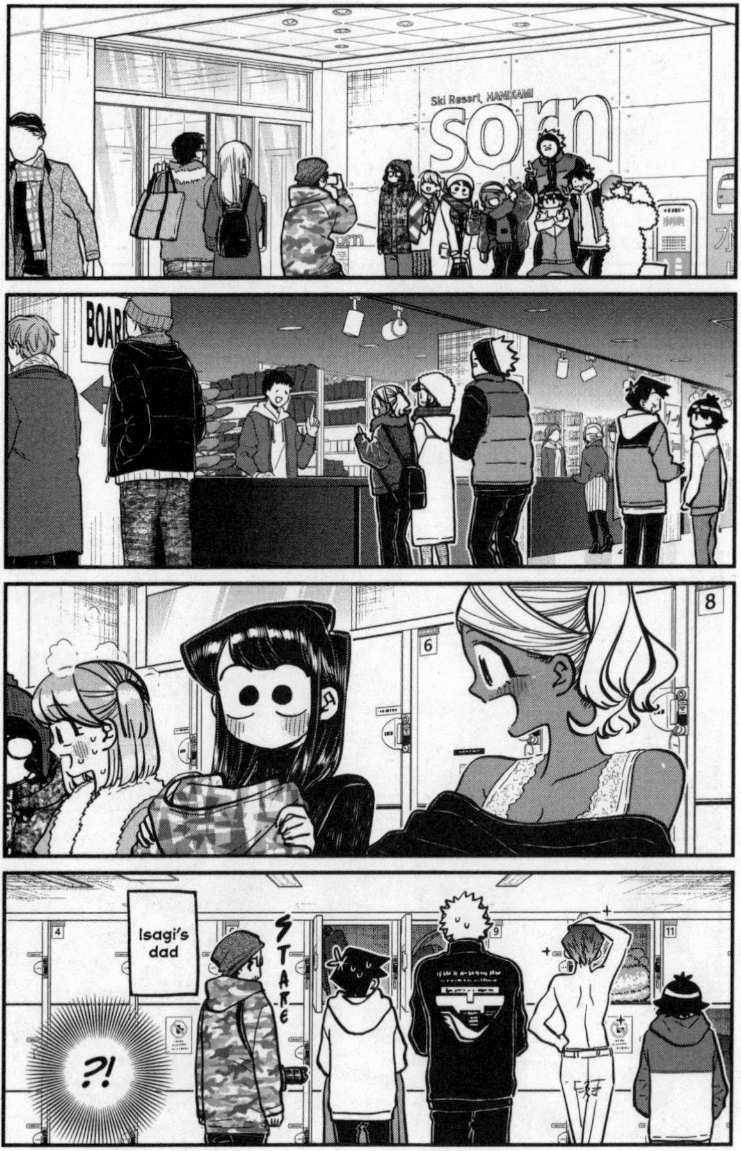

Ski Resort, HAMIKAMI
sorn
BOAR
Isagi's dad
STARE
?!

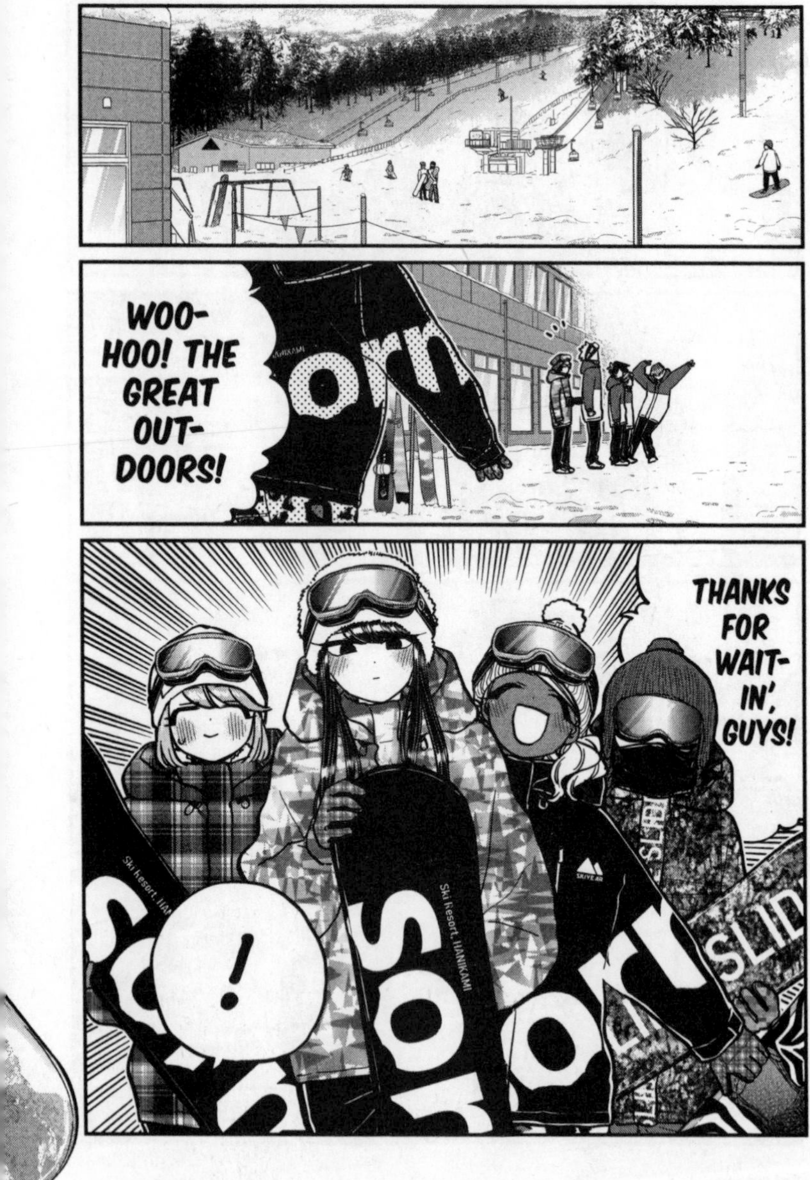
WOO-HOO! THE GREAT OUT-DOORS!
...
THANKS FOR WAIT-IN', GUYS!
!

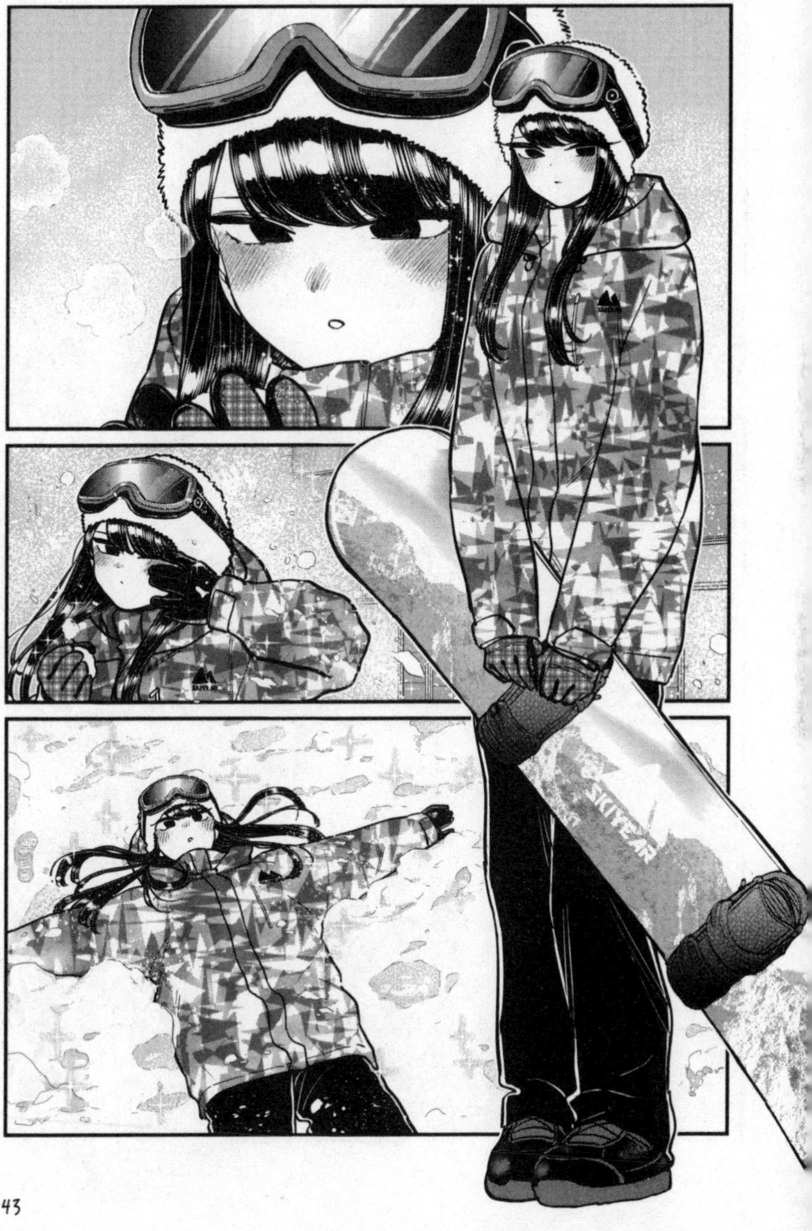
SKIYEAR

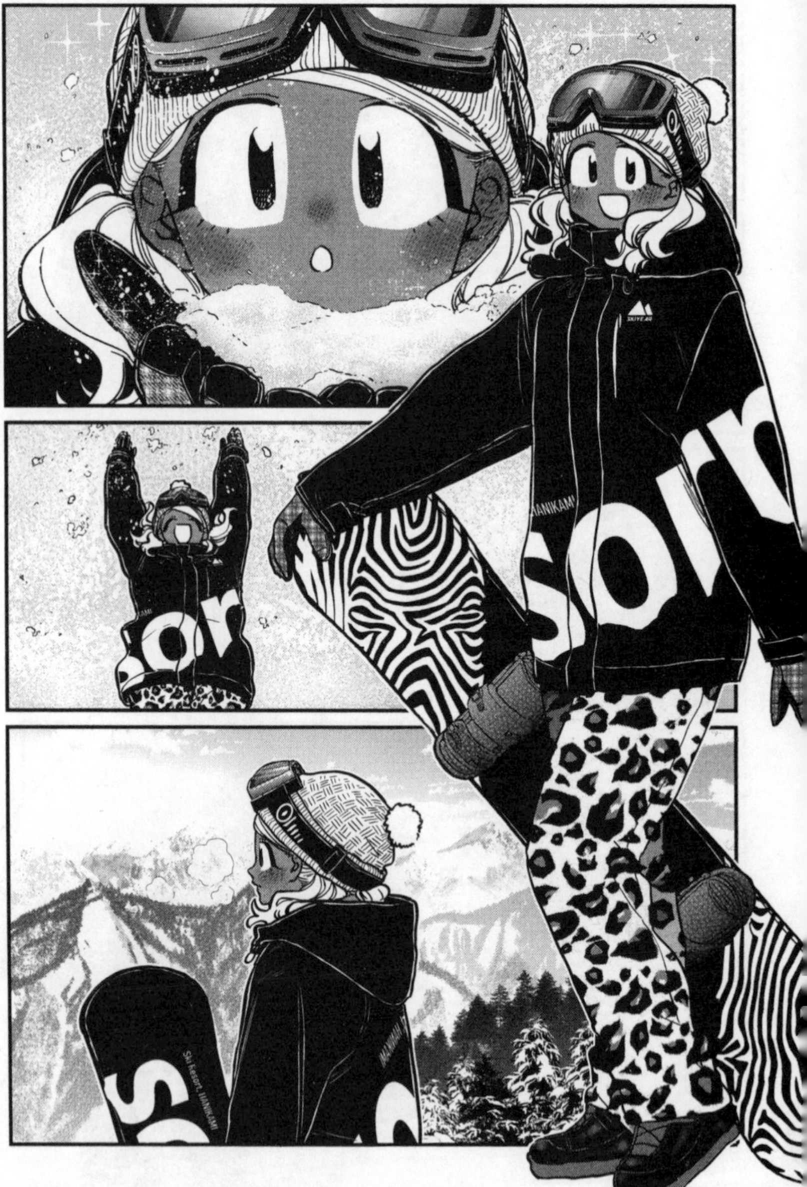

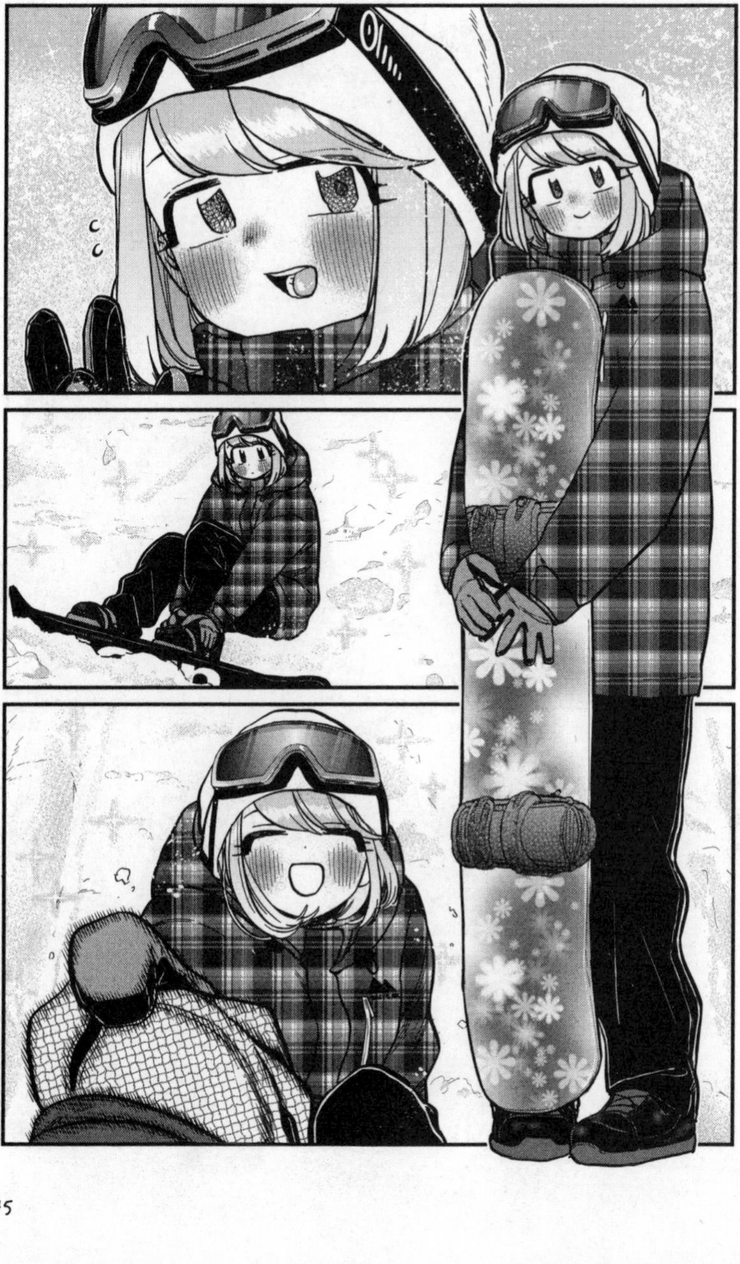

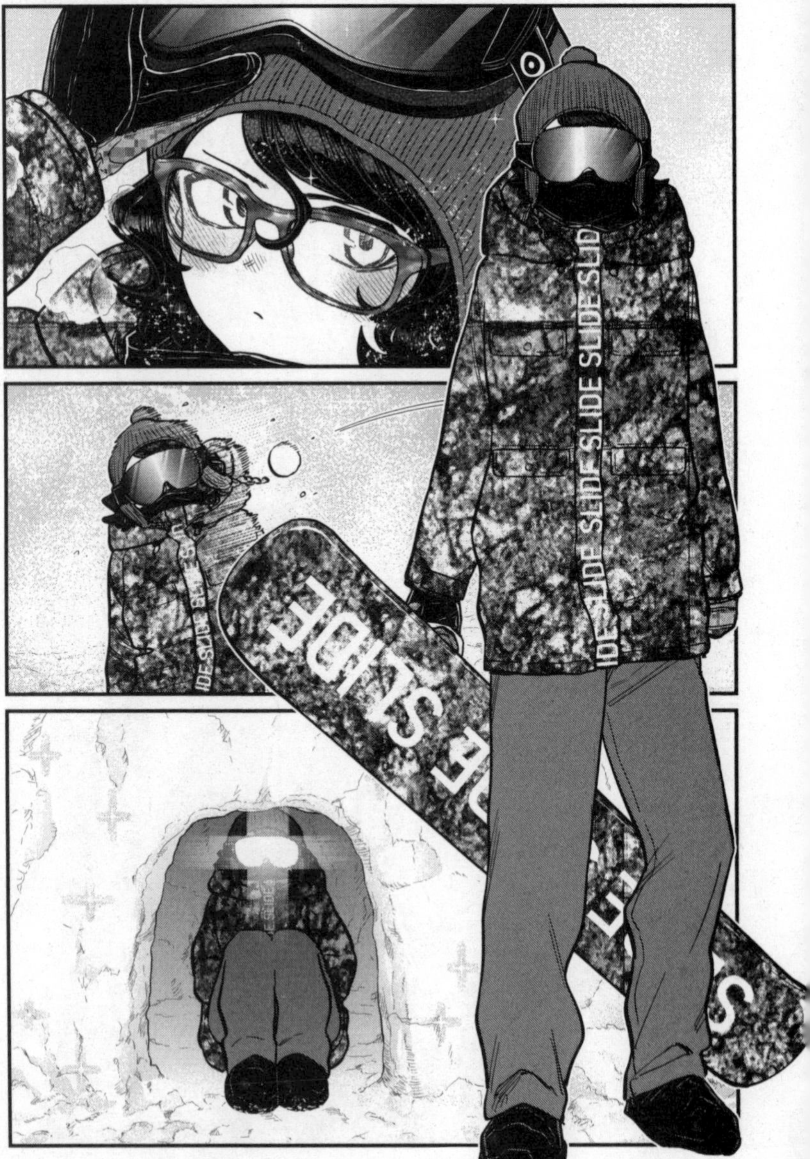
SLIDE SLIDE SLIDE

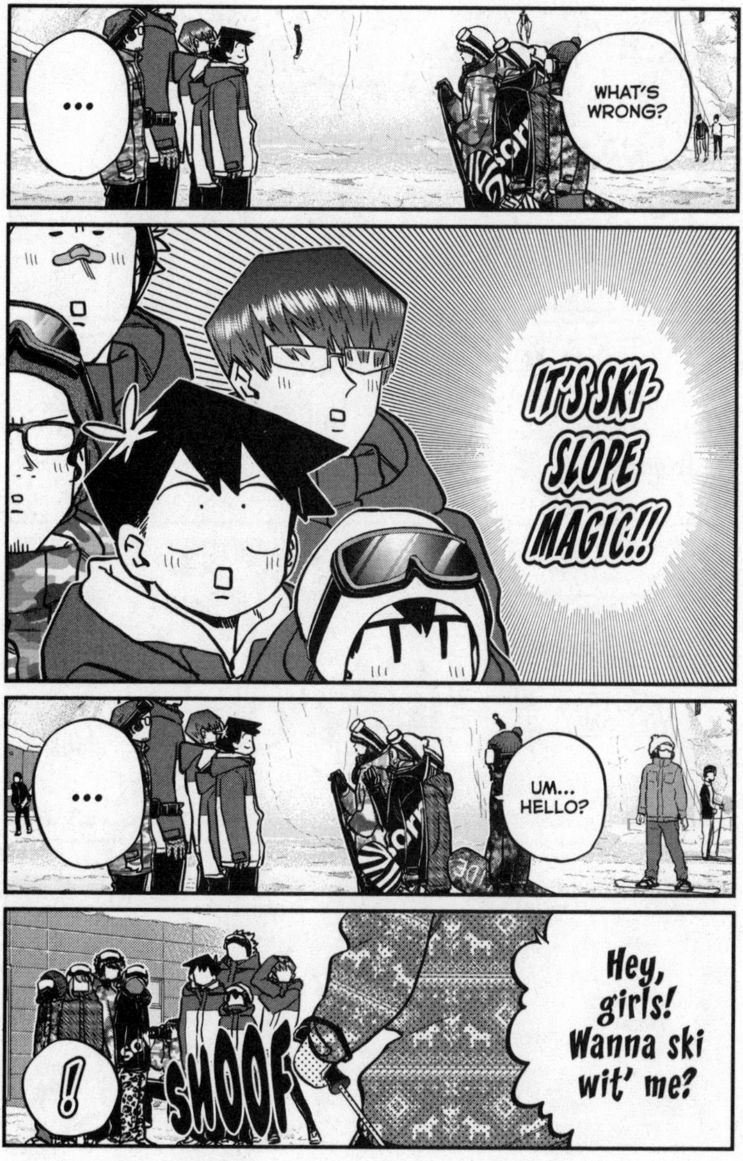
WHAT'S WRONG?
...
IT'S SKI-SLOPE MAGIC!!
UM... HELLO?
...
Hey, girls! Wanna ski wit' me?
SHOOF
!

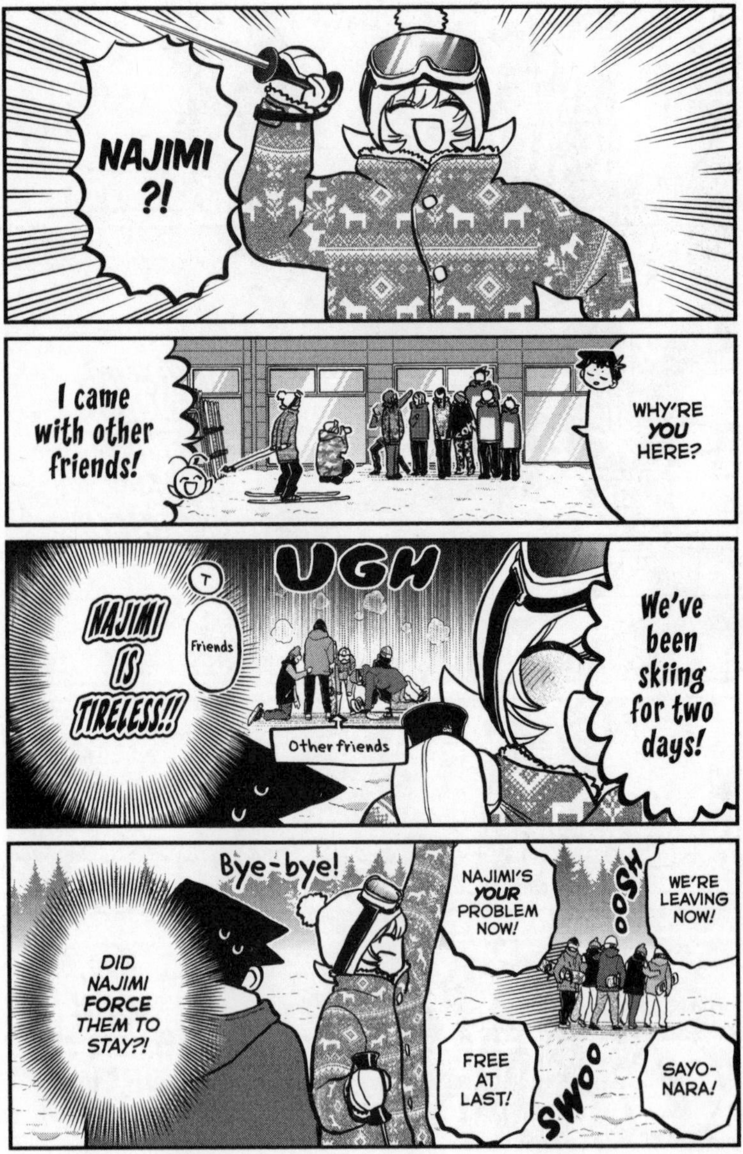
NAJIMI?!
WHY'RE YOU HERE?
I came with other friends!
We've been skiing for two days!
UGH
Friends
Other friends
NAJIMI IS TIRELESS!!
WE'RE LEAVING NOW!
OOSH
NAJIMI'S YOUR PROBLEM NOW!
SAYO-NARA!
SWOO
FREE AT LAST!
Bye-bye!
DID NAJIMI FORCE THEM TO STAY?!

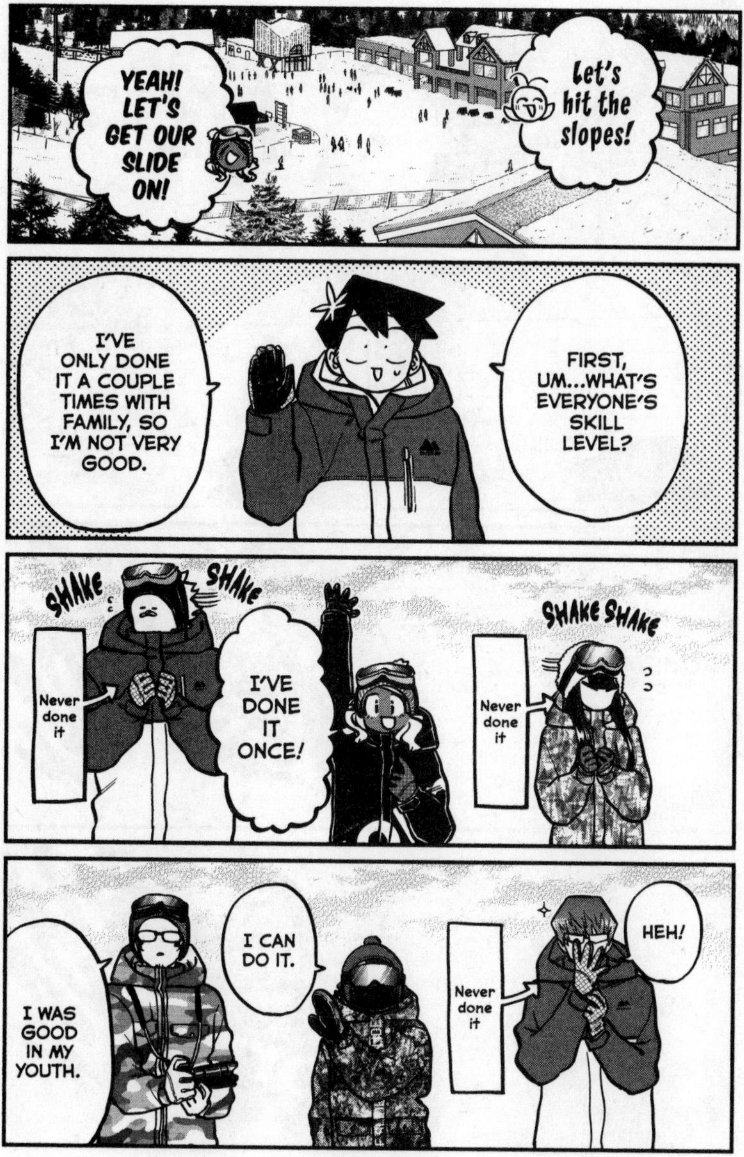
Let's hit the slopes!
YEAH! LET'S GET OUR SLIDE ON!
FIRST, UM...WHAT'S EVERYONE'S SKILL LEVEL?
I'VE ONLY DONE IT A COUPLE TIMES WITH FAMILY, SO I'M NOT VERY GOOD.
SHAKE SHAKE
Never done it
I'VE DONE IT ONCE!
SHAKE
SHAKE
Never done it
HEH!
Never done it
I CAN DO IT.
I WAS GOOD IN MY YOUTH.

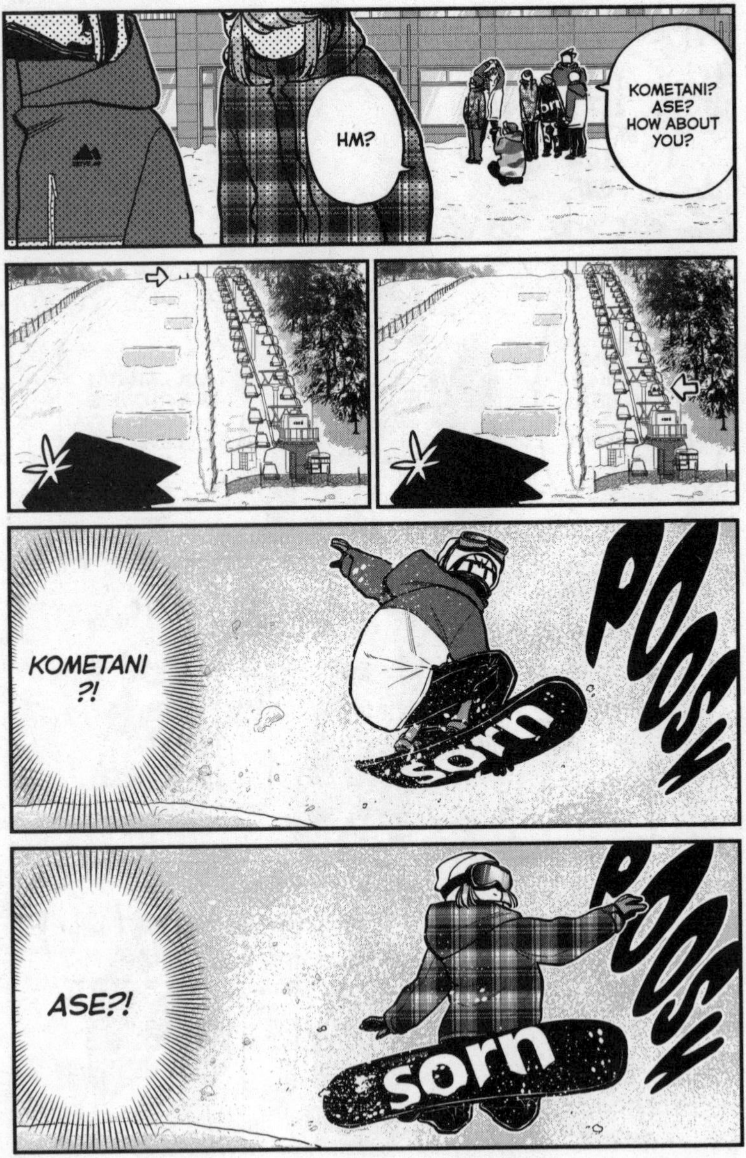
KOMETANI? ASE? HOW ABOUT YOU?
HM?
POOSH
KOMETANI?!
POOSH
ASE?!

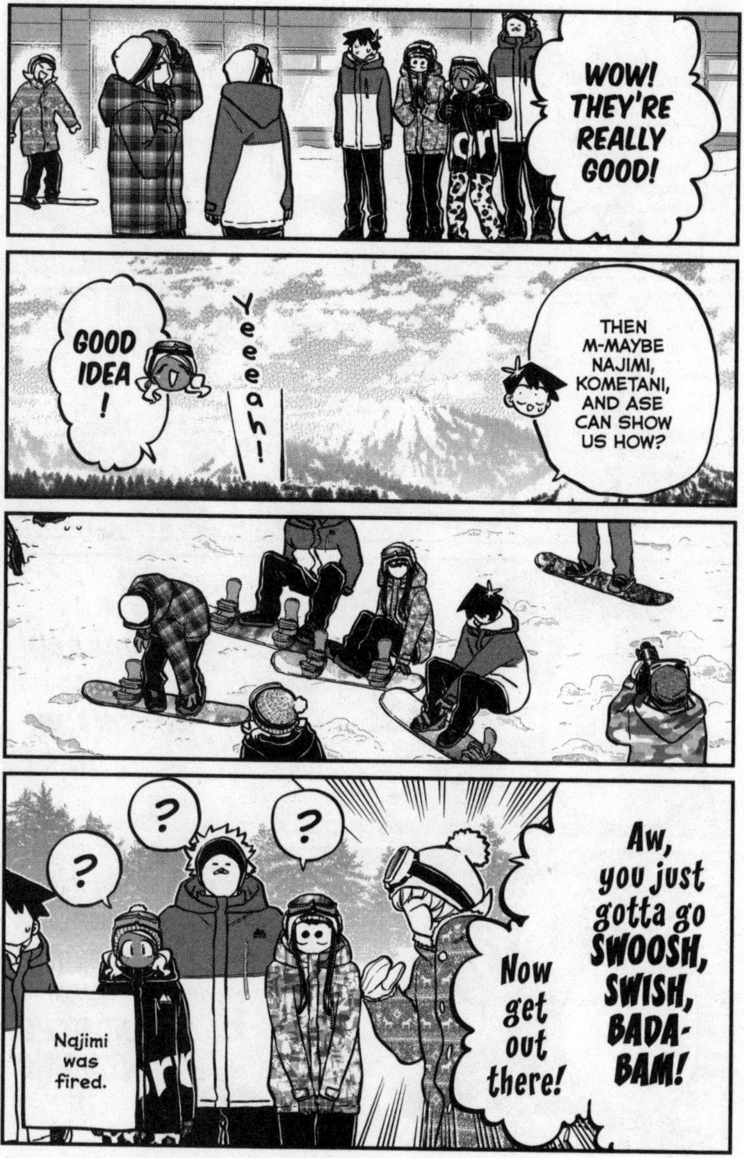
WOW! THEY'RE REALLY GOOD!
THEN M-MAYBE NAJIMI, KOMETANI, AND ASE CAN SHOW US HOW?
Yeeeah!
GOOD IDEA!
Aw, you just gotta go SWOOSH, SWISH, BADA-BAM!
Now get out there!
?
?
?
Najimi was fired.

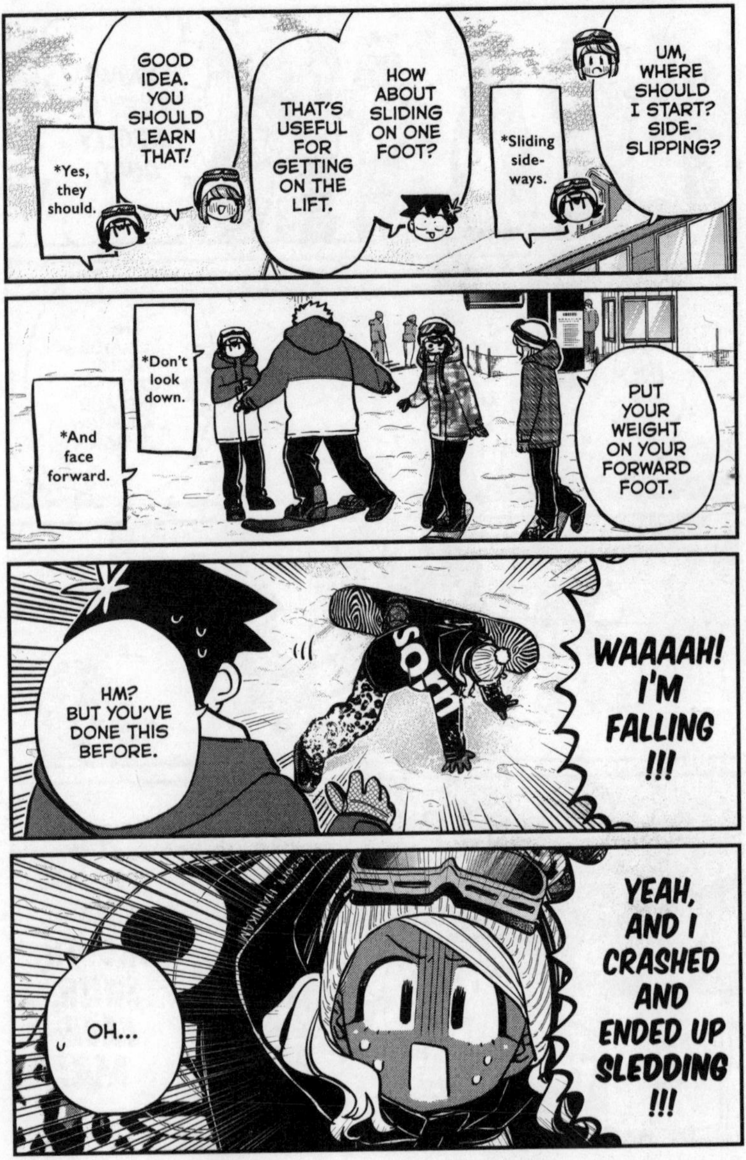
UM, WHERE SHOULD I START? SIDE-SLIPPING?
*Sliding sideways.
HOW ABOUT SLIDING ON ONE FOOT?
THAT'S USEFUL FOR GETTING ON THE LIFT.
GOOD IDEA. YOU SHOULD LEARN THAT!
*Yes, they should.
PUT YOUR WEIGHT ON YOUR FORWARD FOOT.
*Don't look down.
*And face forward.
WAAAAH! I'M FALLING!!!
HM? BUT YOU'VE DONE THIS BEFORE.
YEAH, AND I CRASHED AND ENDED UP SLEDDING!!!
OH...

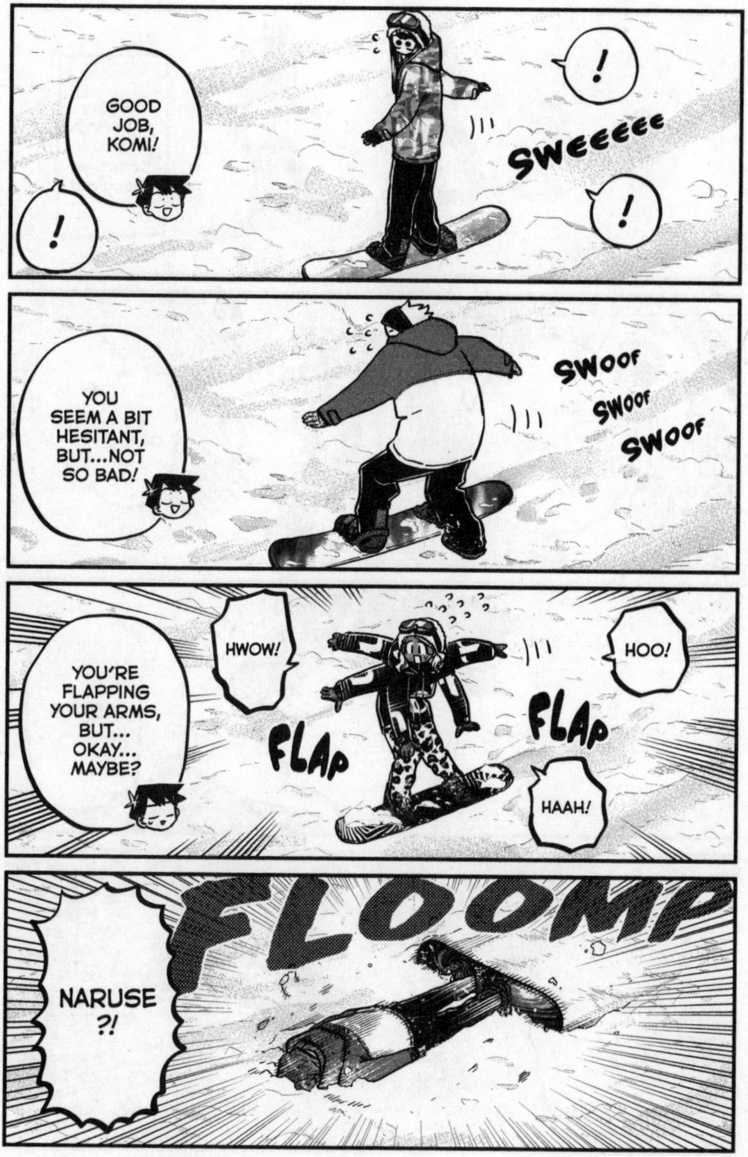

!
SWEEEEE
!
GOOD JOB, KOMI!
!
SWOOF SWOOF SWOOF
YOU SEEM A BIT HESITANT, BUT...NOT SO BAD!
HOO!
FLAP
HAAH!
HWOW!
FLAP
YOU'RE FLAPPING YOUR ARMS, BUT... OKAY... MAYBE?
FLOOMP
NARUSE ?!

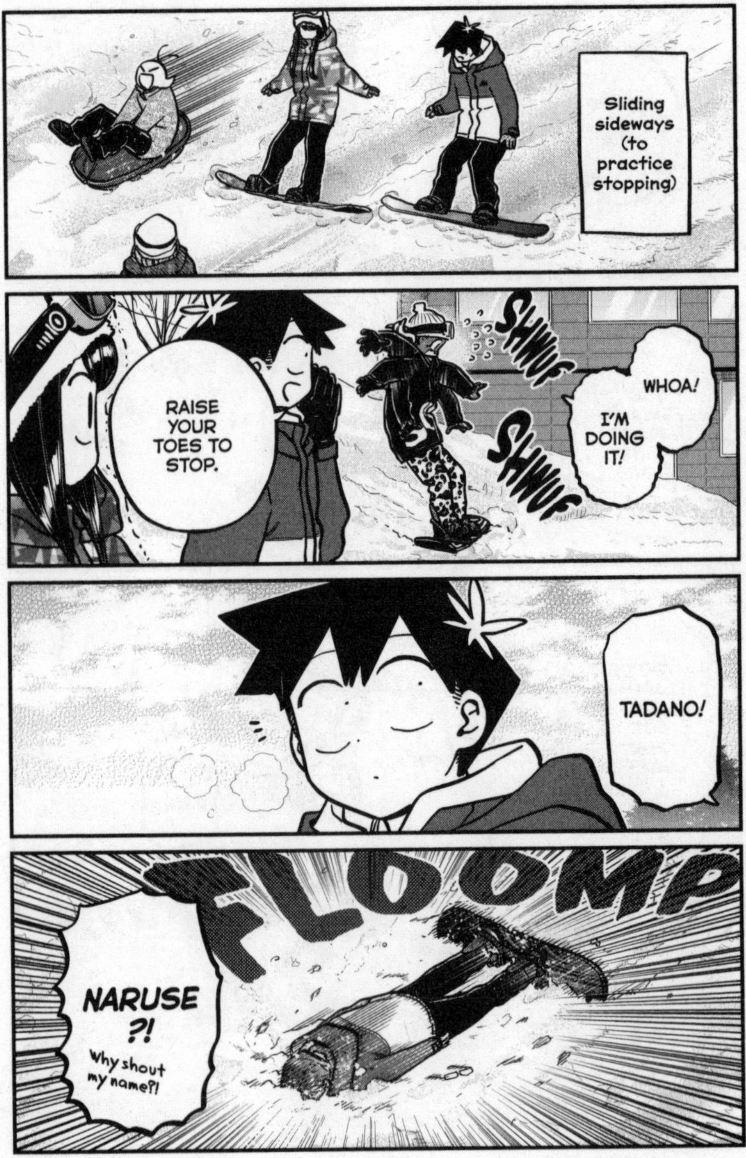
Sliding sideways (to practice stopping)
WHOA!
I'M DOING IT!
SHWUF
SHWUF
SHWUF
RAISE YOUR TOES TO STOP.
TADANO!
FLOOMP
NARUSE ?!
Why shout my name?!

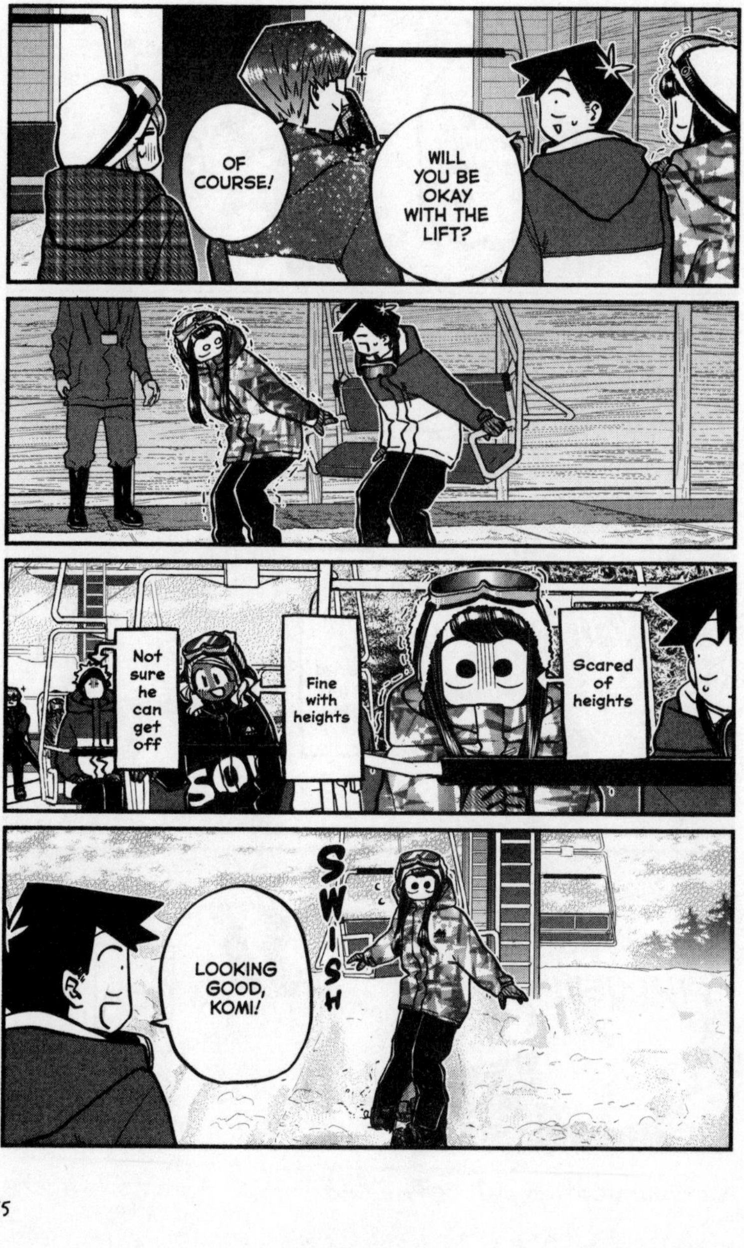
WILL YOU BE OKAY WITH THE LIFT?
OF COURSE!
Scared of heights
Fine with heights
Not sure he can get off
SWISH
LOOKING GOOD, KOMI!

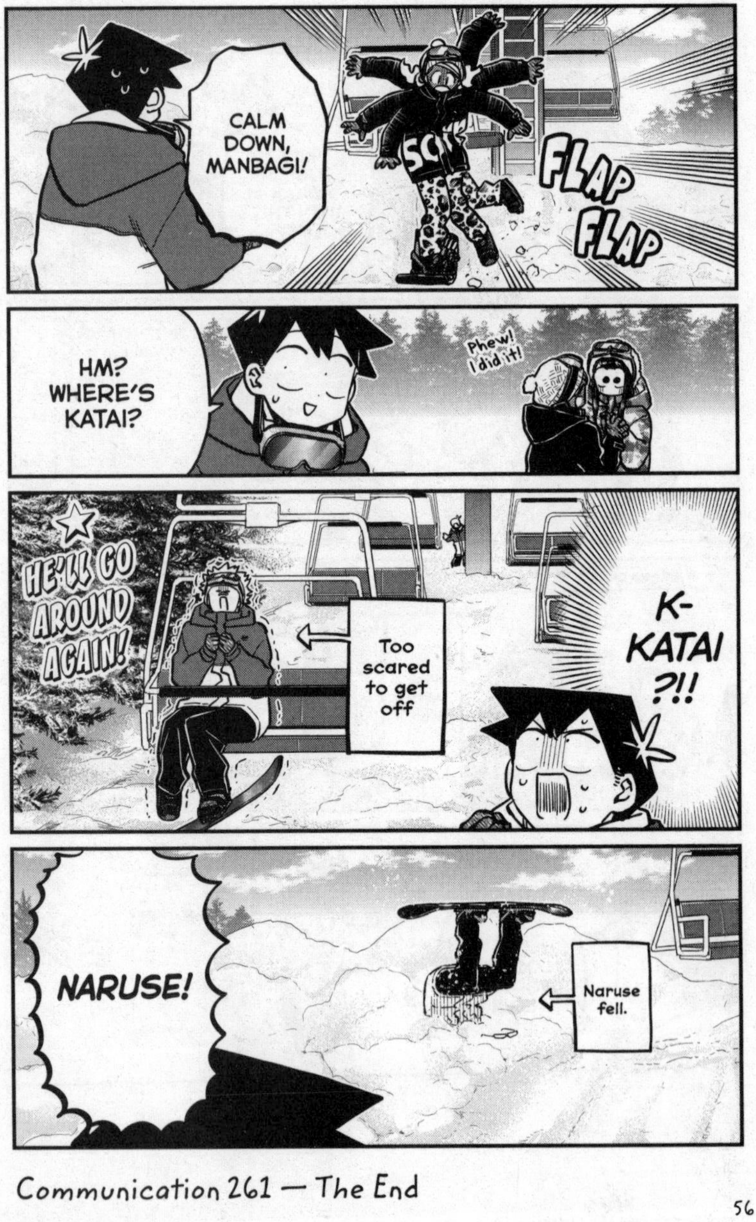
FLAP FLAP
CALM DOWN, MANBAGI!
Phew! I did it!
HM? WHERE'S KATAI?
K-KATAI?!!
Too scared to get off
HE'LL GO AROUND AGAIN!
Naruse fell.
NARUSE!

Communication 261 — The End

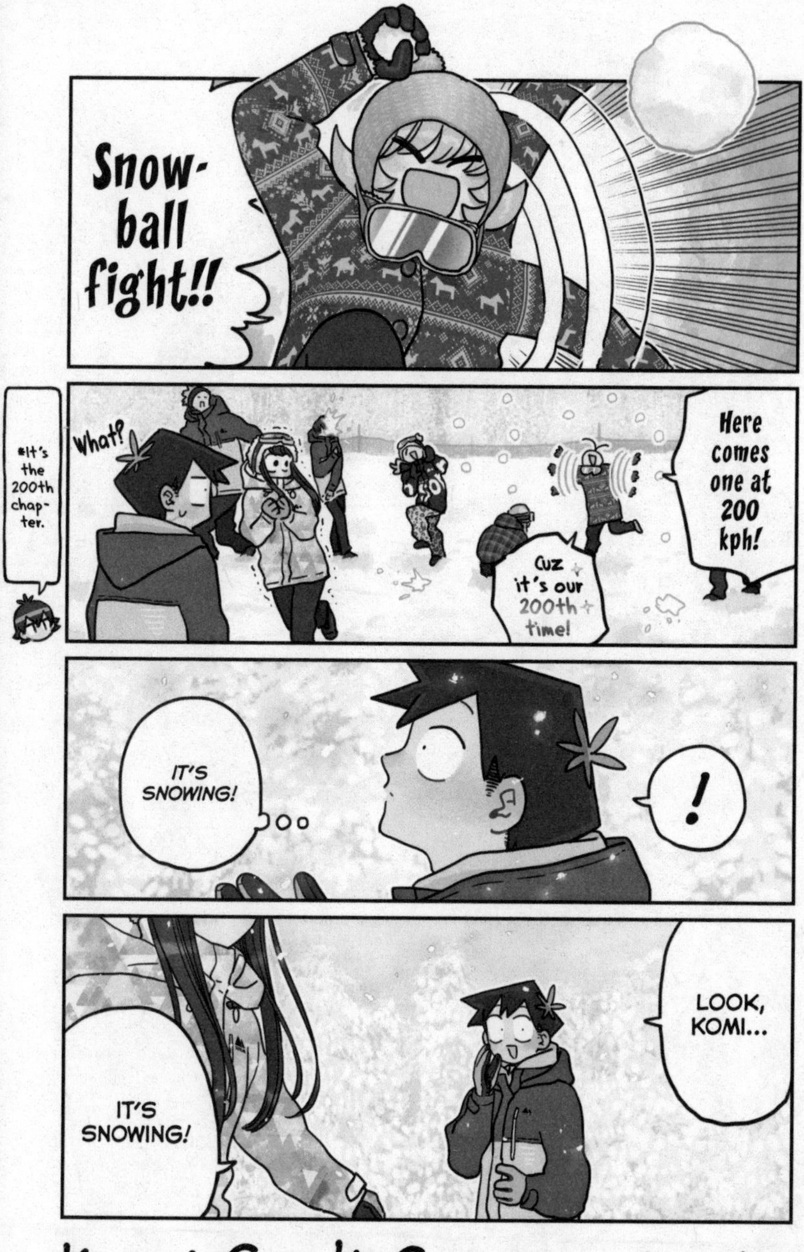
Snow-ball fight!!
Here comes one at 200 kph!
Cuz it's our 200th time!
What?
*It's the 200th chapter.
!
IT'S SNOWING!
LOOK, KOMI...
IT'S SNOWING!

Komi Can't Communicate

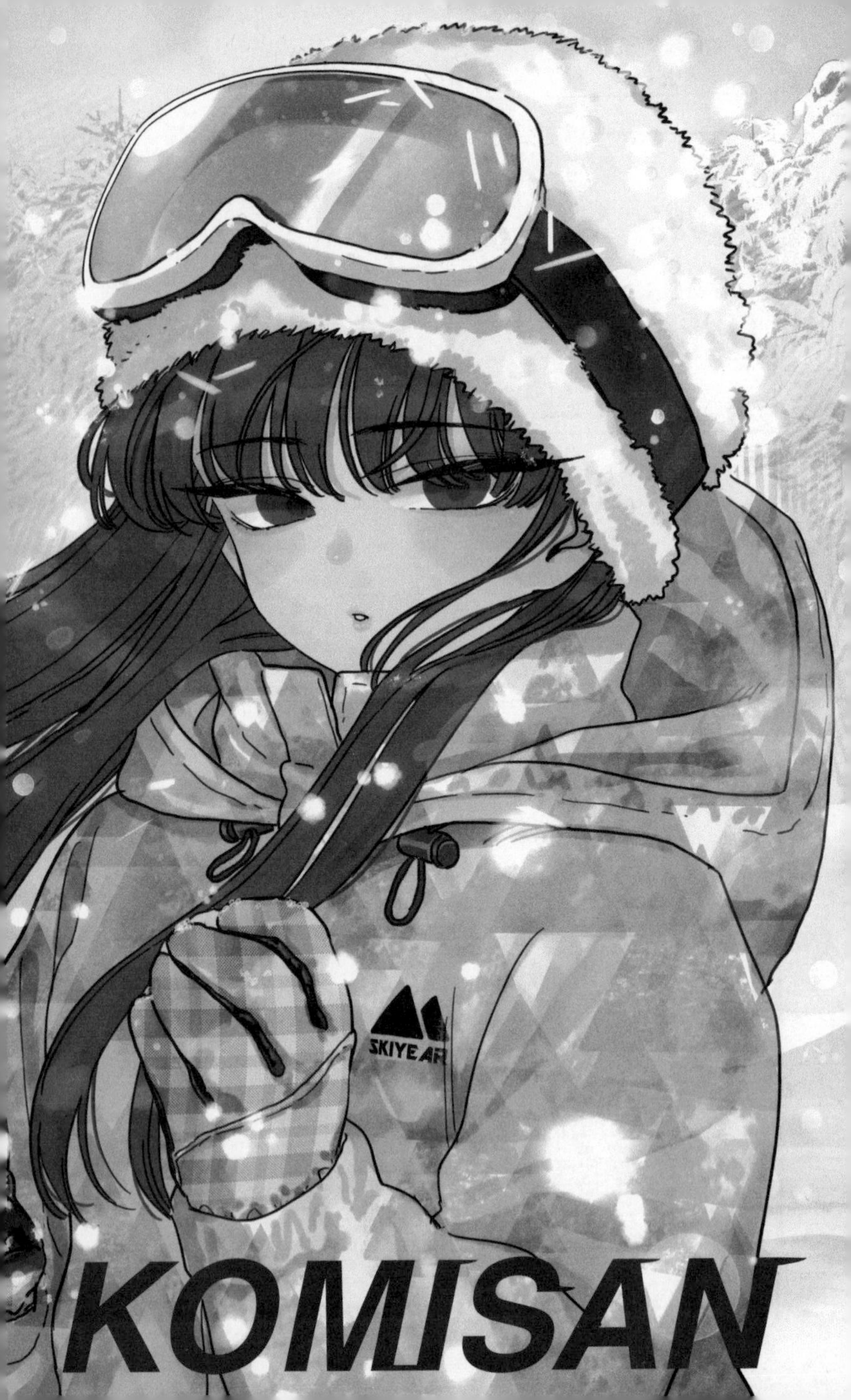
SKIYEAR
KOMISAN

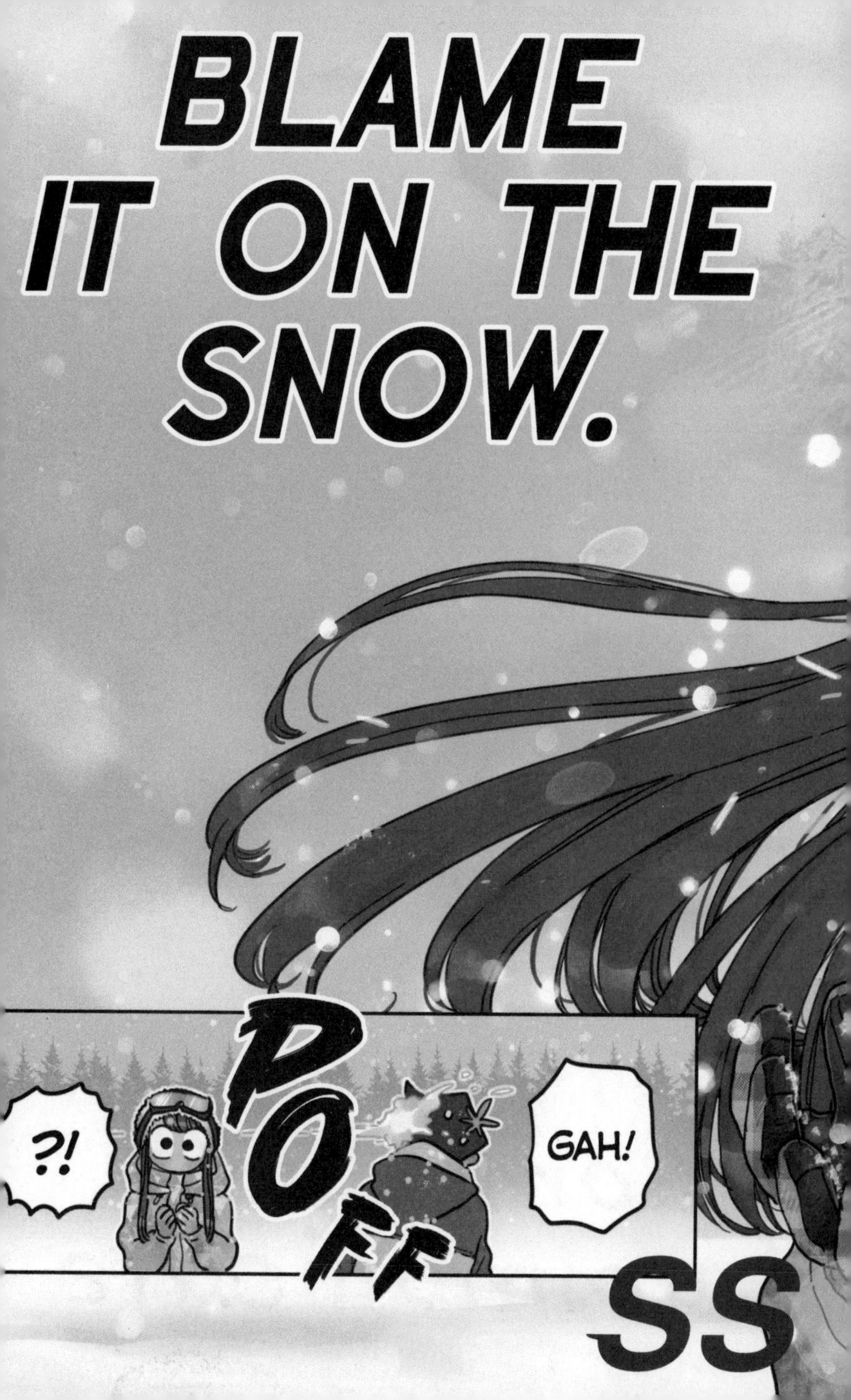
BLAME IT ON THE SNOW.
GAH!
POFF
?!
SS

Komi Can't
Communicate

Komi Can't Communicate

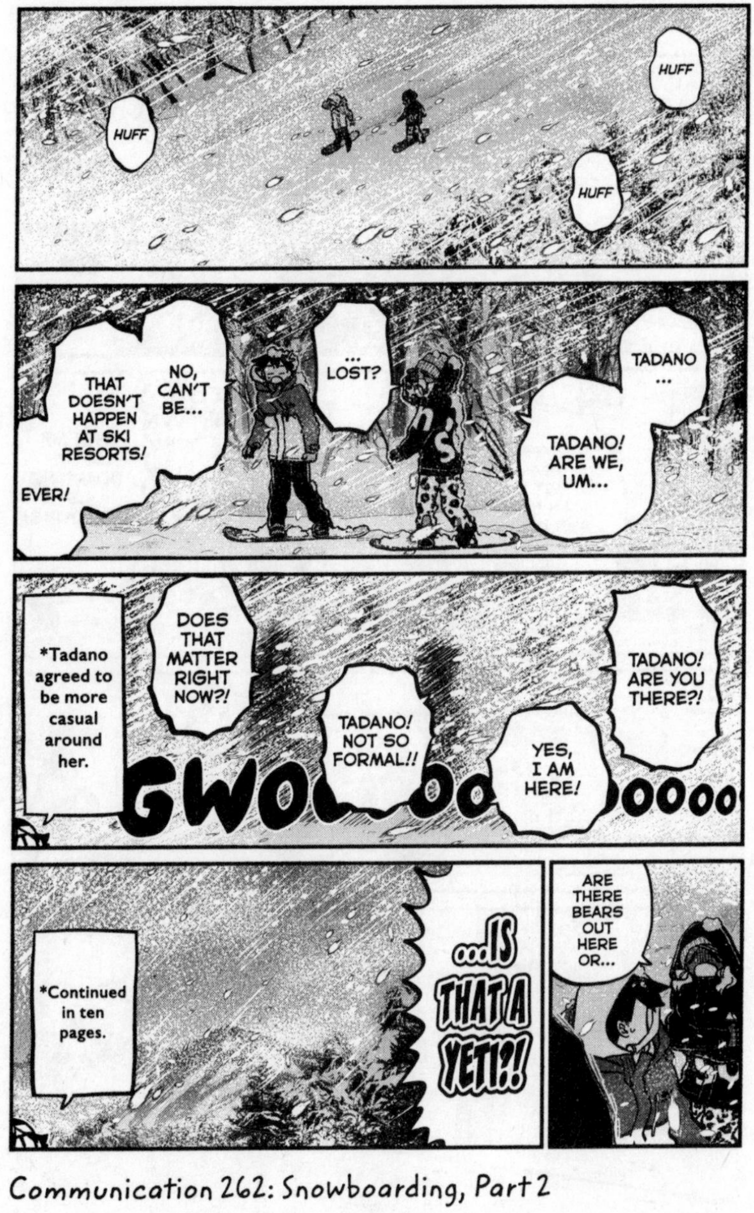

HUFF
HUFF
HUFF
TADANO ...
TADANO! ARE WE, UM...
... LOST?
NO, CAN'T BE...
THAT DOESN'T HAPPEN AT SKI RESORTS!
EVER!
TADANO! ARE YOU THERE?!
YES, I AM HERE!
TADANO! NOT SO FORMAL!!
DOES THAT MATTER RIGHT NOW?!
GWOO OO OOOOO
*Tadano agreed to be more casual around her.
ARE THERE BEARS OUT HERE OR...
...IS THAT A YETI?!
*Continued in ten pages.

Communication 262: Snowboarding, Part 2

Meal Break

WHEW! I'M EXHAUST-ED!
AND HUNGRY!
BUT MY SNOW-BOARDING IS IMPROVING!
!
NODNOD
YES— YEAH, I BET YOU CAN DO THE BUNNY SLOPE WITHOUT FALLING NOW.
!
NODNOD

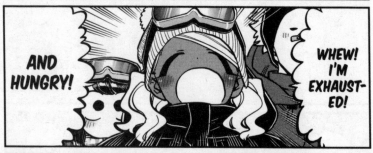

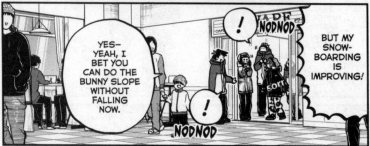

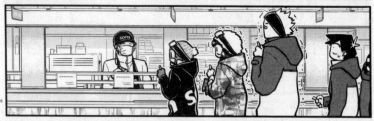

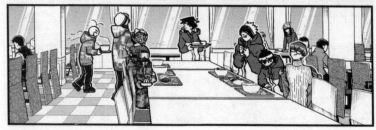

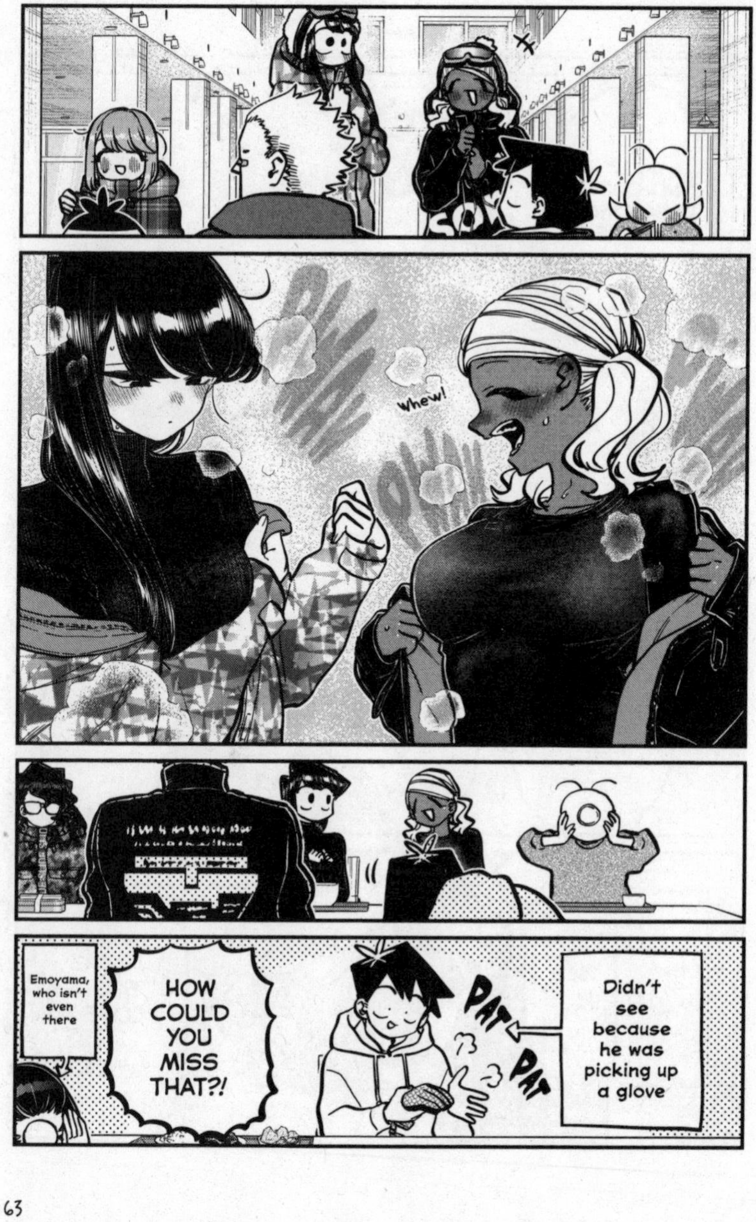
Whew!
Didn't see because he was picking up a glove
PAT
PAT
HOW COULD YOU MISS THAT?!
Emoyama, who isn't even there

Intervention

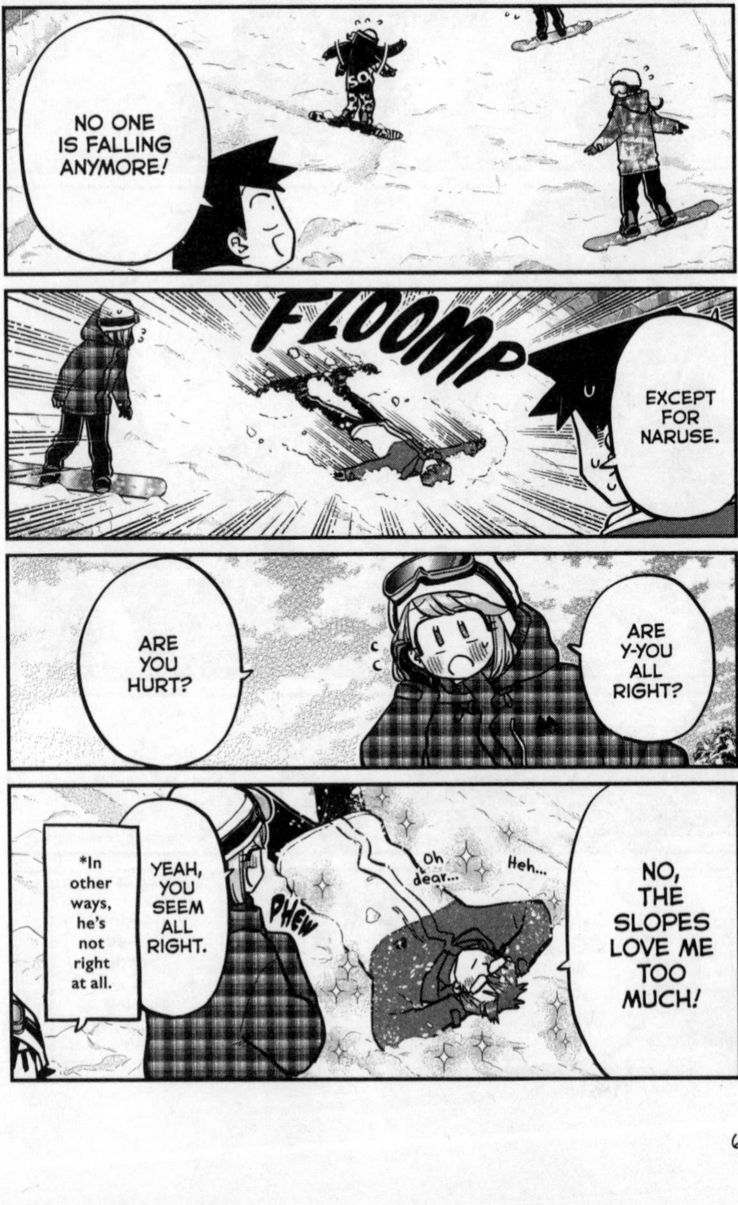
NO ONE IS FALLING ANYMORE!
EXCEPT FOR NARUSE.
FLOOMP
ARE Y-YOU ALL RIGHT?
ARE YOU HURT?
NO, THE SLOPES LOVE ME TOO MUCH!
Heh...
Oh dear...
PHEW
YEAH, YOU SEEM ALL RIGHT.
*In other ways, he's not right at all.

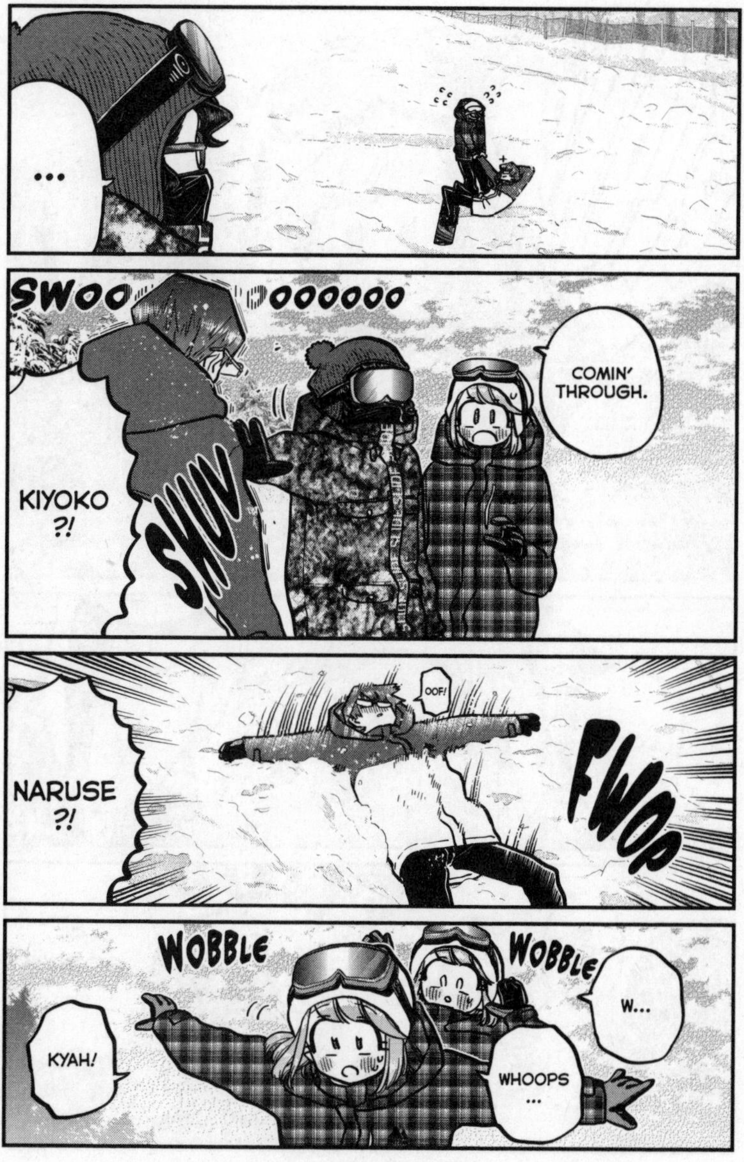
...
COMIN' THROUGH.
SWOO OOOOOO
SHUV
KIYOKO ?!
FWOP
OOF!
NARUSE ?!
W...
WOBBLE WOBBLE
WHOOPS ...
KYAH!

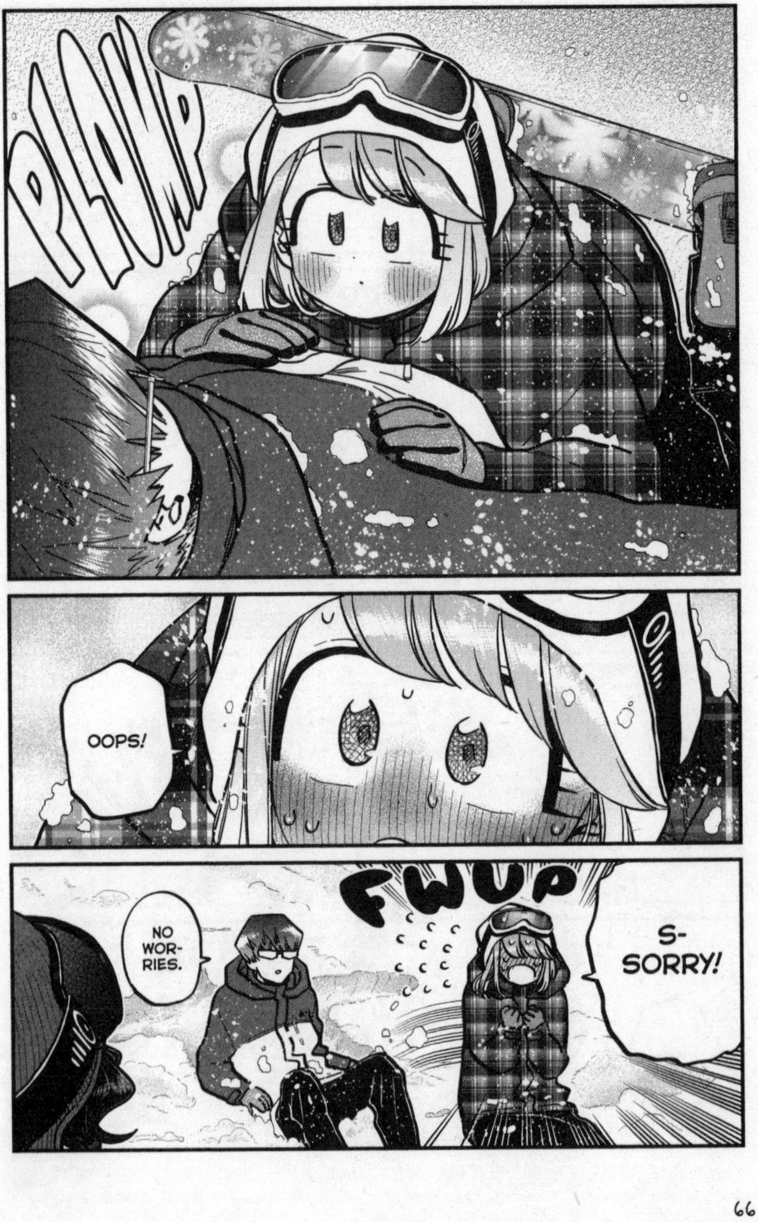
PLOMP
OOPS!
FWUP
S-SORRY!
NO WORRIES.

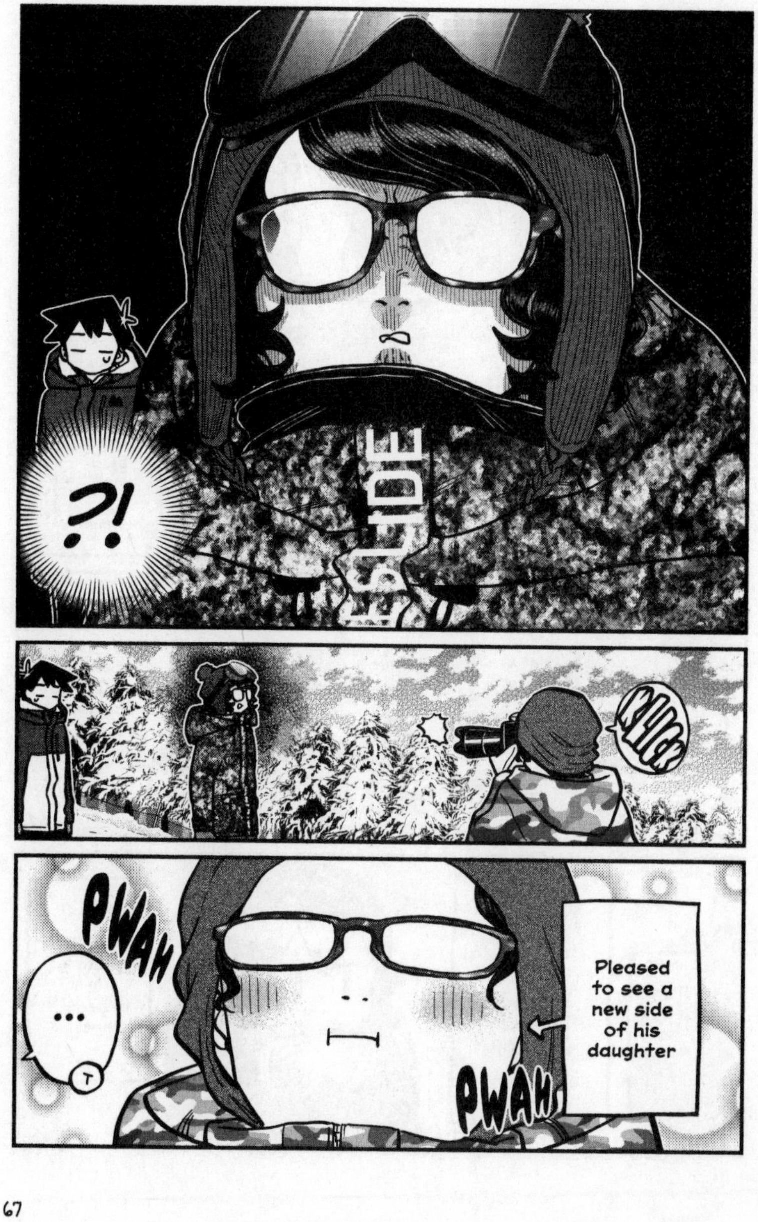
?!
SLIDE
KLICK
Pleased to see a new side of his daughter
PWAH
PWAH
...
T

The Usual

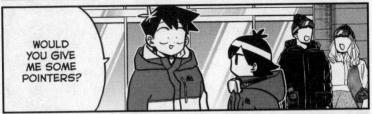

WOULD YOU GIVE ME SOME POINTERS?
*Twist your body and rest on your back foot.
*Keep your head up.
*Yes, like that.
YOU'RE A GOOD TEACHER, KOMETANI.
*But not as good as you.
HUH? ME?
*I couldn't put myself in a beginner's shoes...
*...but everyone improved thanks to your help.
*Except for Naruse.

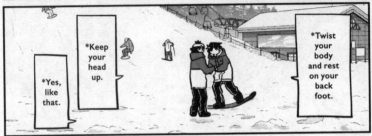

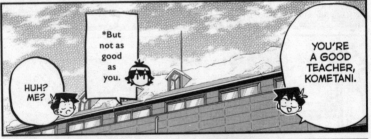

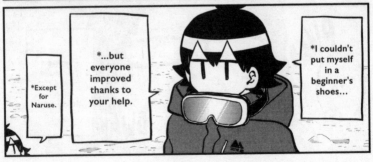

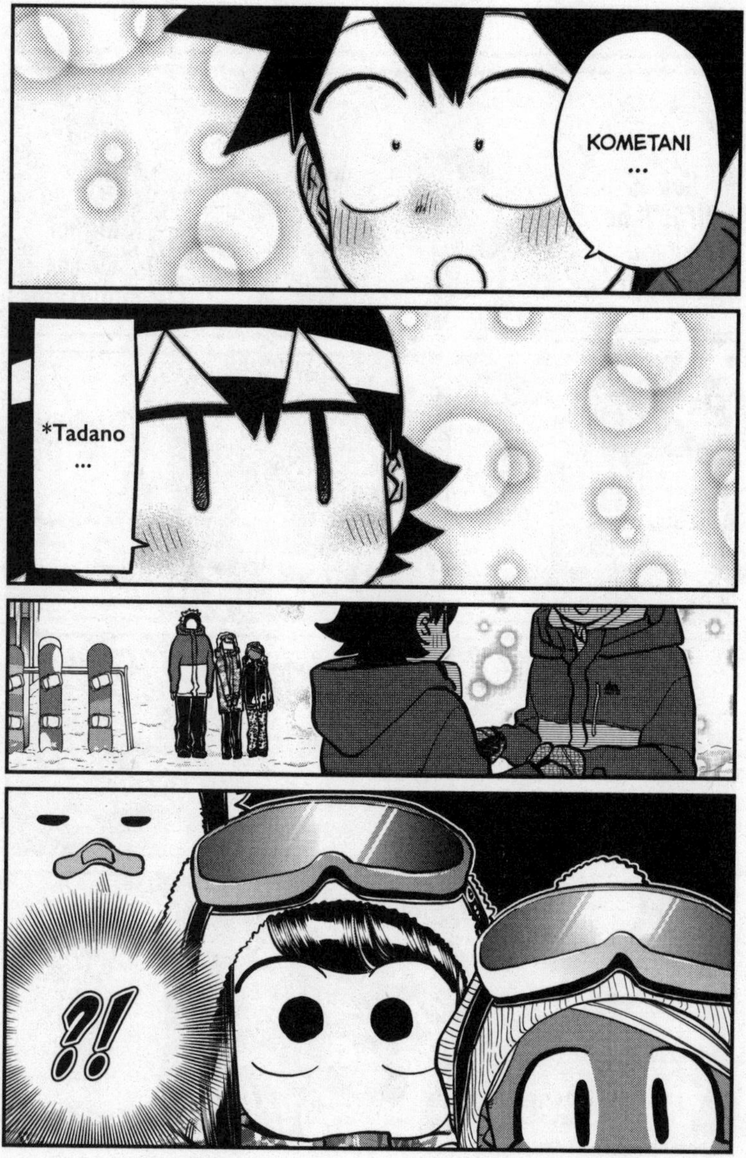
KOMETANI
...
*Tadano
...
?!

Lost?

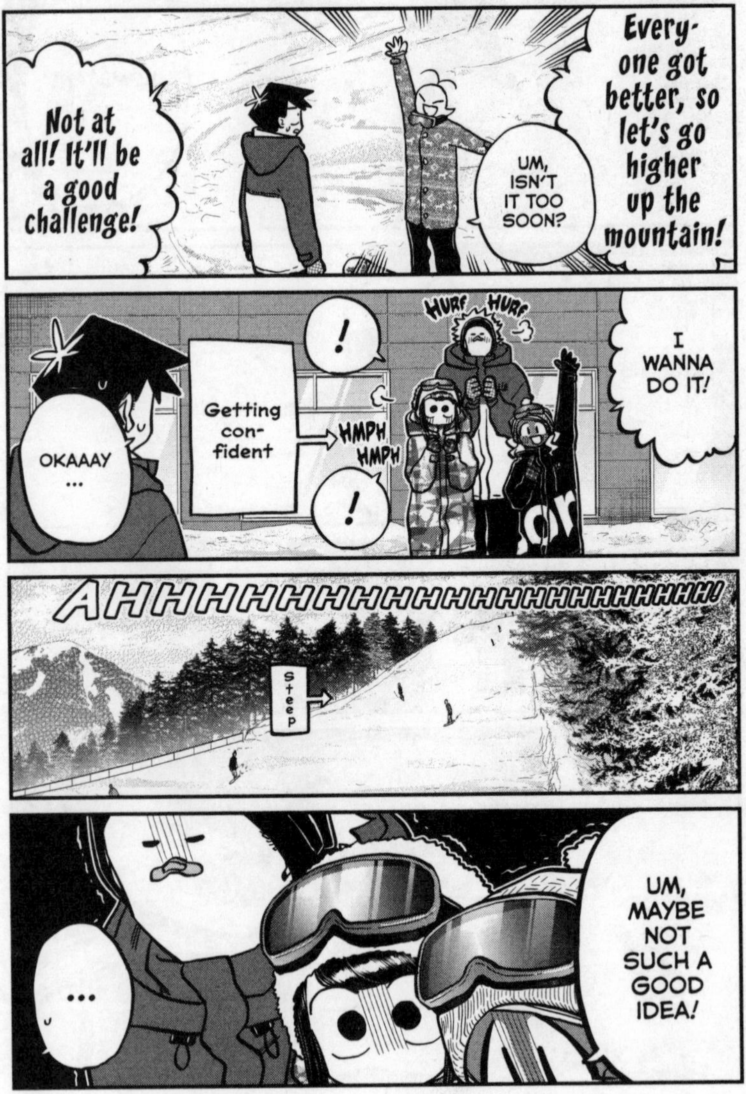
Every-one got better, so let's go higher up the mountain!
UM, ISN'T IT TOO SOON?
Not at all! It'll be a good challenge!
I WANNA DO IT!
HURF HURF
!
Getting con-fident
HMPH HMPH
!
OKAAAY ...
AHHHHHHHHHHHHHHHHHHHHHHHHH!
Steep
UM, MAYBE NOT SUCH A GOOD IDEA!
...

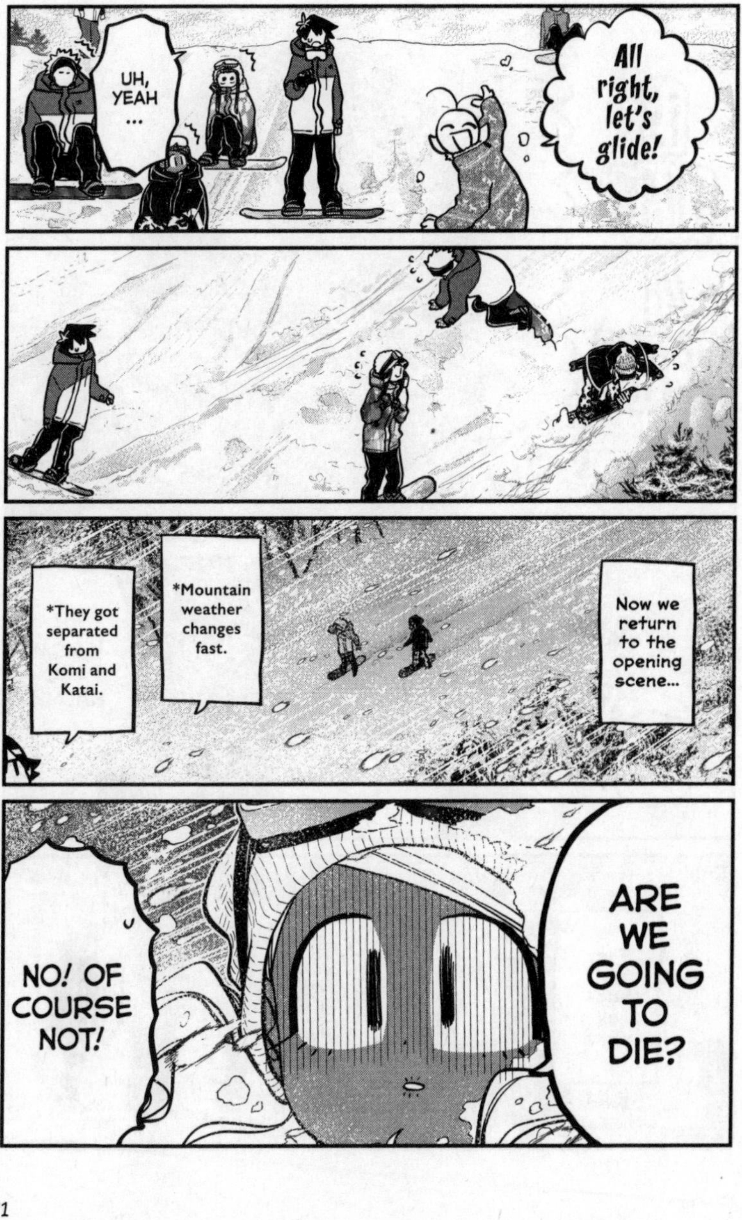
All right, let's glide!
UH, YEAH ...
Now we return to the opening scene...
*Mountain weather changes fast.
*They got separated from Komi and Katai.
ARE WE GOING TO DIE?
NO! OF COURSE NOT!

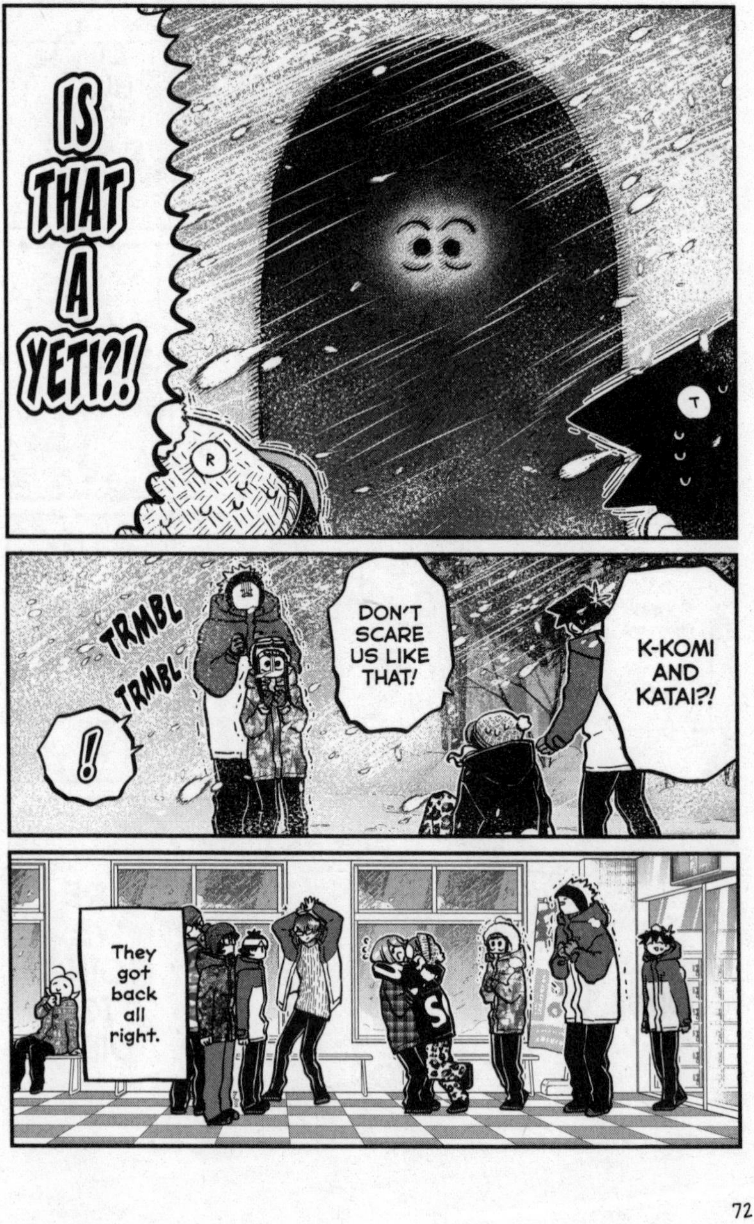
IS THAT A YETI?!
K-KOMI AND KATAI?!
DON'T SCARE US LIKE THAT!
TRMBL
TRMBL
!
They got back all right.

Returning Home

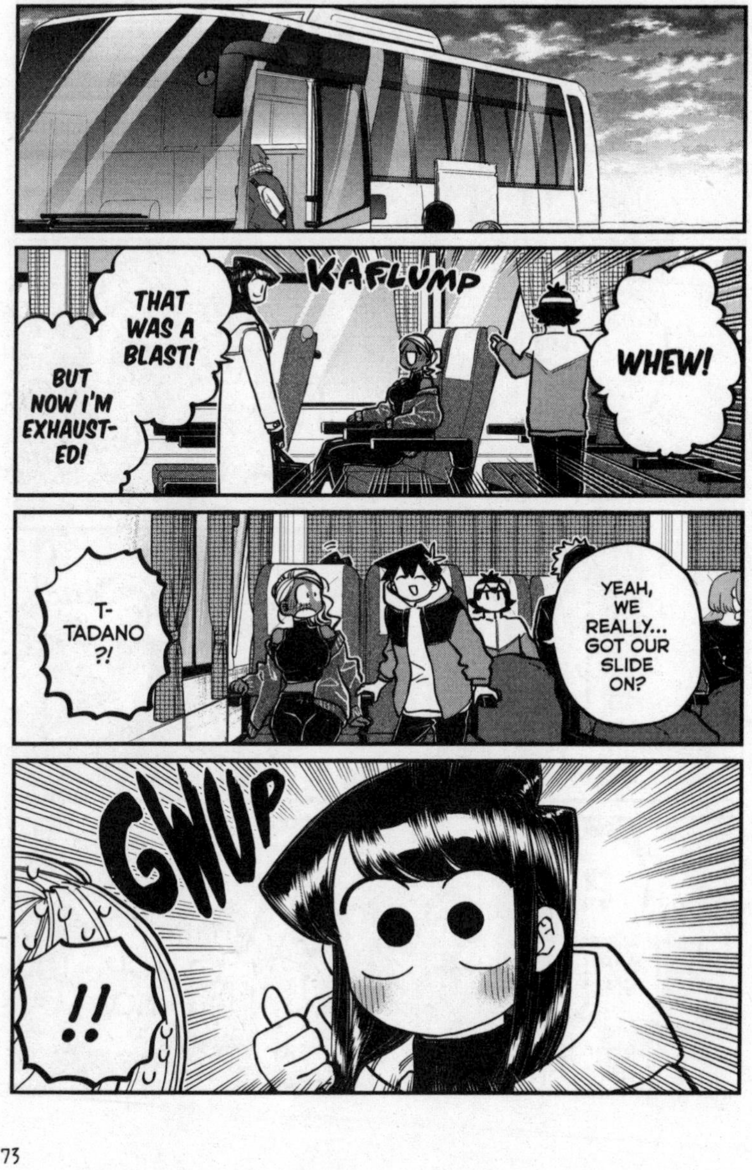

WHEW!
KAFLUMP
THAT WAS A BLAST!
BUT NOW I'M EXHAUST-ED!
YEAH, WE REALLY... GOT OUR SLIDE ON?
T-TADANO?!
GWUP
!!

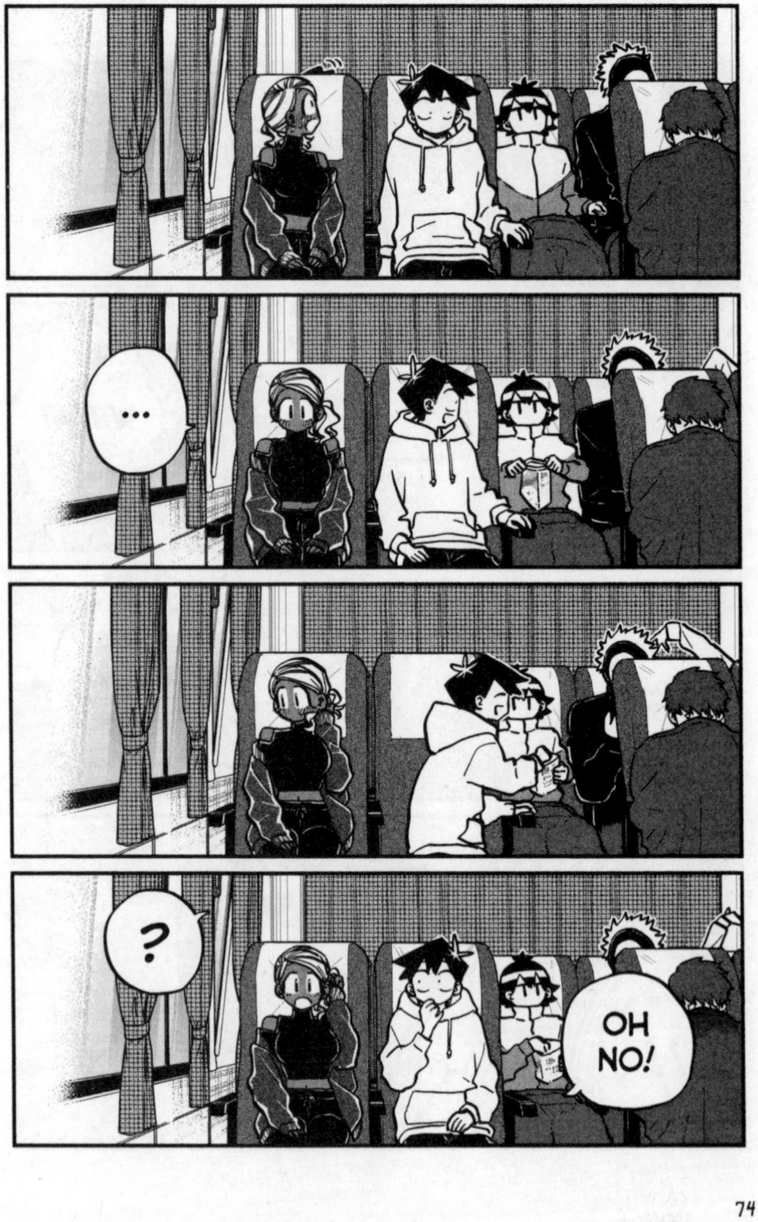
...
OH NO!
?

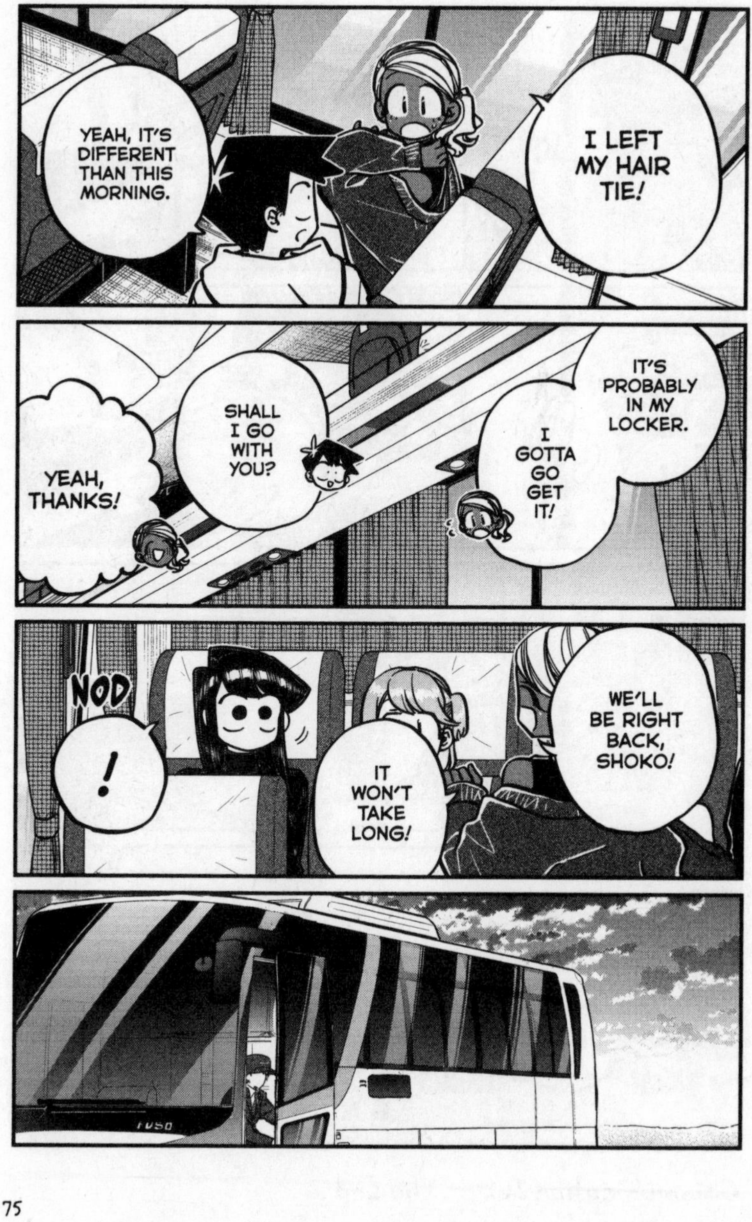
I LEFT MY HAIR TIE!
YEAH, IT'S DIFFERENT THAN THIS MORNING.
IT'S PROBABLY IN MY LOCKER.
I GOTTA GO GET IT!
SHALL I GO WITH YOU?
YEAH, THANKS!
WE'LL BE RIGHT BACK, SHOKO!
IT WON'T TAKE LONG!
NOD
!
FUSO

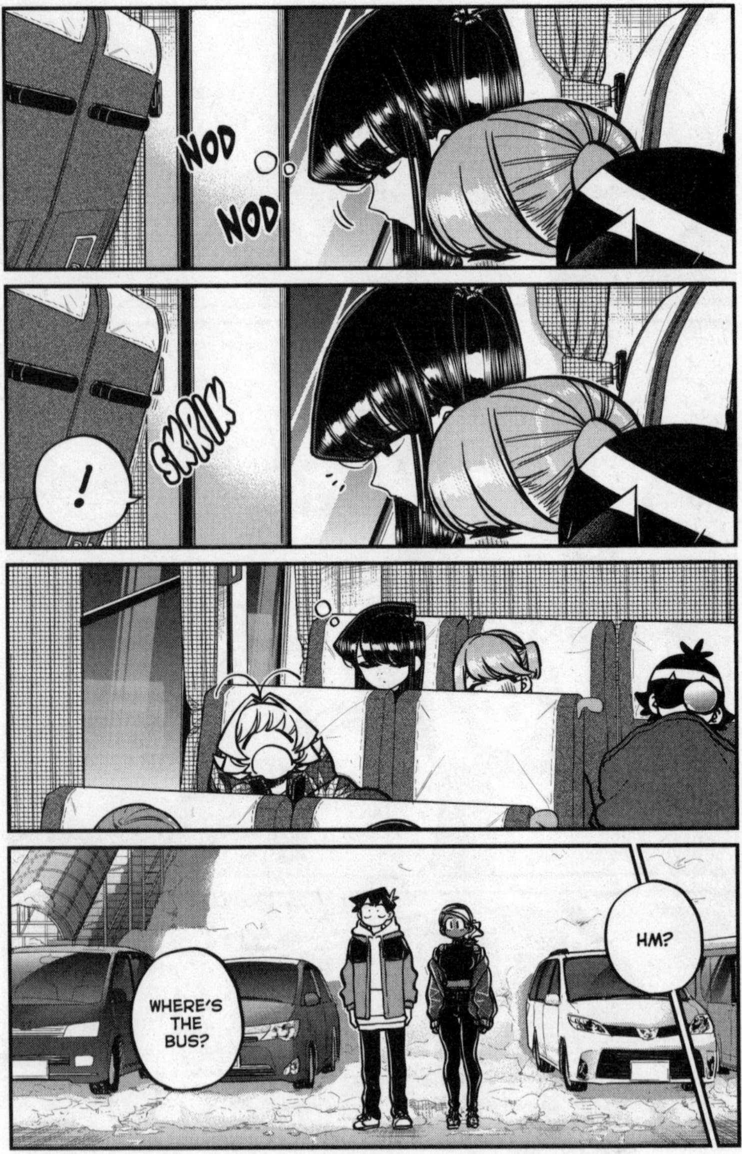
NOD
NOD
SKRIK
!
HM?
WHERE'S THE BUS?

Communication 262 — The End

Komi Can't Communicate

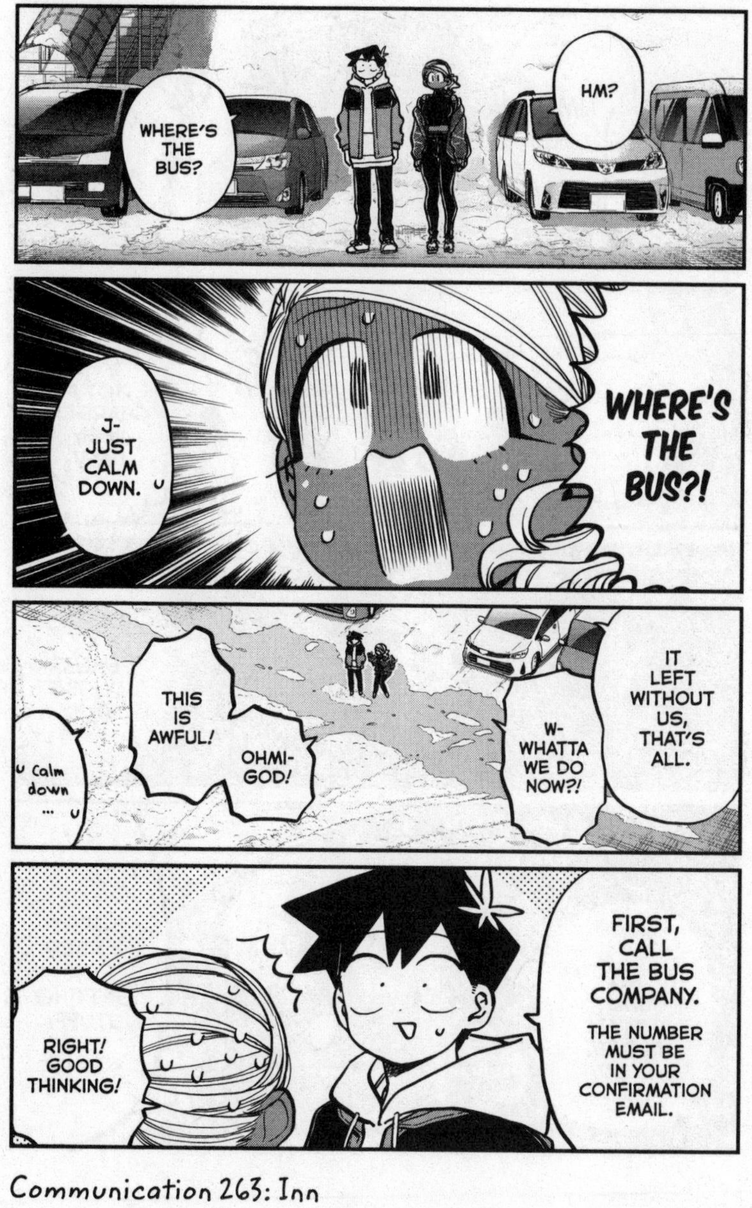
HM?
WHERE'S THE BUS?
WHERE'S THE BUS?!
J- JUST CALM DOWN.
IT LEFT WITHOUT US, THAT'S ALL.
W- WHATTA WE DO NOW?!
OHMI- GOD!
THIS IS AWFUL!
Calm down ...
FIRST, CALL THE BUS COMPANY.
THE NUMBER MUST BE IN YOUR CONFIRMATION EMAIL.
RIGHT! GOOD THINKING!

Communication 263: Inn

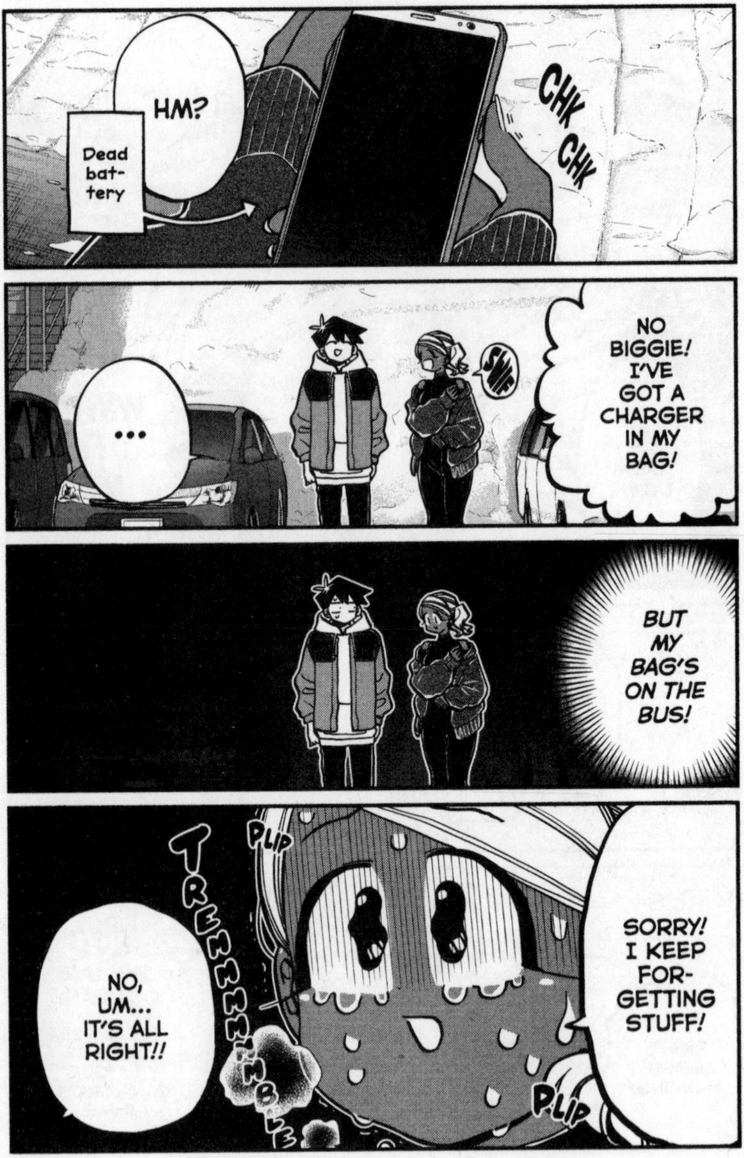
CHK CHK
HM?
Dead battery
NO BIGGIE! I'VE GOT A CHARGER IN MY BAG!
SNIF
...
BUT MY BAG'S ON THE BUS!
SORRY! I KEEP FORGETTING STUFF!
PLIP
PLIP
TREMMMMMMBLE
NO, UM... IT'S ALL RIGHT!!

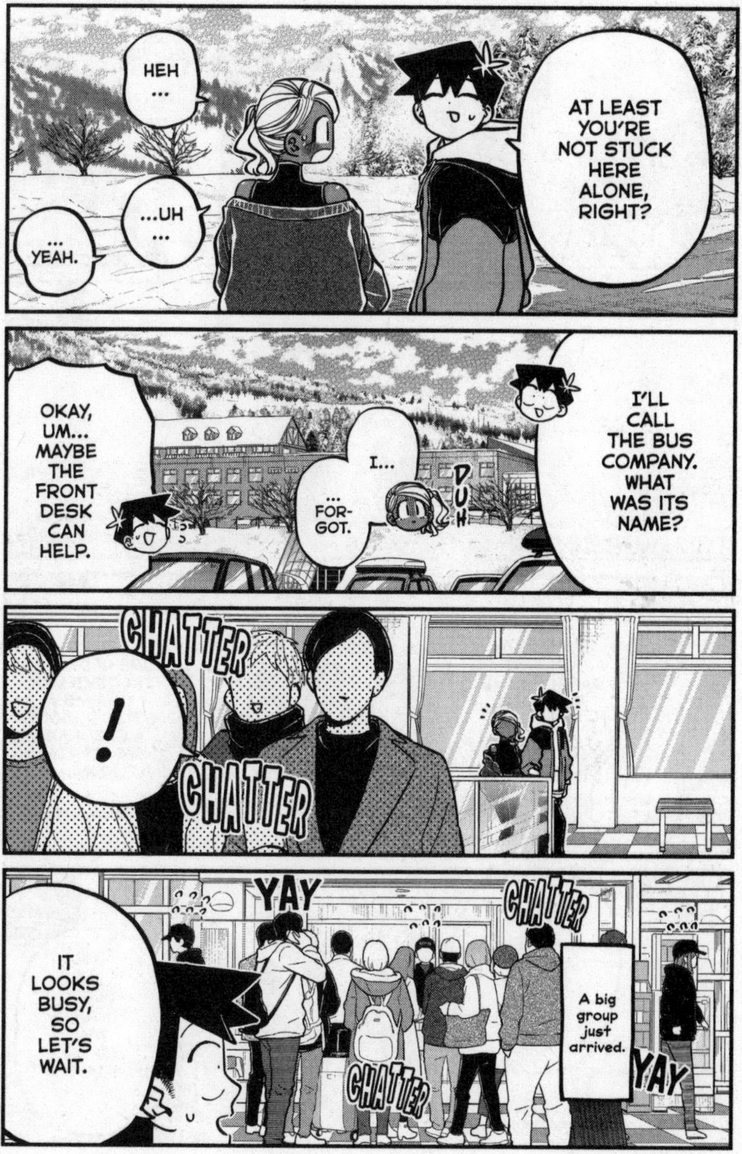

AT LEAST YOU'RE NOT STUCK HERE ALONE, RIGHT?
HEH ...
...UH ...
... YEAH.
I'LL CALL THE BUS COMPANY. WHAT WAS ITS NAME?
DUH
I... ... FOR-GOT.
OKAY, UM... MAYBE THE FRONT DESK CAN HELP.
CHATTER
CHATTER
!
CHATTER
YAY
A big group just arrived.
YAY
CHATTER
IT LOOKS BUSY, SO LET'S WAIT.

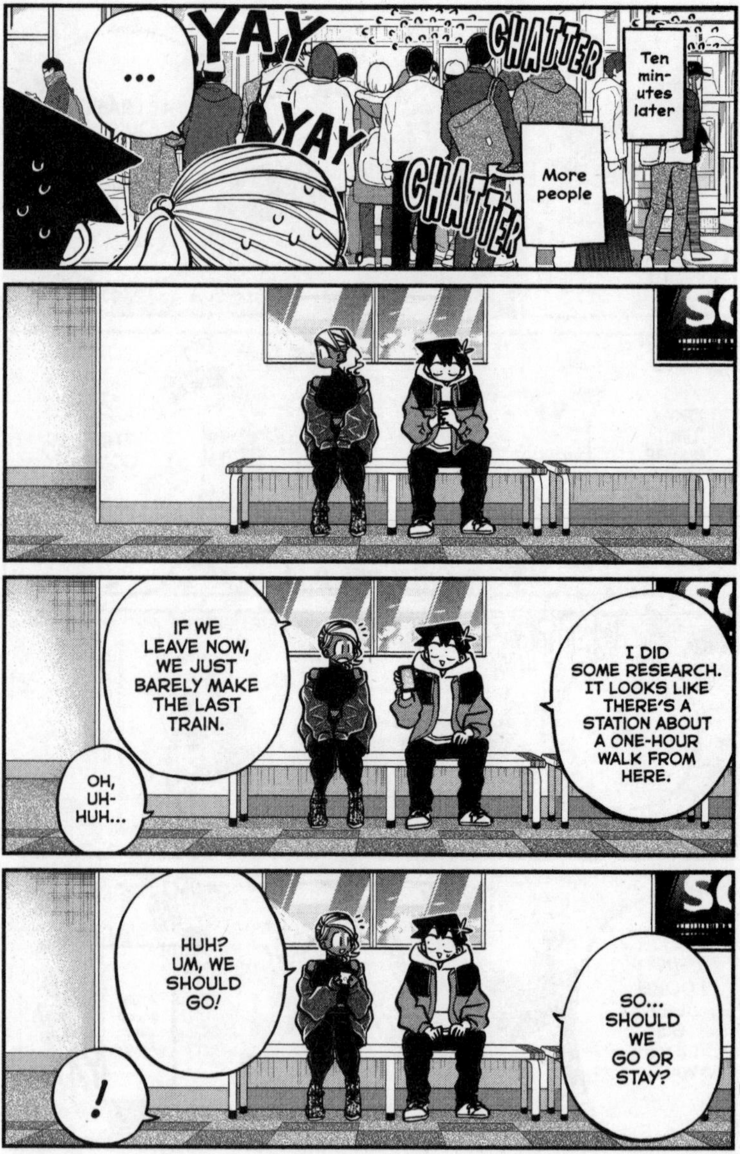
Ten min-utes later
CHATTER
More people
CHATTER
YAY
YAY
...
I DID SOME RESEARCH. IT LOOKS LIKE THERE'S A STATION ABOUT A ONE-HOUR WALK FROM HERE.
IF WE LEAVE NOW, WE JUST BARELY MAKE THE LAST TRAIN.
OH, UH-HUH...
SO... SHOULD WE GO OR STAY?
HUH? UM, WE SHOULD GO!
!

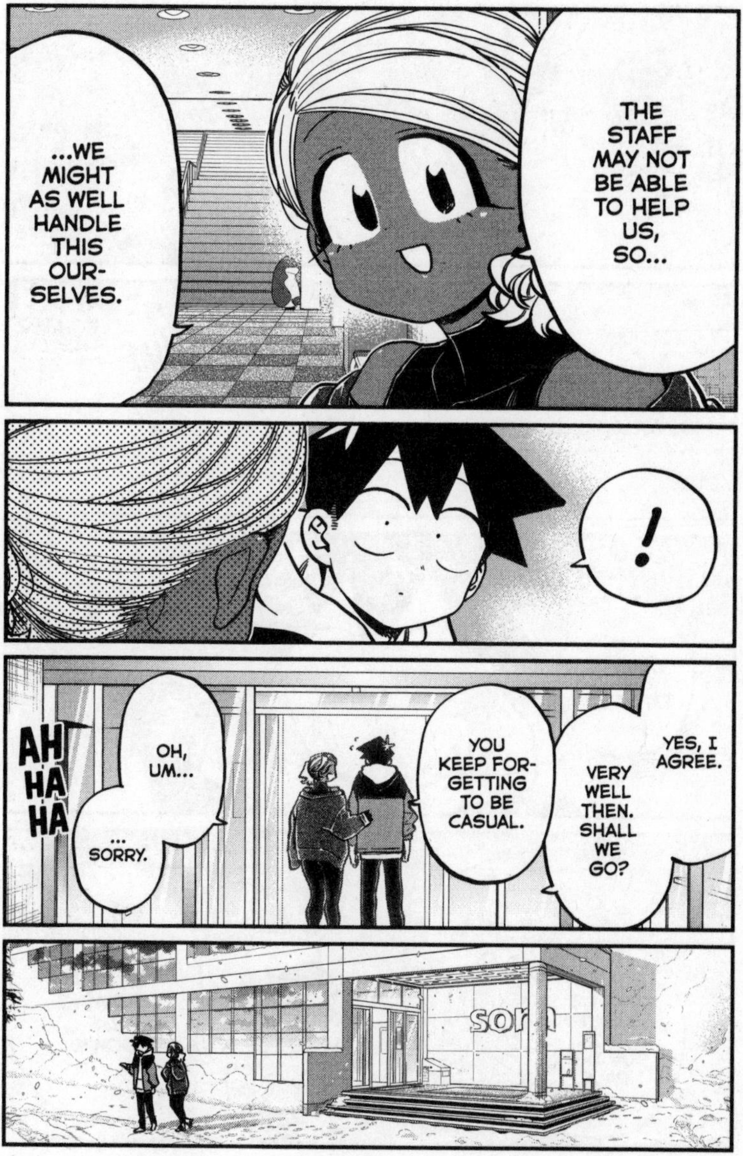
THE STAFF MAY NOT BE ABLE TO HELP US, SO...
...WE MIGHT AS WELL HANDLE THIS OUR-SELVES.
!
YES, I AGREE.
VERY WELL THEN. SHALL WE GO?
YOU KEEP FOR-GETTING TO BE CASUAL.
OH, UM...
...SORRY.
AH HA HA

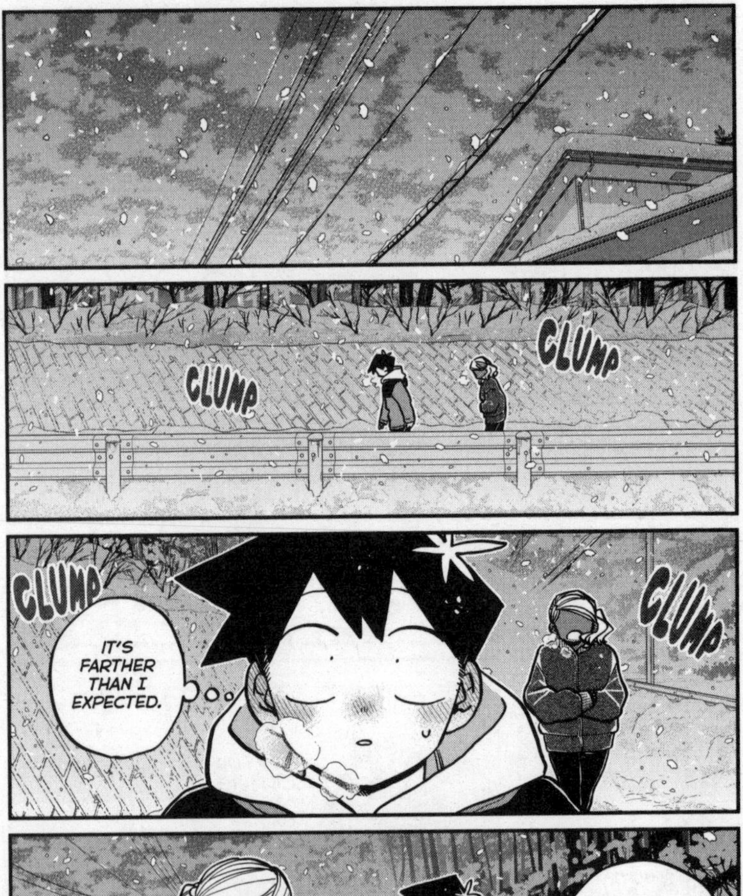
CLUMP
CLUMP
CLUMP
CLUMP
IT'S FARTHER THAN I EXPECTED.
AND THE SNOW IS SLOWING US DOWN.
UM, WE SHOULD PICK UP THE PACE.

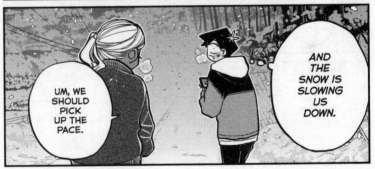

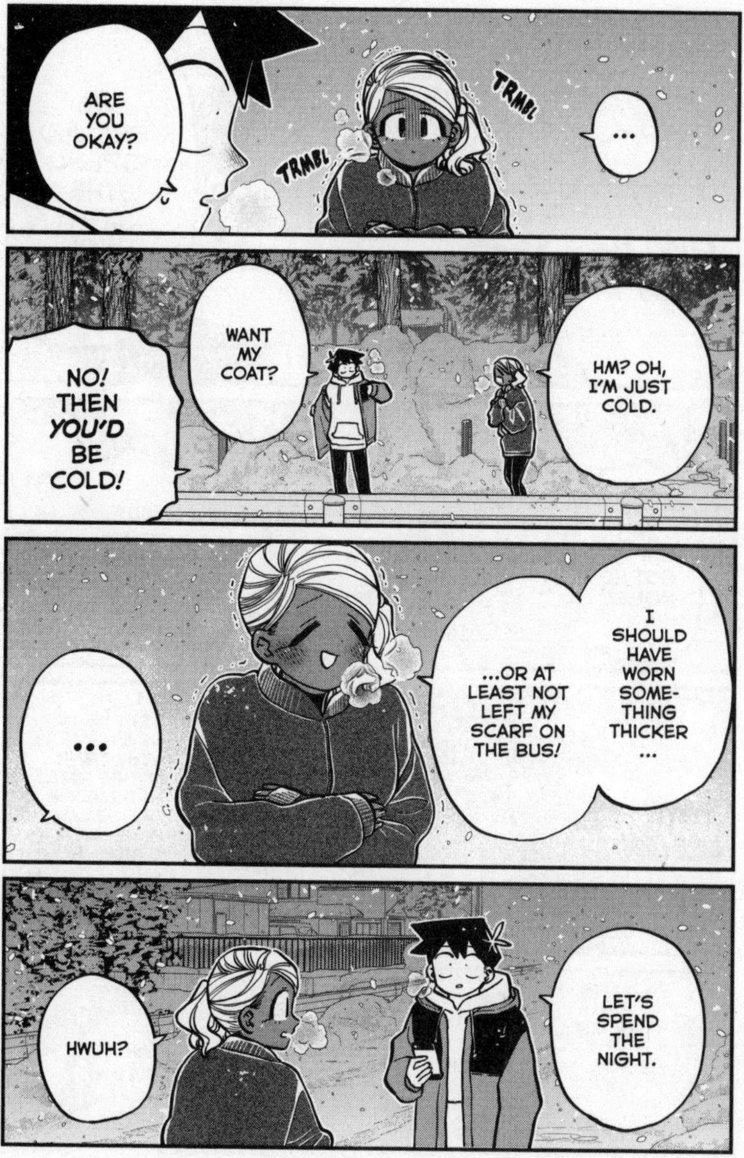
...
TRMBL
TRMBL
ARE YOU OKAY?
HM? OH, I'M JUST COLD.
WANT MY COAT?
NO! THEN *YOU'D* BE COLD!
I SHOULD HAVE WORN SOME-THING THICKER...
...OR AT LEAST NOT LEFT MY SCARF ON THE BUS!
...
LET'S SPEND THE NIGHT.
HWUH?

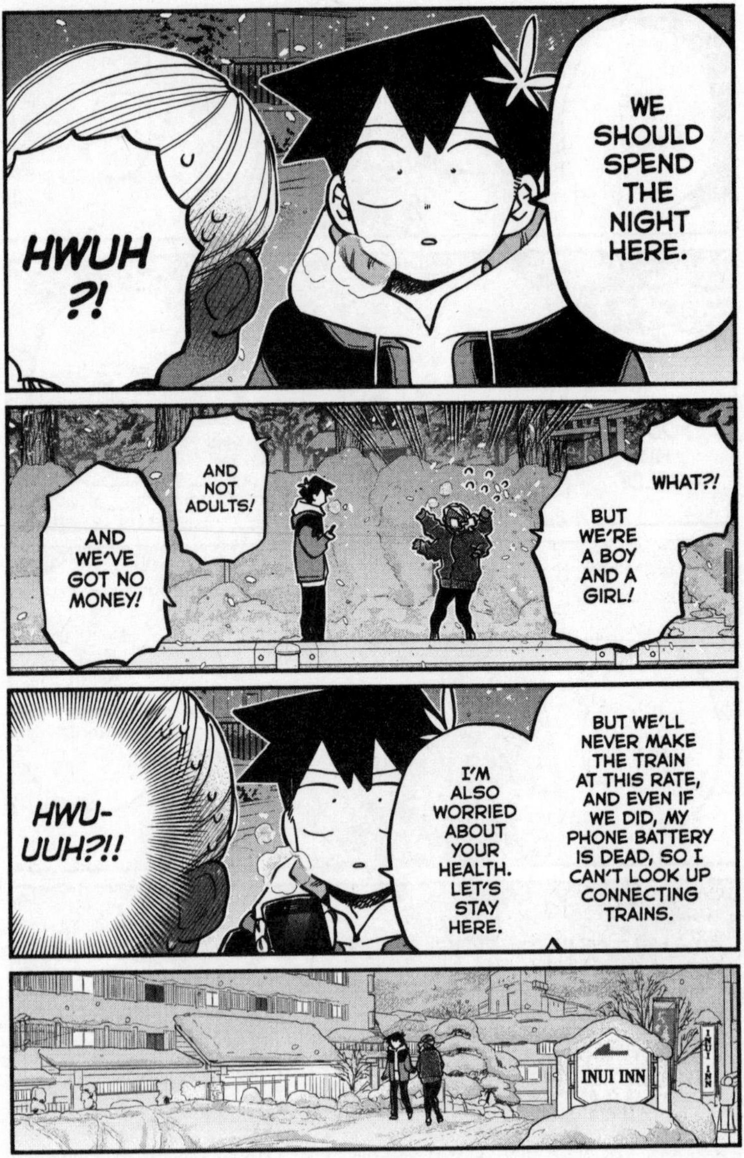
WE SHOULD SPEND THE NIGHT HERE.
HWUH ?!
WHAT?!
BUT WE'RE A BOY AND A GIRL!
AND NOT ADULTS!
AND WE'VE GOT NO MONEY!
BUT WE'LL NEVER MAKE THE TRAIN AT THIS RATE, AND EVEN IF WE DID, MY PHONE BATTERY IS DEAD, SO I CAN'T LOOK UP CONNECTING TRAINS.
I'M ALSO WORRIED ABOUT YOUR HEALTH. LET'S STAY HERE.
HWU-UUH?!!
INUI INN
INUI INN

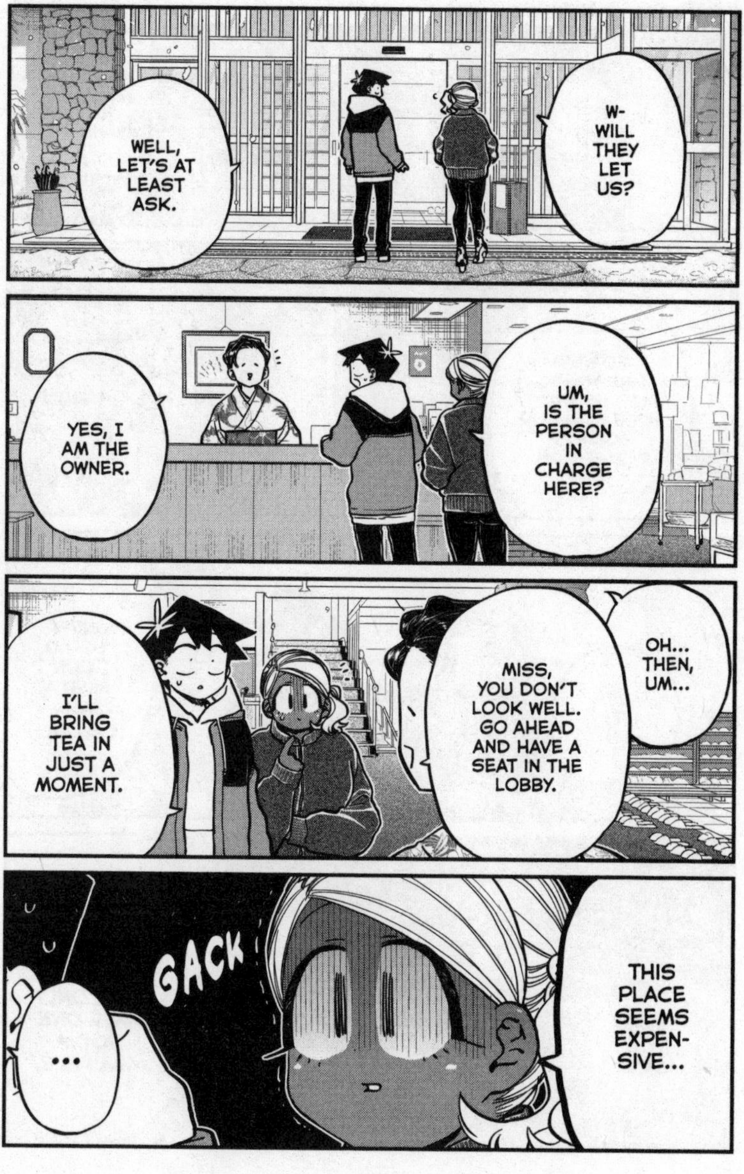
W-WILL THEY LET US?
WELL, LET'S AT LEAST ASK.
UM, IS THE PERSON IN CHARGE HERE?
YES, I AM THE OWNER.
OH... THEN, UM...
MISS, YOU DON'T LOOK WELL. GO AHEAD AND HAVE A SEAT IN THE LOBBY.
I'LL BRING TEA IN JUST A MOMENT.
THIS PLACE SEEMS EXPENSIVE...
GACK
...

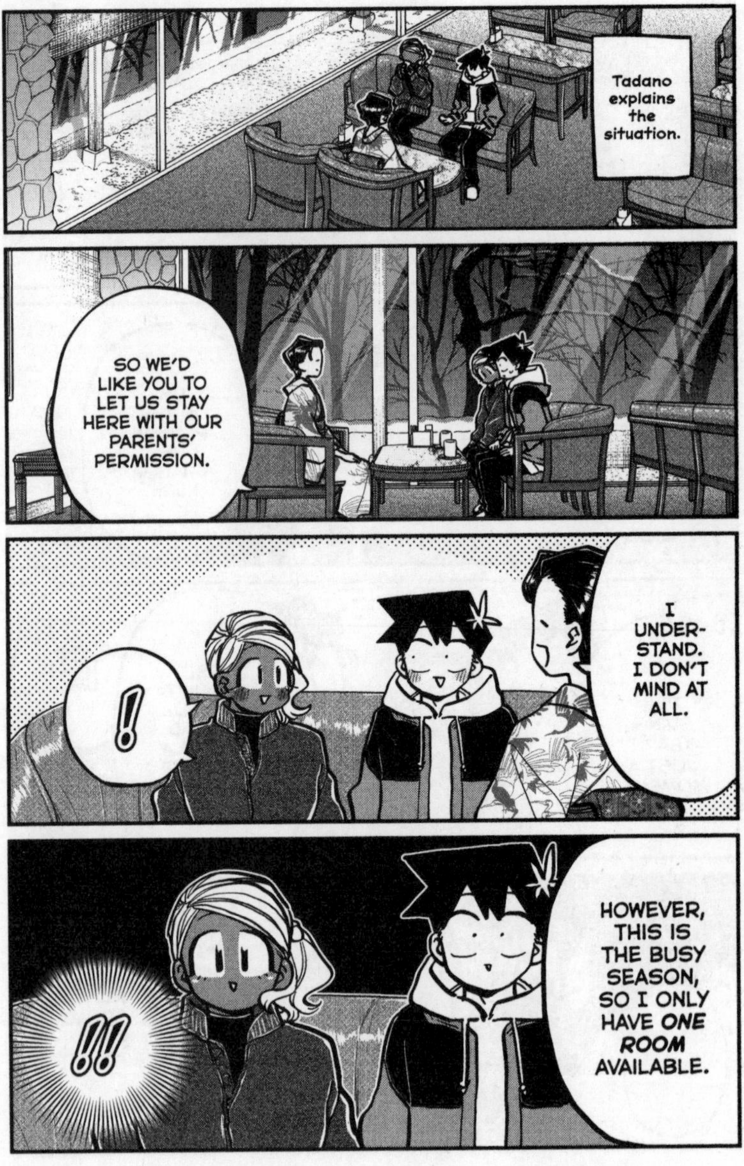
Tadano explains the situation.
SO WE'D LIKE YOU TO LET US STAY HERE WITH OUR PARENTS' PERMISSION.
I UNDERSTAND. I DON'T MIND AT ALL.
!
HOWEVER, THIS IS THE BUSY SEASON, SO I ONLY HAVE *ONE ROOM* AVAILABLE.
!!

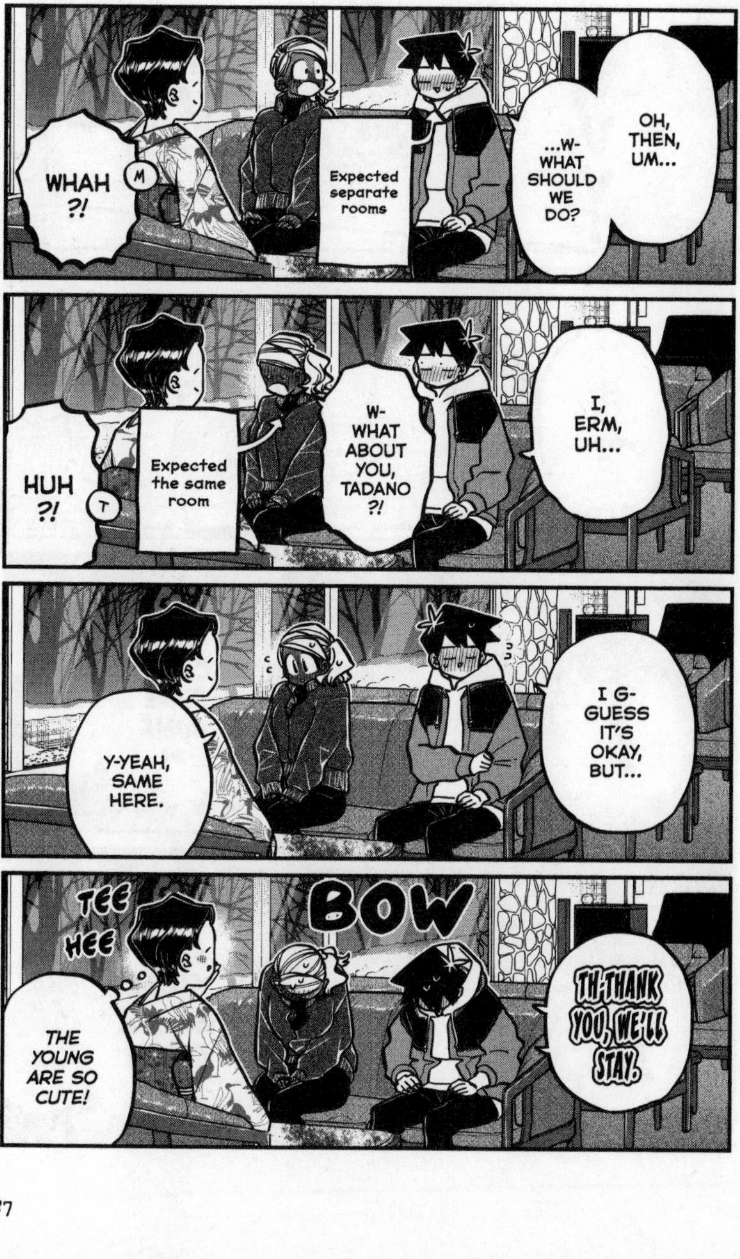

OH, THEN, UM...
...W-WHAT SHOULD WE DO?
Expected separate rooms
M
WHAH ?!
I, ERM, UH...
W-WHAT ABOUT YOU, TADANO ?!
Expected the same room
T
HUH ?!
I G-GUESS IT'S OKAY, BUT...
Y-YEAH, SAME HERE.
BOW
TH-THANK YOU, WE'LL STAY.
TEE HEE
THE YOUNG ARE SO CUTE!

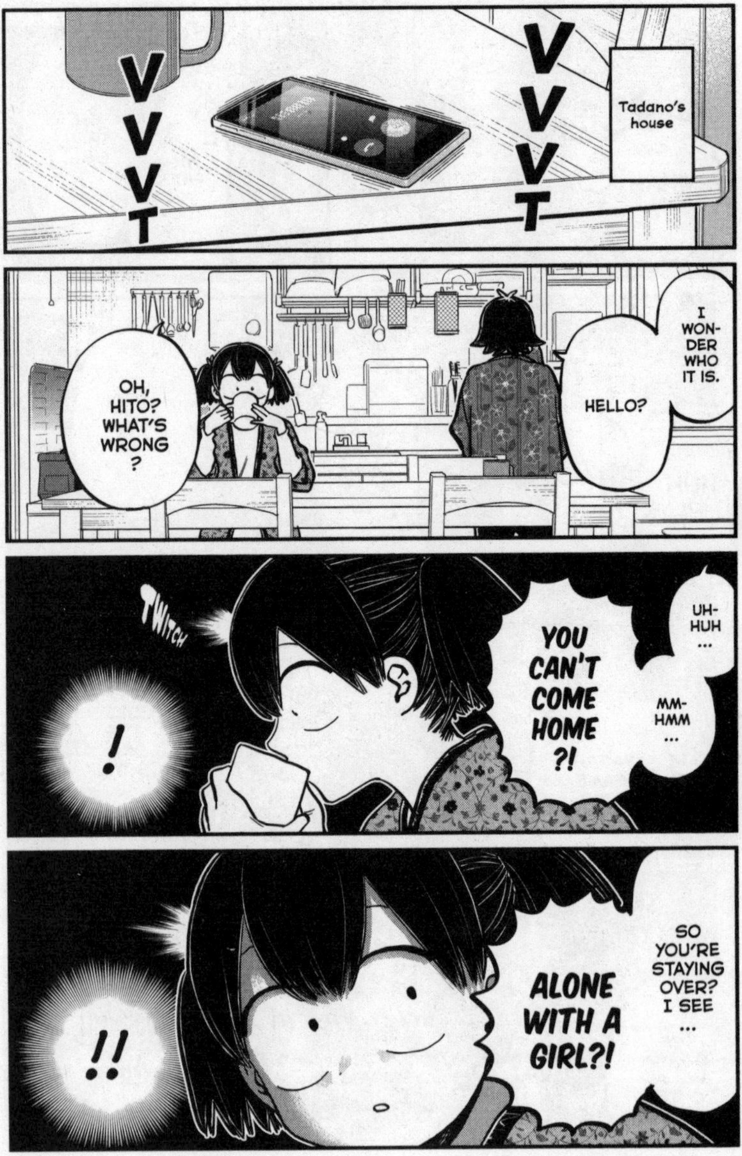
Tadano's house
VVVT
VVVT
I WONDER WHO IT IS.
HELLO?
OH, HITO? WHAT'S WRONG?
UH-HUH ...
MM-HMM ...
YOU CAN'T COME HOME?!
TWITCH
!
SO YOU'RE STAYING OVER? I SEE ...
ALONE WITH A GIRL?!
!!

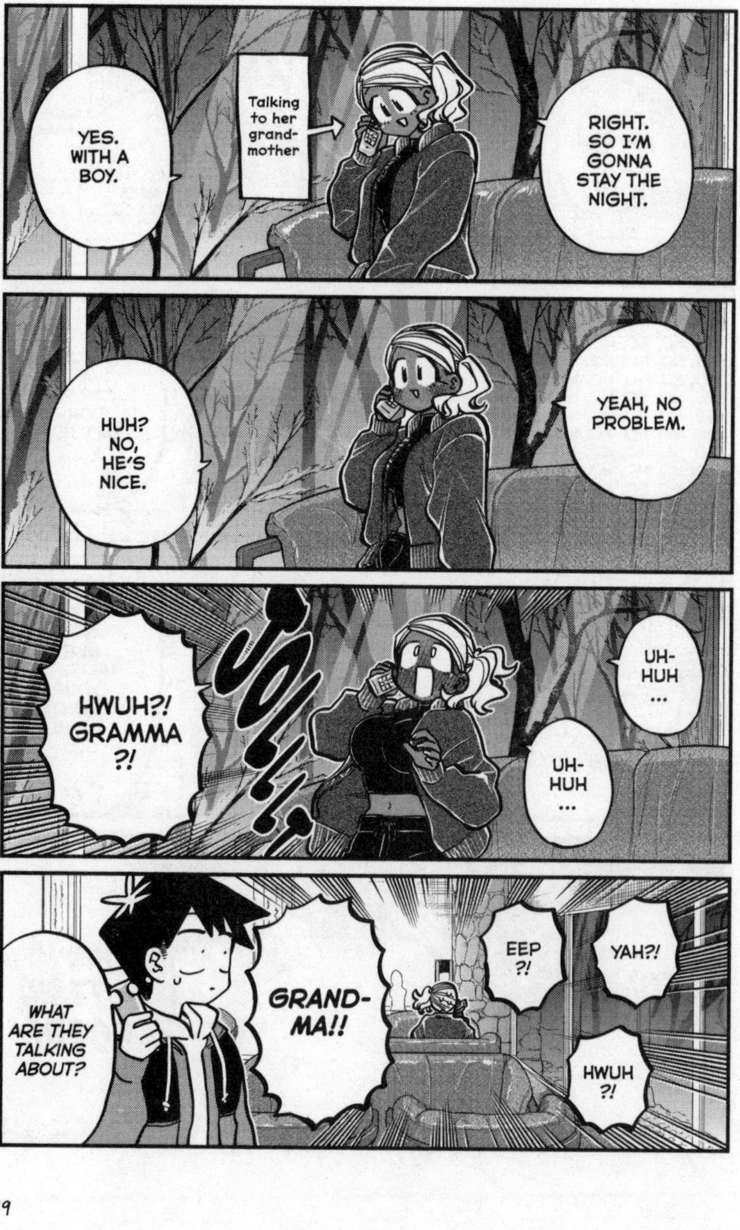
RIGHT. SO I'M GONNA STAY THE NIGHT.
Talking to her grandmother
YES. WITH A BOY.
YEAH, NO PROBLEM.
HUH? NO, HE'S NICE.
UH-HUH ...
UH-HUH ...
HWUH?! GRAMMA ?!
YAH?!
EEP ?!
HWUH ?!
GRAND-MA!!
WHAT ARE THEY TALKING ABOUT?

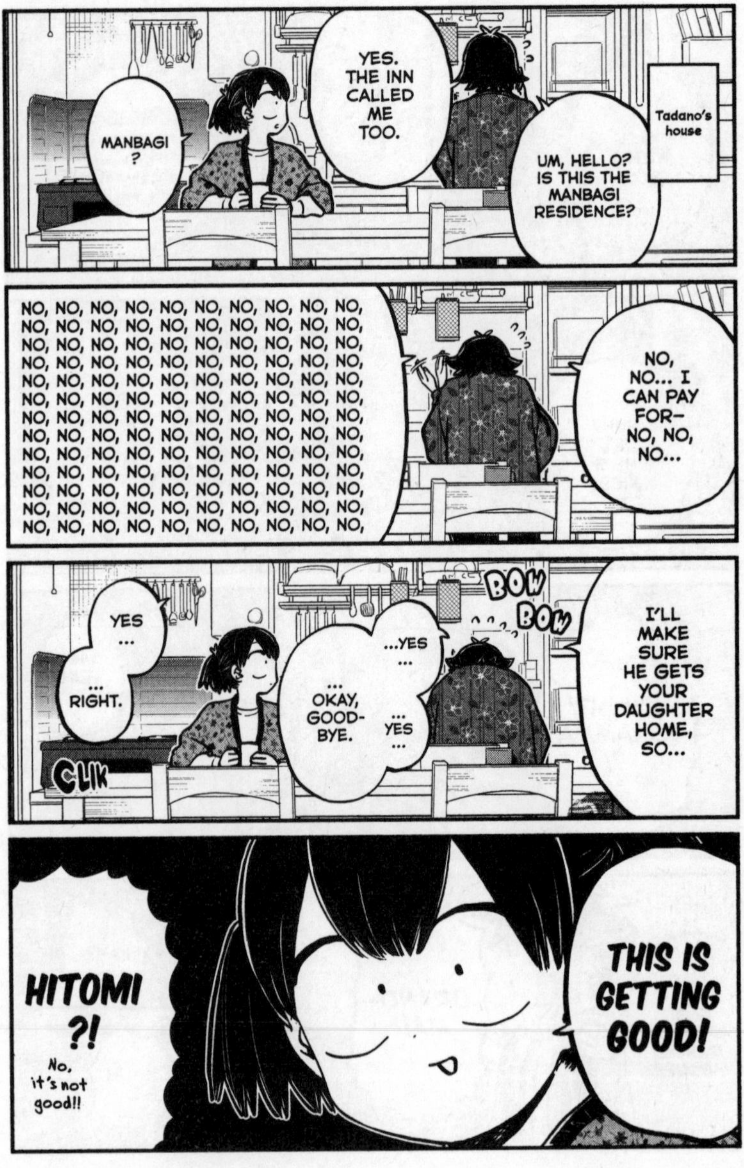
Tadano's house
UM, HELLO? IS THIS THE MANBAGI RESIDENCE?
YES. THE INN CALLED ME TOO.
MANBAGI ?
NO, NO... I CAN PAY FOR— NO, NO, NO...
NO, NO,
I'LL MAKE SURE HE GETS YOUR DAUGHTER HOME, SO...
BOW BOW
...YES ... ... YES ...
... OKAY, GOOD-BYE.
YES ... ... RIGHT.
CLIK
THIS IS GETTING GOOD!
HITOMI ?!
No, it's not good!!

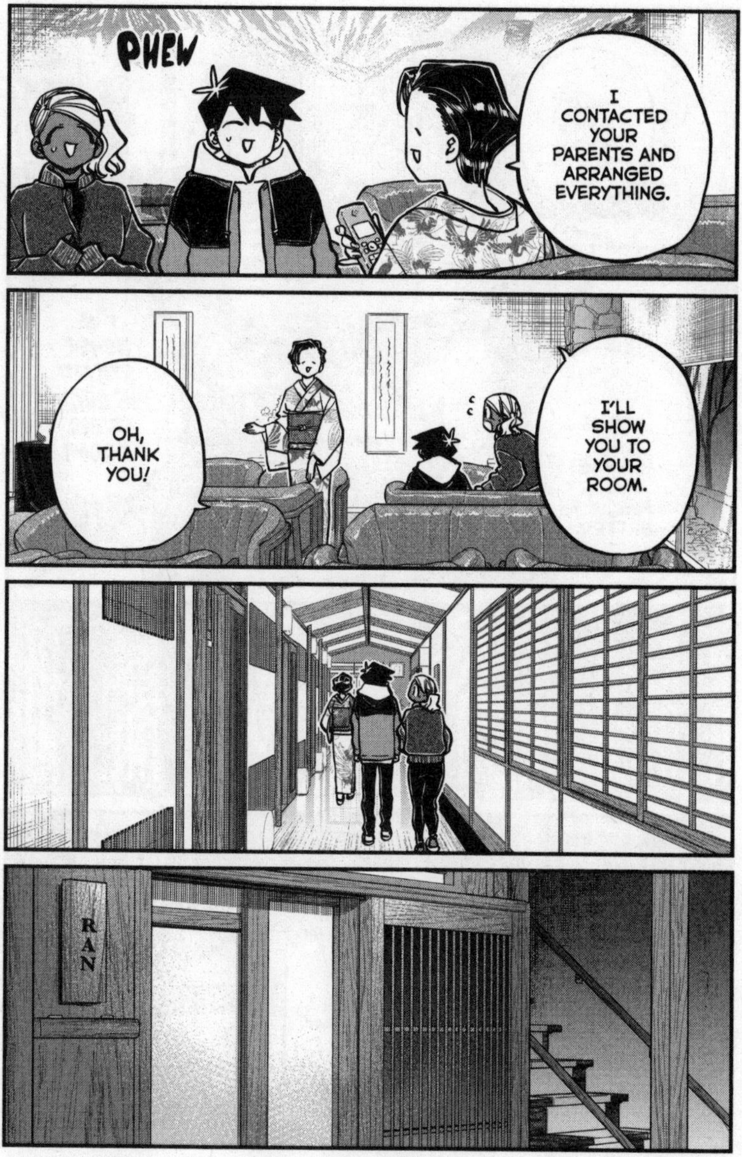
I CONTACTED YOUR PARENTS AND ARRANGED EVERYTHING.
PHEW
I'LL SHOW YOU TO YOUR ROOM.
OH, THANK YOU!
RAN

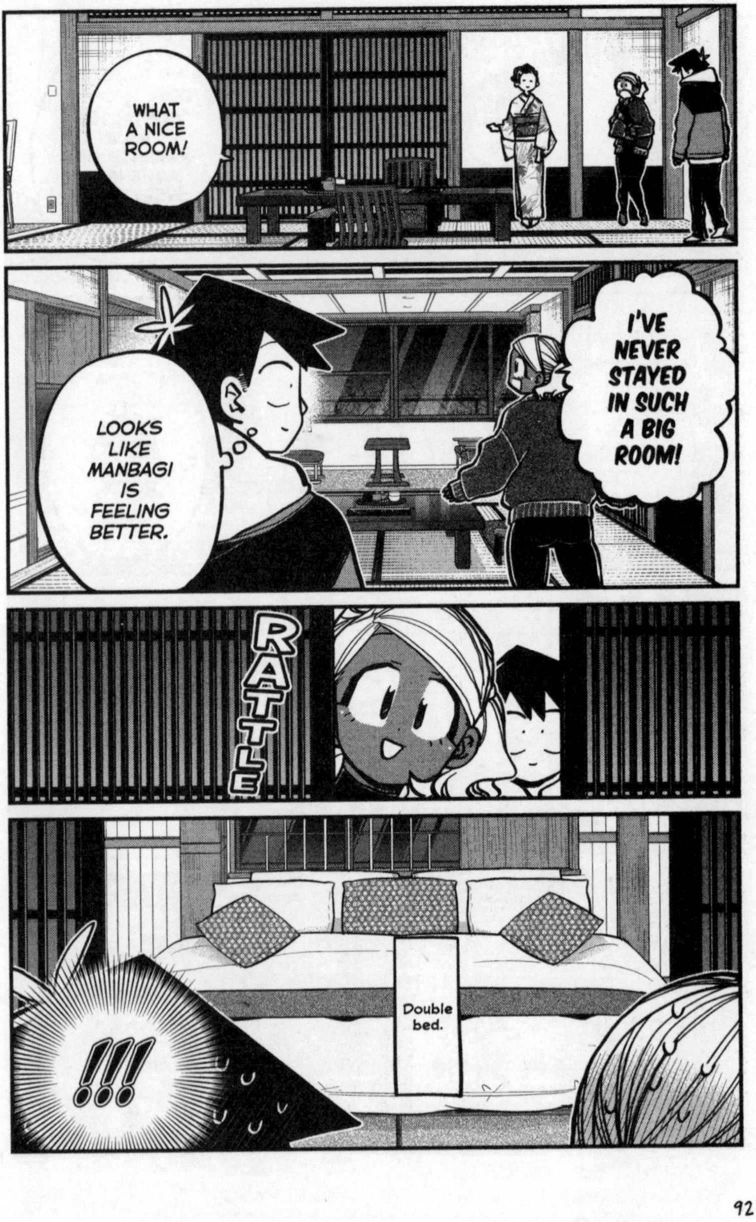
WHAT A NICE ROOM!
I'VE NEVER STAYED IN SUCH A BIG ROOM!
LOOKS LIKE MANBAGI IS FEELING BETTER.
RATTLE
Double bed.
!!!

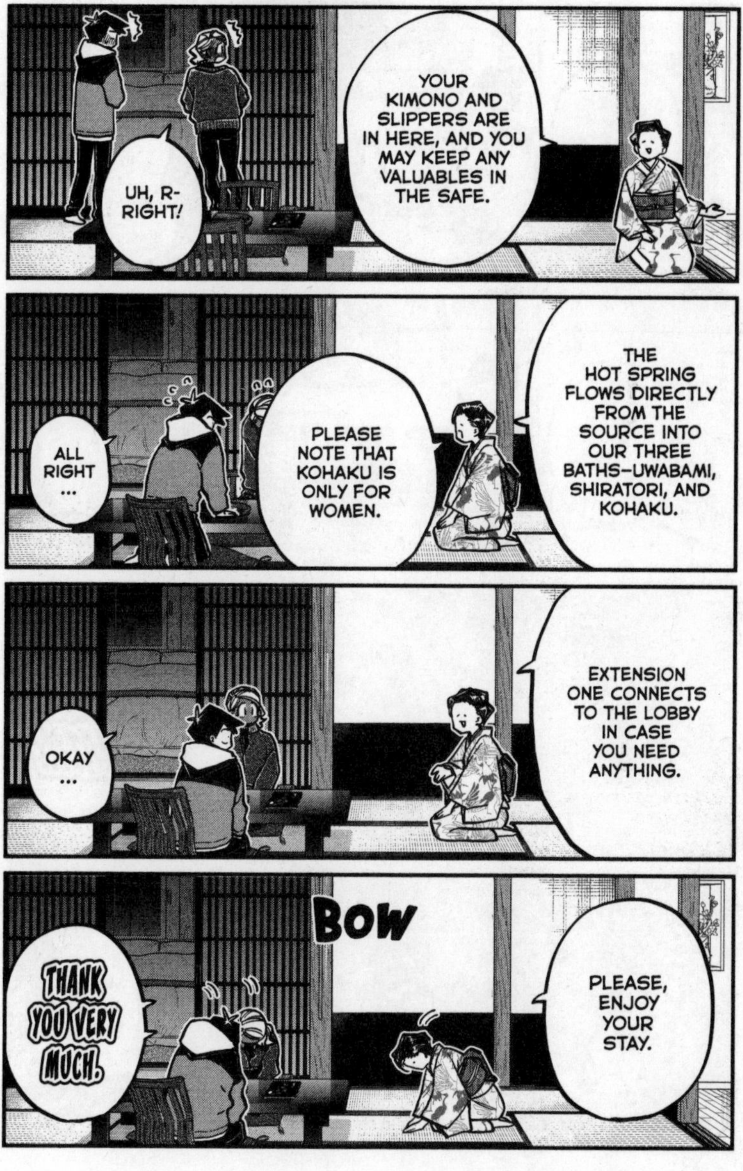
YOUR KIMONO AND SLIPPERS ARE IN HERE, AND YOU MAY KEEP ANY VALUABLES IN THE SAFE.
UH, R-RIGHT!
THE HOT SPRING FLOWS DIRECTLY FROM THE SOURCE INTO OUR THREE BATHS—UWABAMI, SHIRATORI, AND KOHAKU.
PLEASE NOTE THAT KOHAKU IS ONLY FOR WOMEN.
ALL RIGHT ...
EXTENSION ONE CONNECTS TO THE LOBBY IN CASE YOU NEED ANYTHING.
OKAY ...
PLEASE, ENJOY YOUR STAY.
BOW
THANK YOU VERY MUCH.

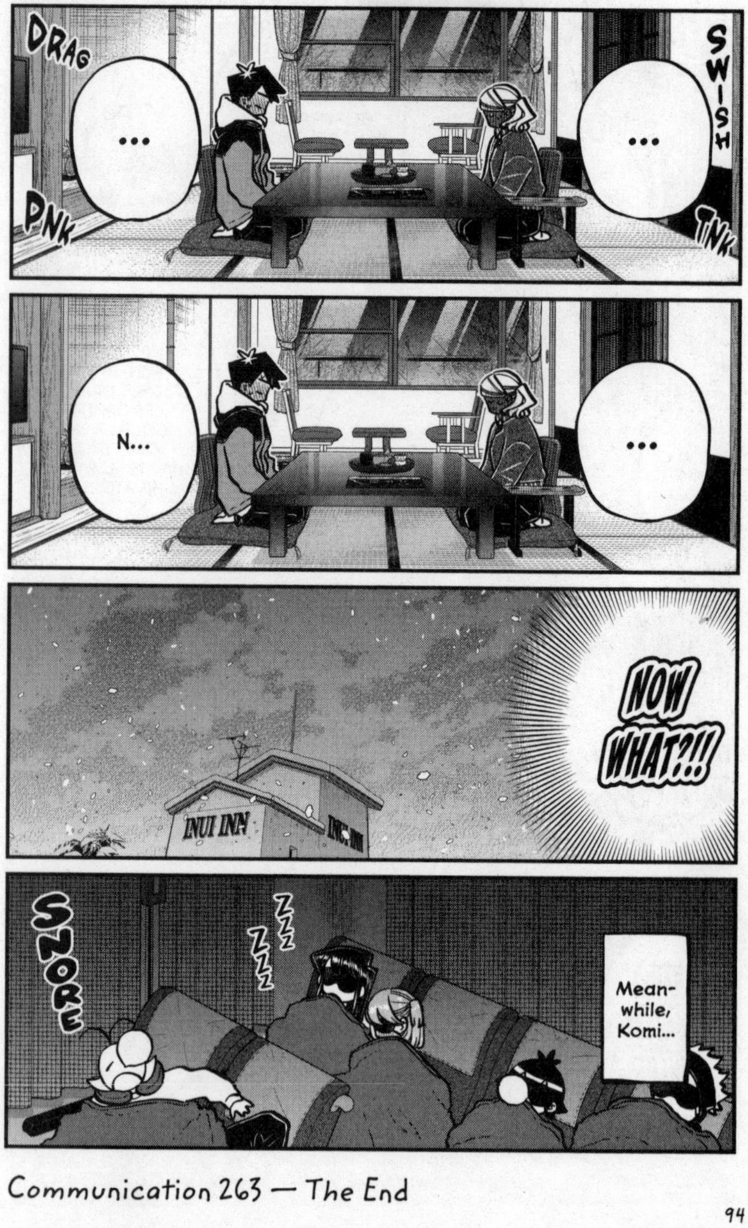
SWISH
...
TNK
DRAG
...
PNK
...
N...
NOW WHAT?!!
INUI INN
Mean-while, Komi...
ZZZ
SNORE

Communication 263 — The End

Komi Can't Communicate

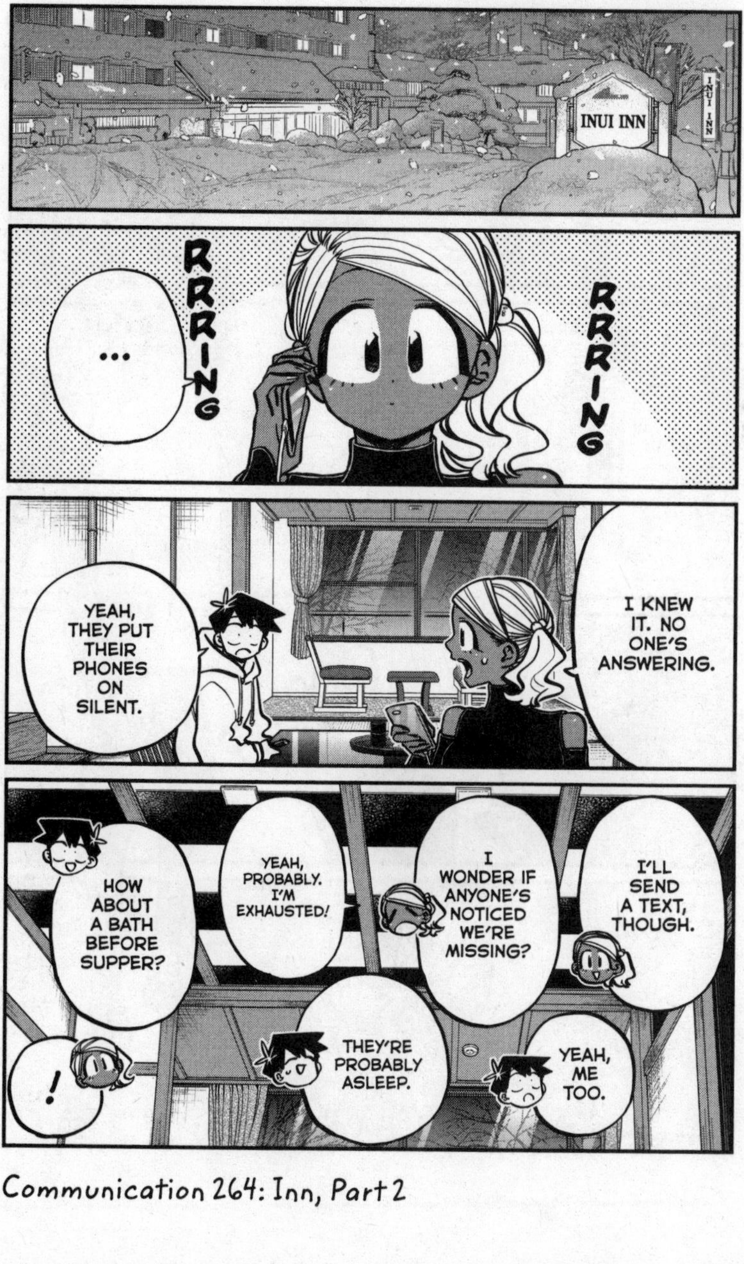
INUI INN
INUI INN
RRRING
...
RRRING
I KNEW IT. NO ONE'S ANSWERING.
YEAH, THEY PUT THEIR PHONES ON SILENT.
I'LL SEND A TEXT, THOUGH.
YEAH, ME TOO.
I WONDER IF ANYONE'S NOTICED WE'RE MISSING?
THEY'RE PROBABLY ASLEEP.
YEAH, PROBABLY. I'M EXHAUSTED!
HOW ABOUT A BATH BEFORE SUPPER?
!

Communication 264: Inn, Part 2

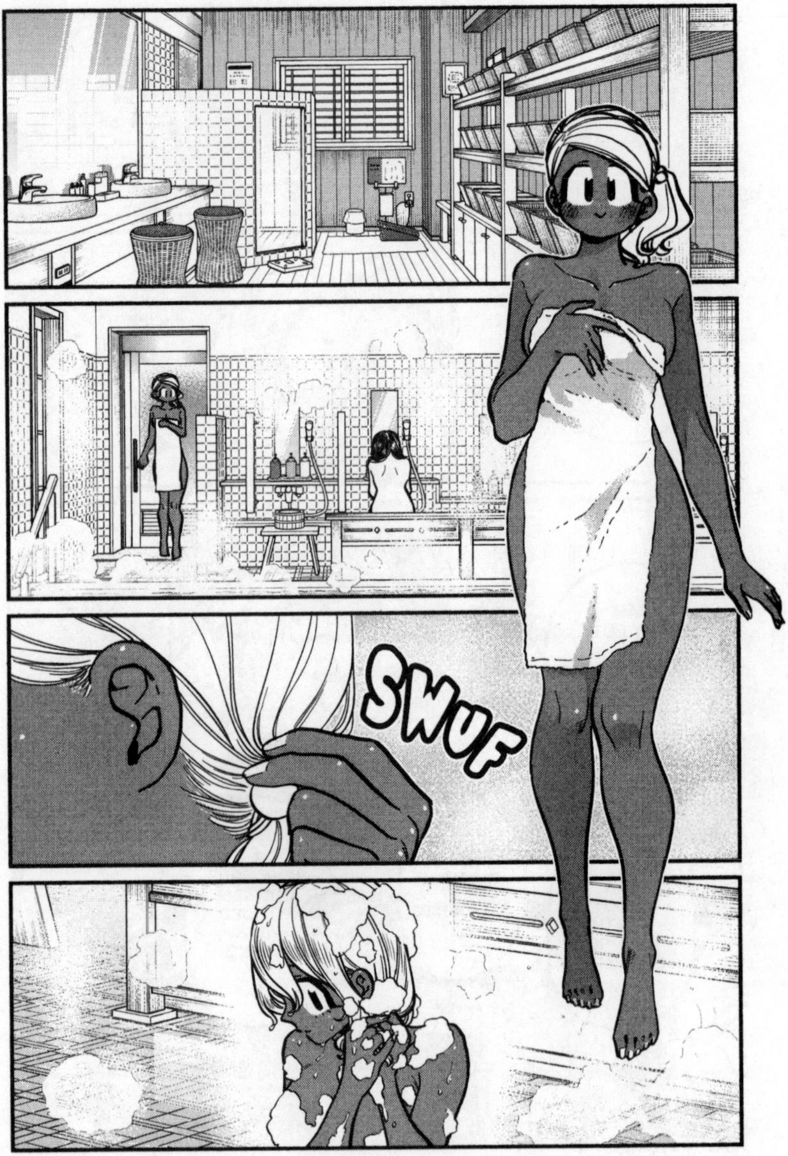
SWUF

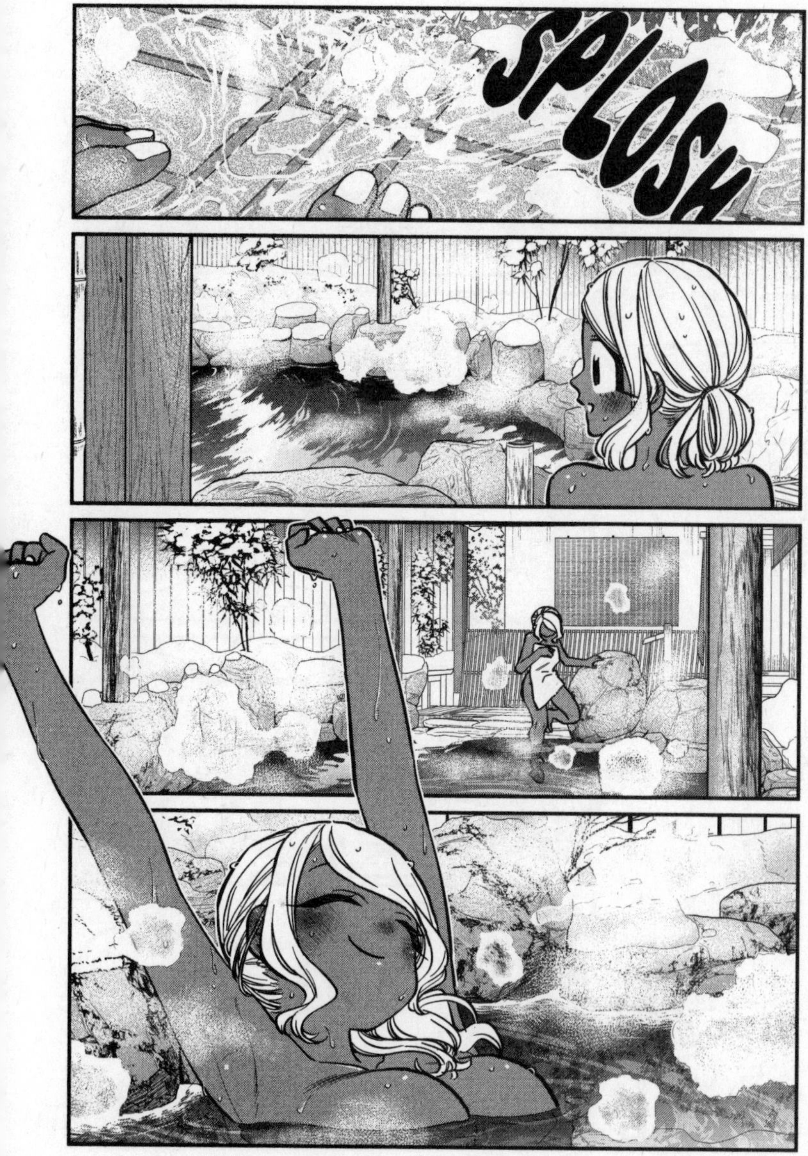
SPLOSH

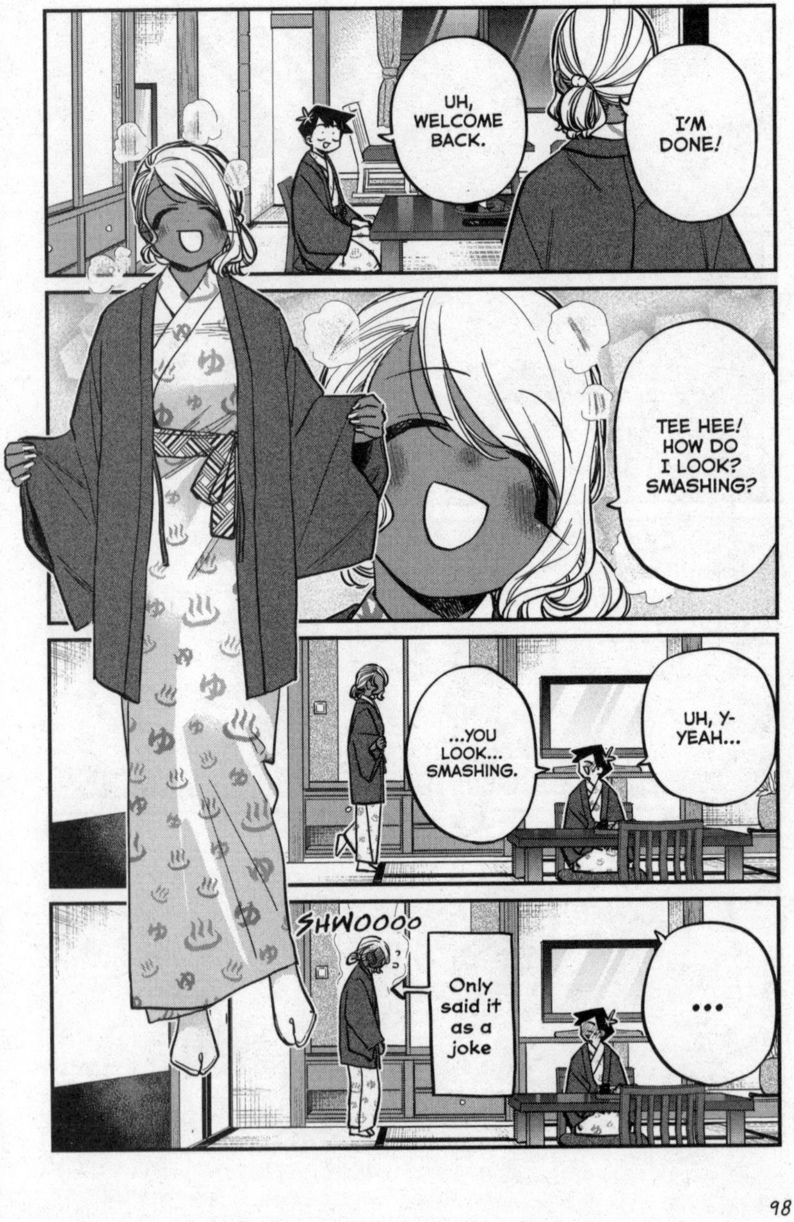
I'M DONE!
UH, WELCOME BACK.
TEE HEE! HOW DO I LOOK? SMASHING?
UH, Y-YEAH...
...YOU LOOK... SMASHING.
...
SHWOOOO
Only said it as a joke

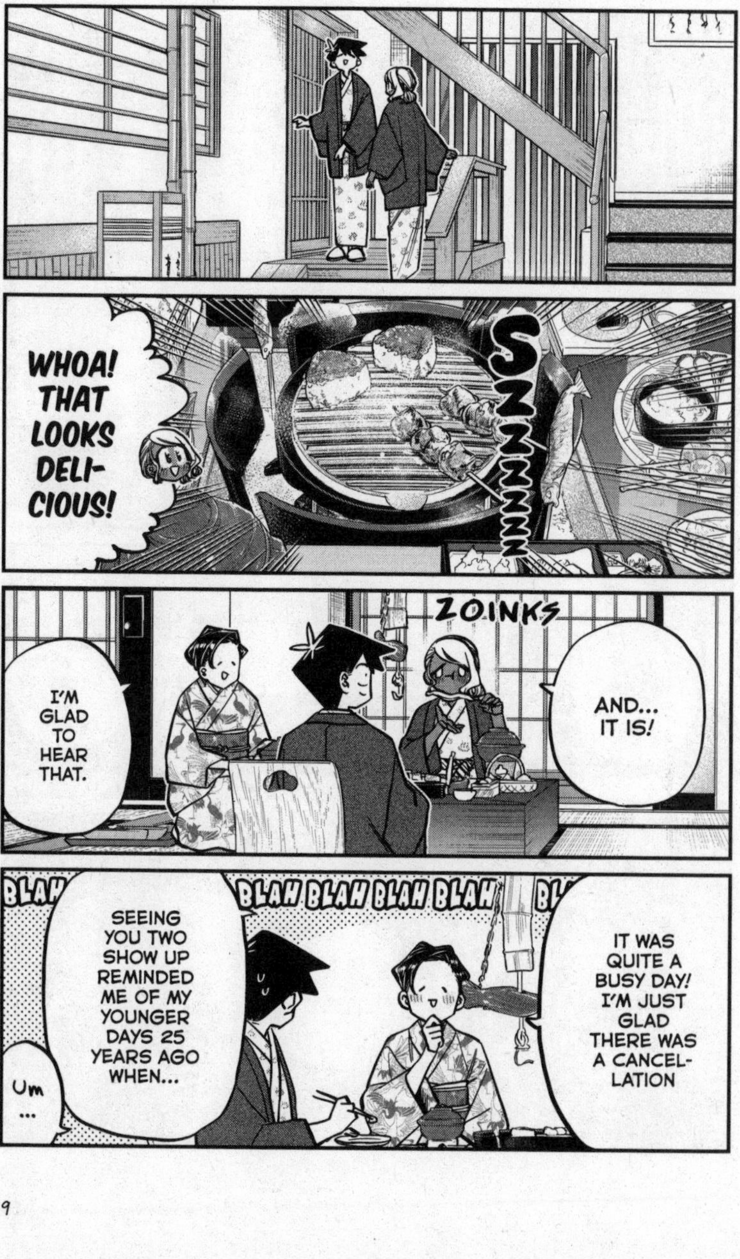
SZZZZZZZ
WHOA! THAT LOOKS DELI-CIOUS!
ZOINKS
AND... IT IS!
I'M GLAD TO HEAR THAT.
BLAH BLAH BLAH BLAH BLAH BLAH
IT WAS QUITE A BUSY DAY! I'M JUST GLAD THERE WAS A CANCEL-LATION
SEEING YOU TWO SHOW UP REMINDED ME OF MY YOUNGER DAYS 25 YEARS AGO WHEN...
Um ...

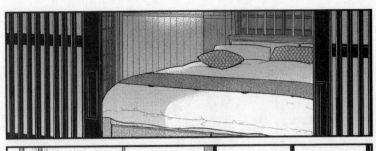

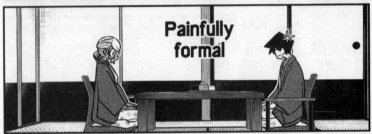

Painfully formal

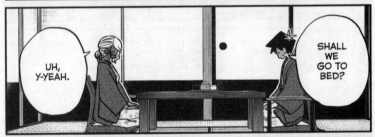

SHALL WE GO TO BED?

UH, Y-YEAH.

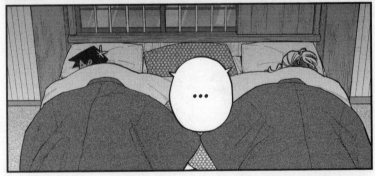

...

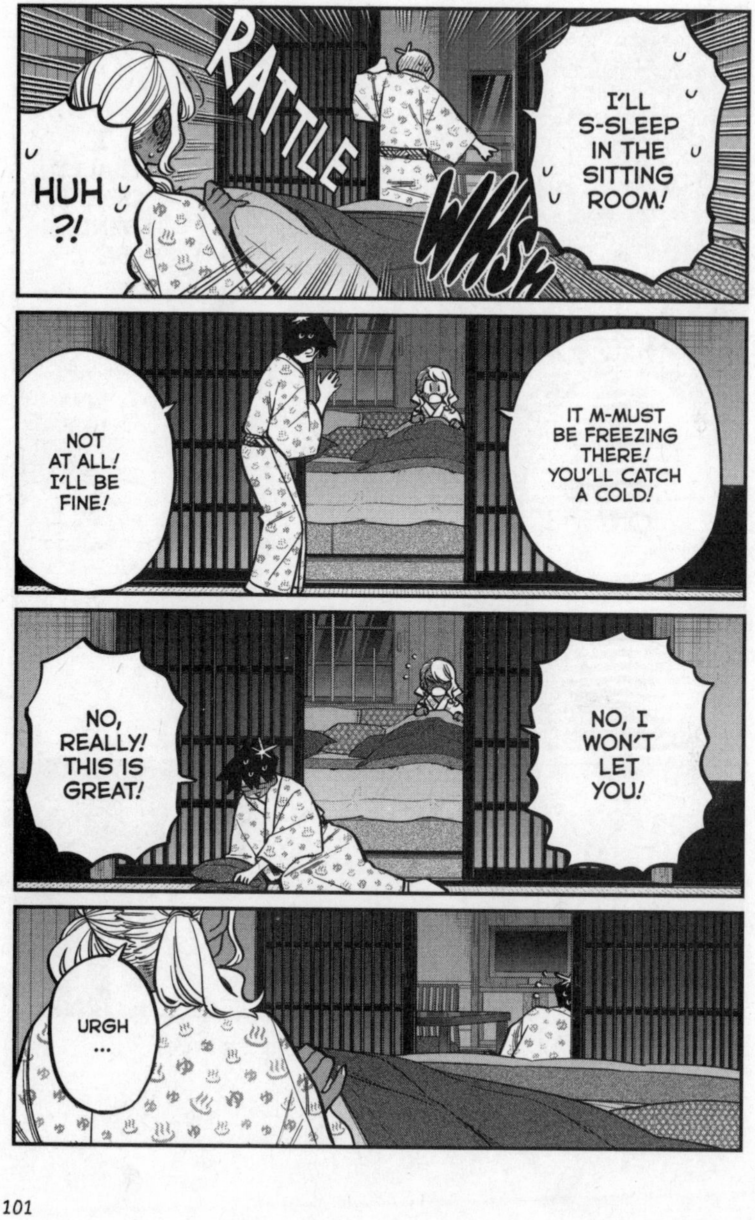
I'LL S-SLEEP IN THE SITTING ROOM!
RATTLE
WHSH
HUH ?!
IT M-MUST BE FREEZING THERE! YOU'LL CATCH A COLD!
NOT AT ALL! I'LL BE FINE!
NO, I WON'T LET YOU!
NO, REALLY! THIS IS GREAT!
URGH ...

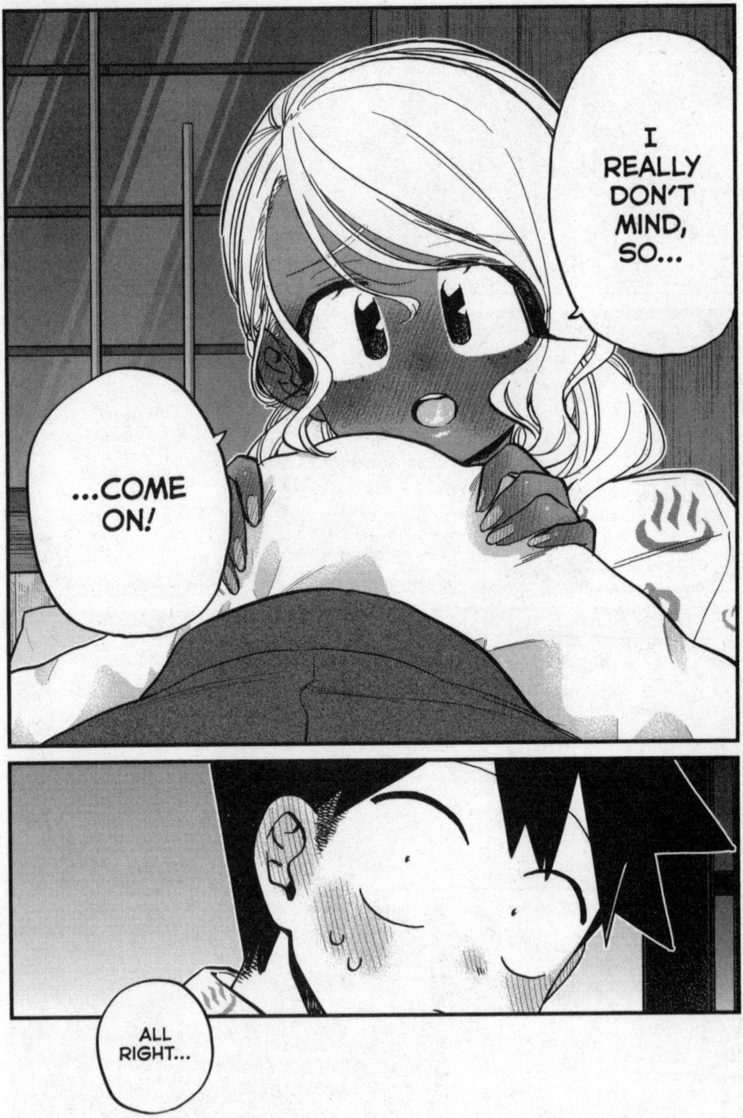
I REALLY DON'T MIND, SO...
...COME ON!
ALL RIGHT...

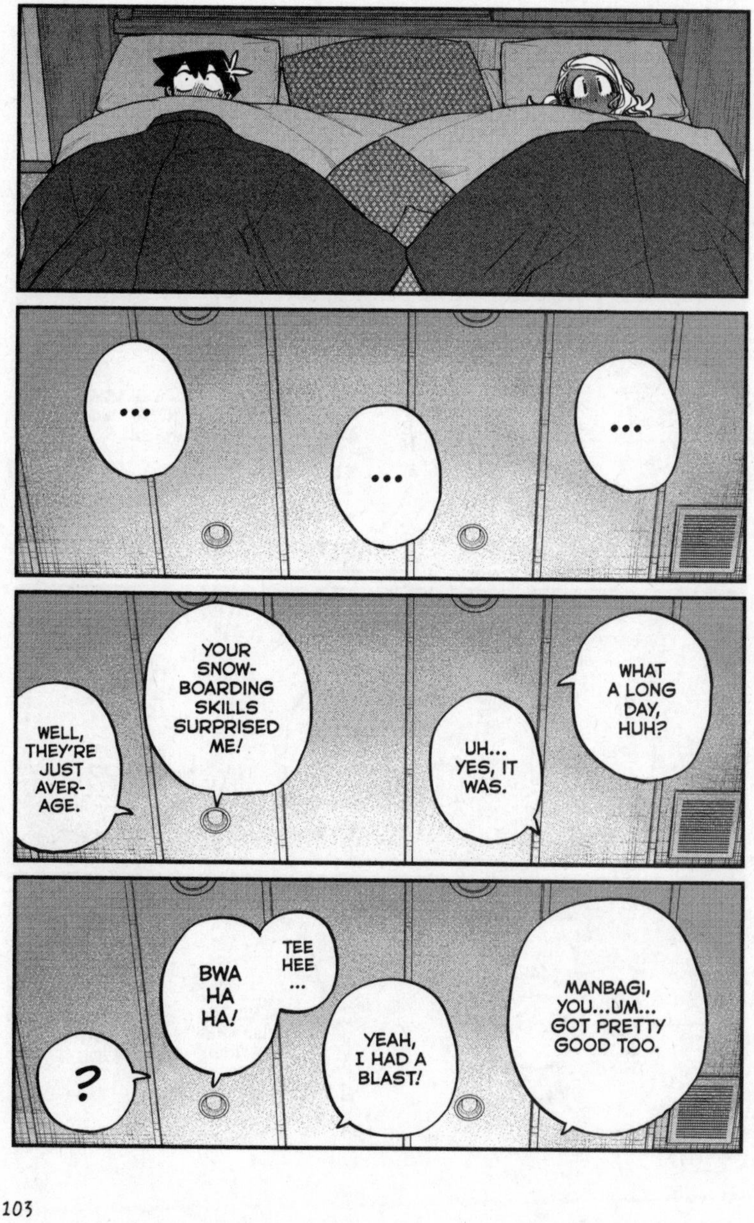
...
...
...
WHAT A LONG DAY, HUH?
UH... YES, IT WAS.
YOUR SNOW-BOARDING SKILLS SURPRISED ME!
WELL, THEY'RE JUST AVER-AGE.
MANBAGI, YOU...UM... GOT PRETTY GOOD TOO.
YEAH, I HAD A BLAST!
TEE HEE ...
BWA HA HA!
?

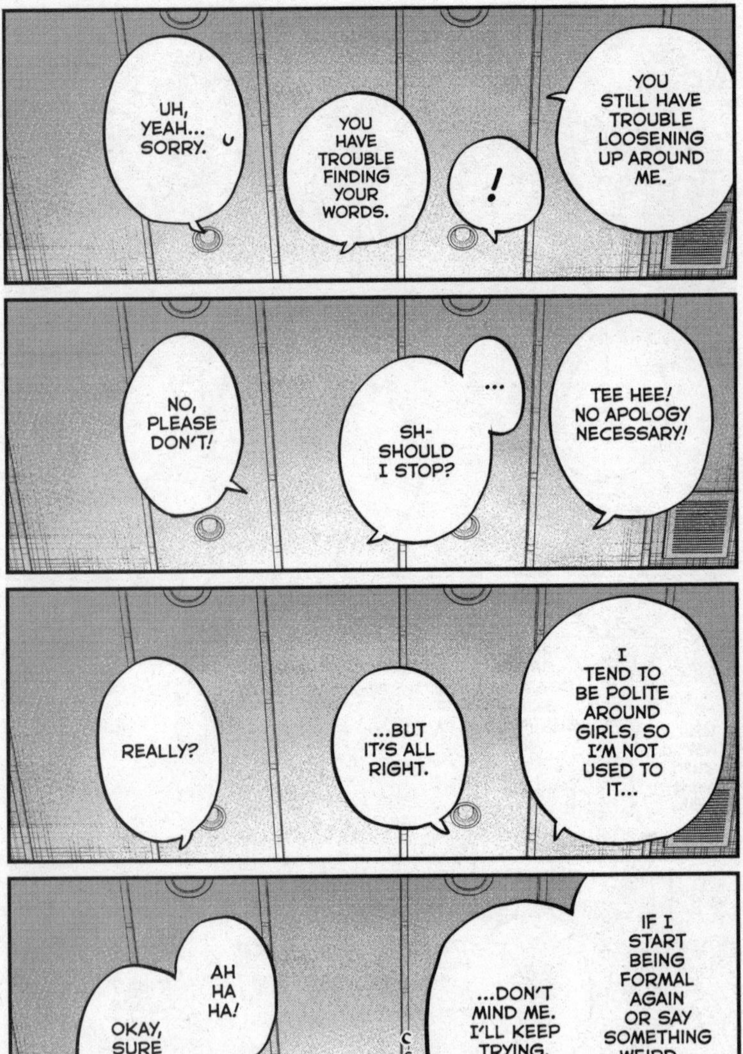
YOU STILL HAVE TROUBLE LOOSENING UP AROUND ME.
!
YOU HAVE TROUBLE FINDING YOUR WORDS.
UH, YEAH... SORRY.
TEE HEE! NO APOLOGY NECESSARY!
...
SH- SHOULD I STOP?
NO, PLEASE DON'T!
I TEND TO BE POLITE AROUND GIRLS, SO I'M NOT USED TO IT...
...BUT IT'S ALL RIGHT.
REALLY?
IF I START BEING FORMAL AGAIN OR SAY SOMETHING WEIRD...
...DON'T MIND ME. I'LL KEEP TRYING.
AH HA HA!
OKAY, SURE THING!

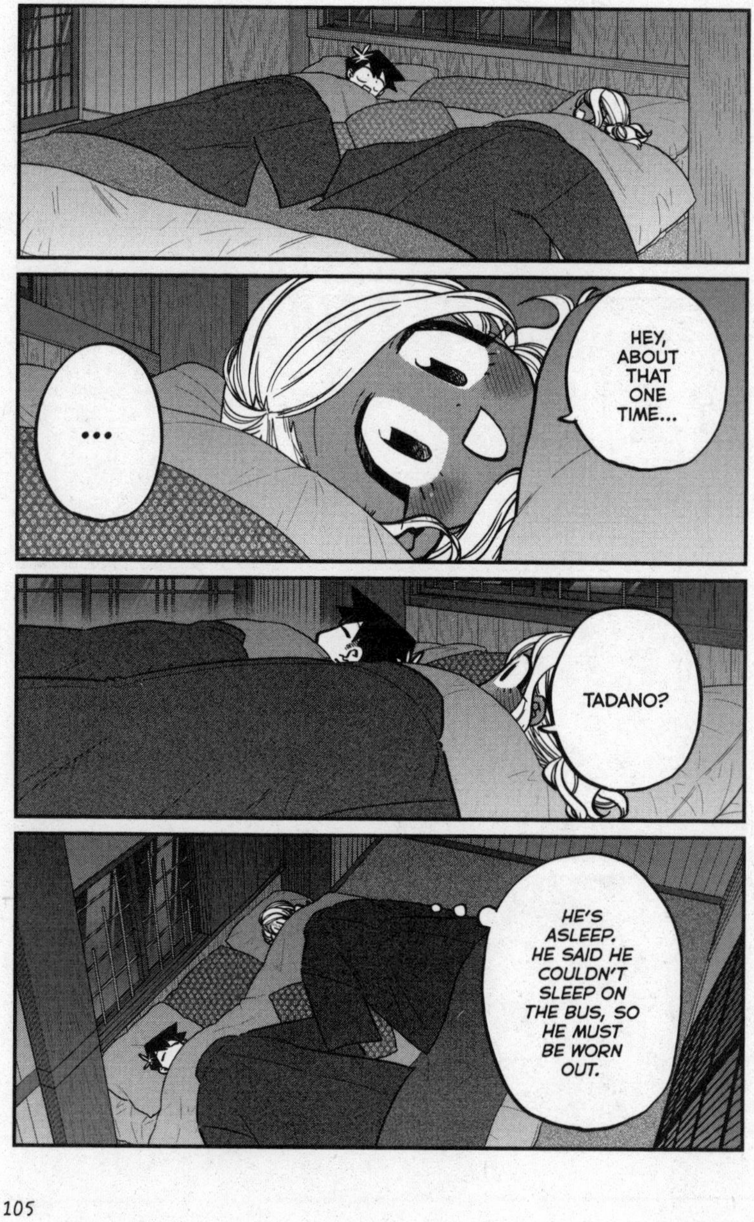
HEY, ABOUT THAT ONE TIME...
...
TADANO?
HE'S ASLEEP. HE SAID HE COULDN'T SLEEP ON THE BUS, SO HE MUST BE WORN OUT.

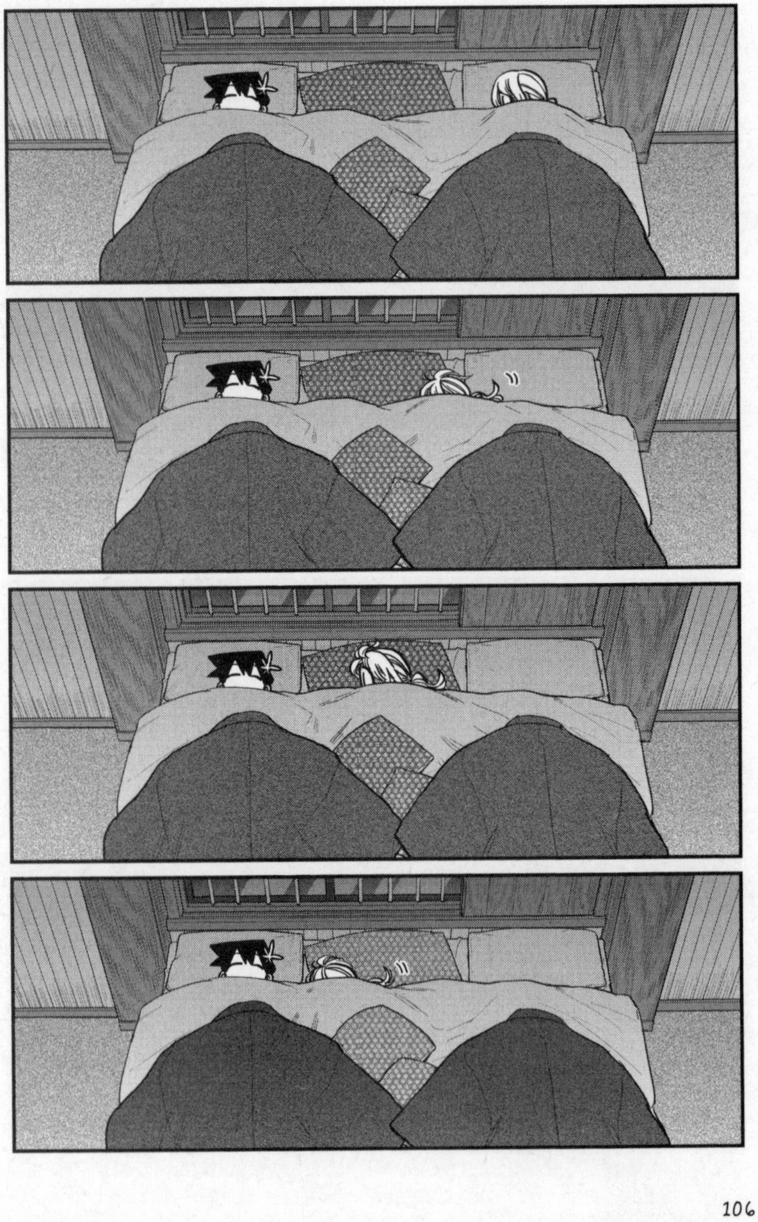

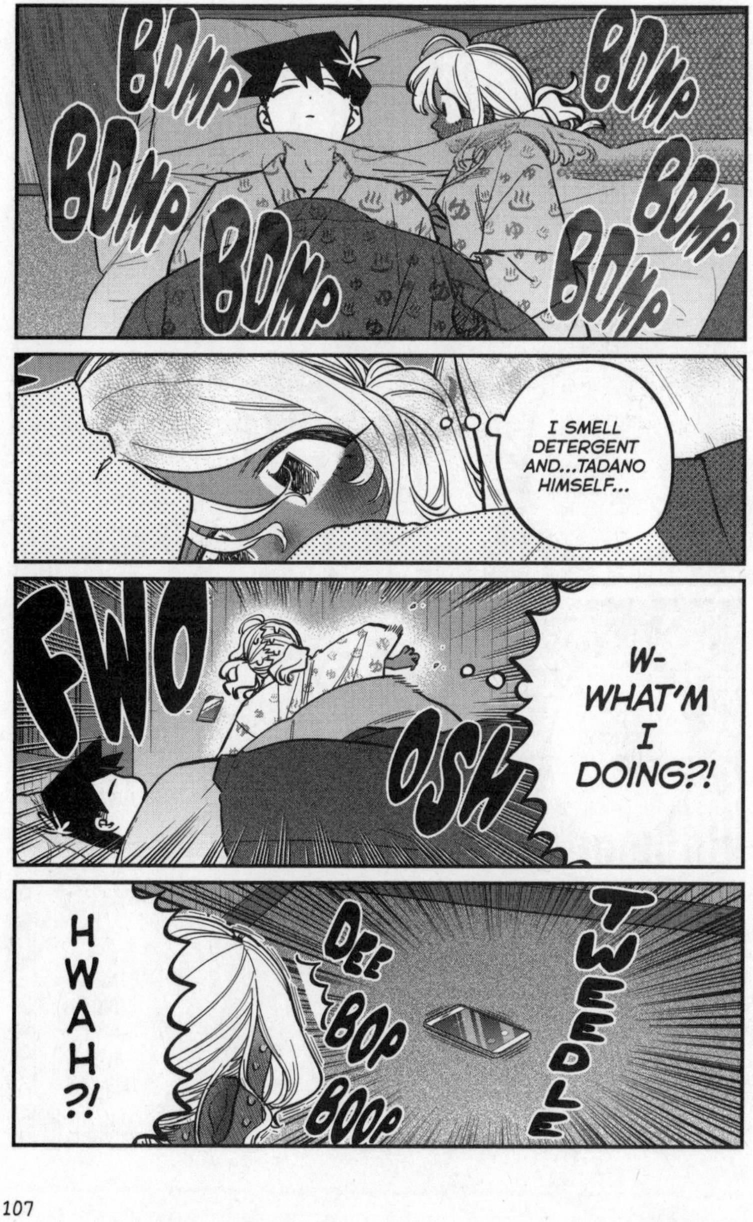
BOMP
BOMP
BOMP
BOMP
BOMP
BOMP
I SMELL DETERGENT AND...TADANO HIMSELF...
W-WHAT'M I DOING?!
FWO
OSH
TWEEDLE
DEE BOP BOP BOOP
HWAH?!

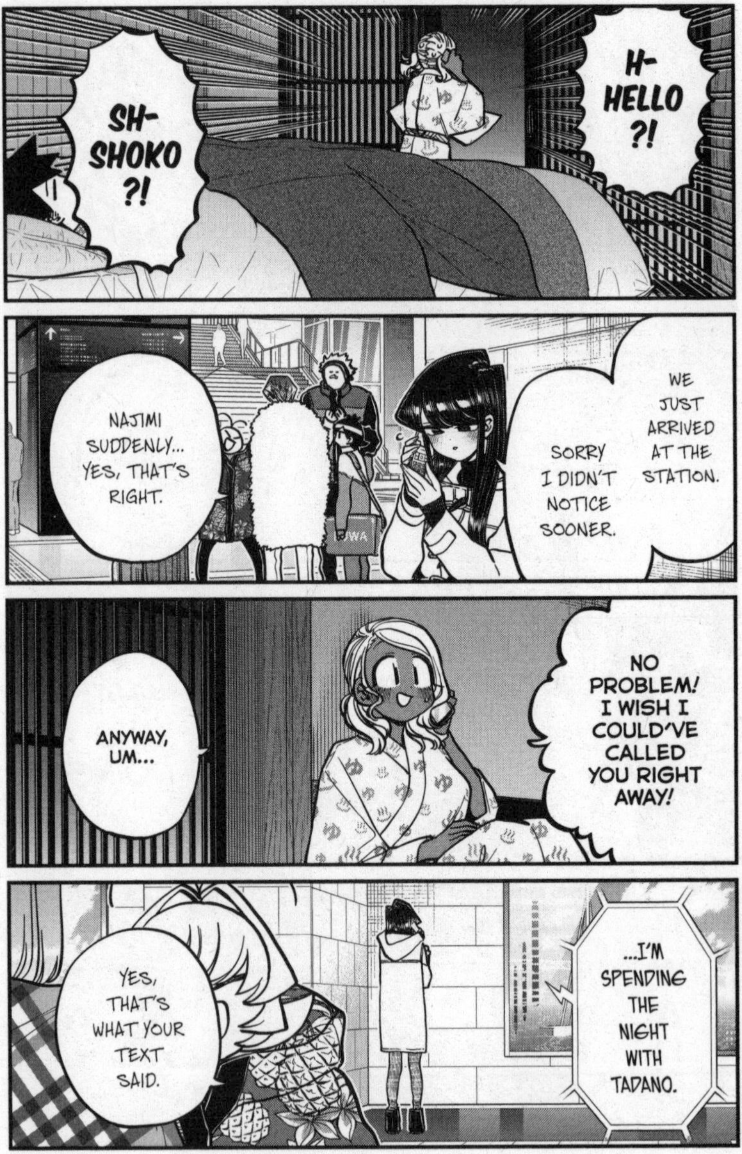
H-HELLO?!
SH-SHOKO?!
WE JUST ARRIVED AT THE STATION.
SORRY I DIDN'T NOTICE SOONER.
NAJIMI SUDDENLY... YES, THAT'S RIGHT.
NO PROBLEM! I WISH I COULD'VE CALLED YOU RIGHT AWAY!
ANYWAY, UM...
...I'M SPENDING THE NIGHT WITH TADANO.
YES, THAT'S WHAT YOUR TEXT SAID.

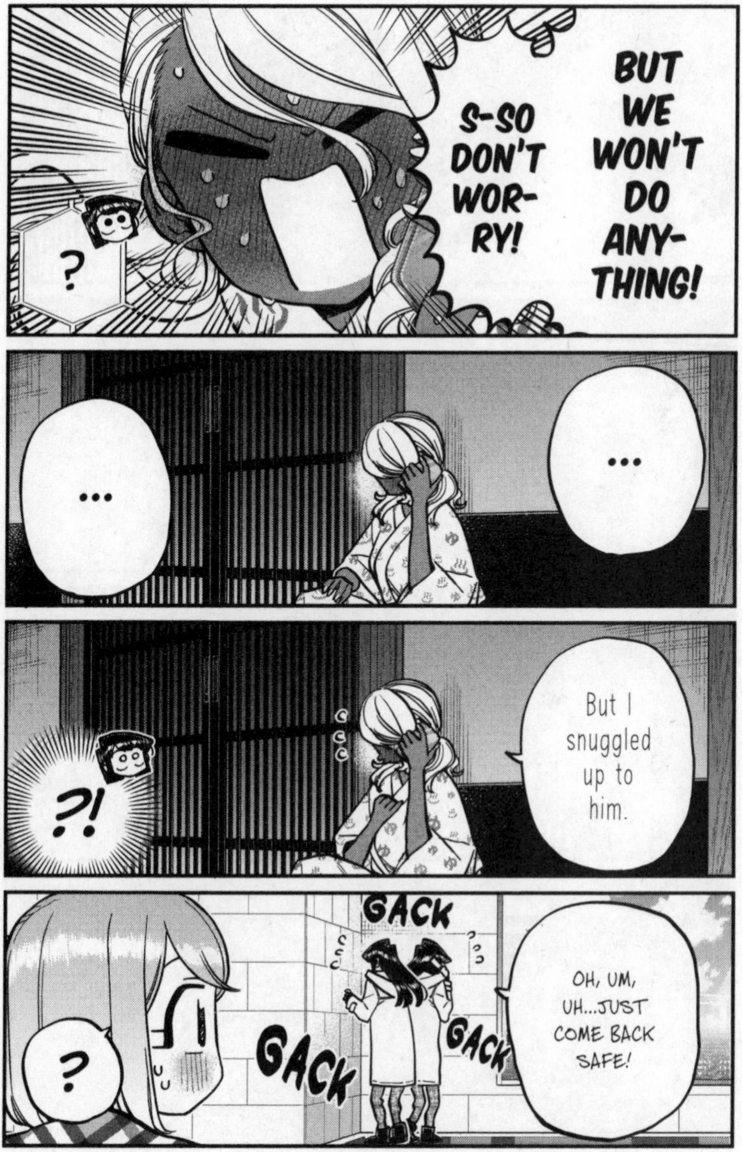
BUT WE WON'T DO ANY-THING!
S-SO DON'T WOR-RY!
?
...
...
But I snuggled up to him.
?!
OH, UM, UH...JUST COME BACK SAFE!
GACK
GACK
GACK
?

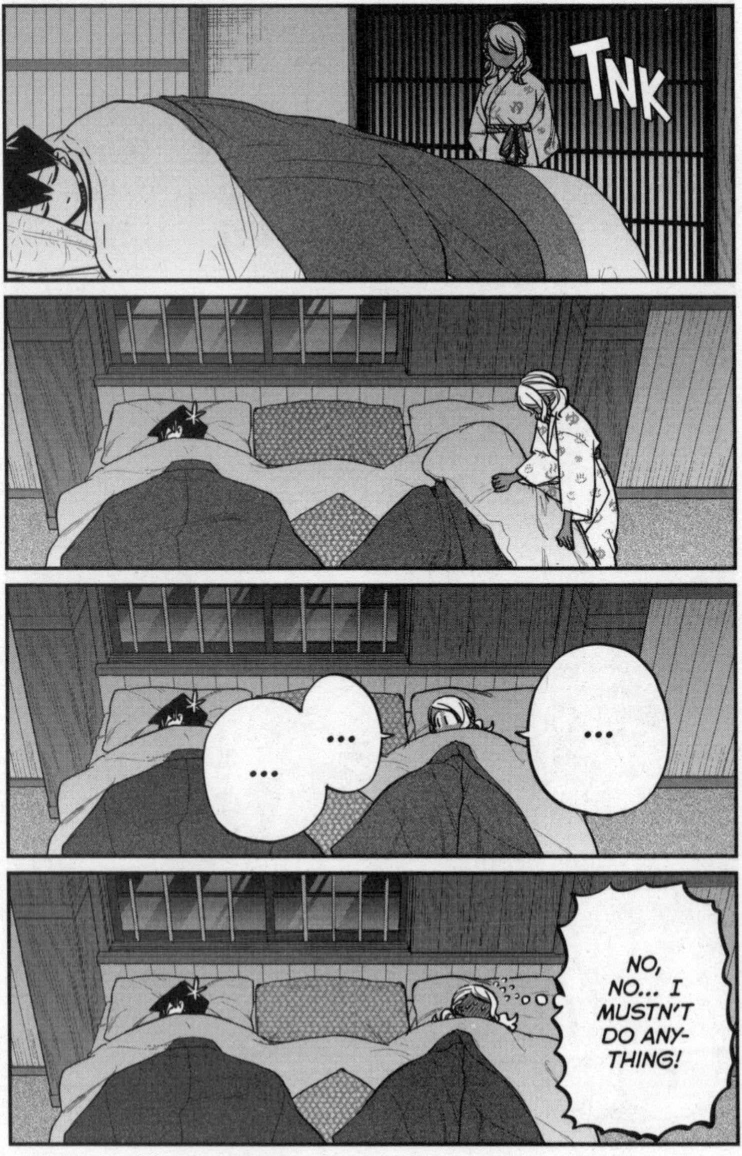
TNK
...
...
...
NO, NO... I MUSTN'T DO ANYTHING!

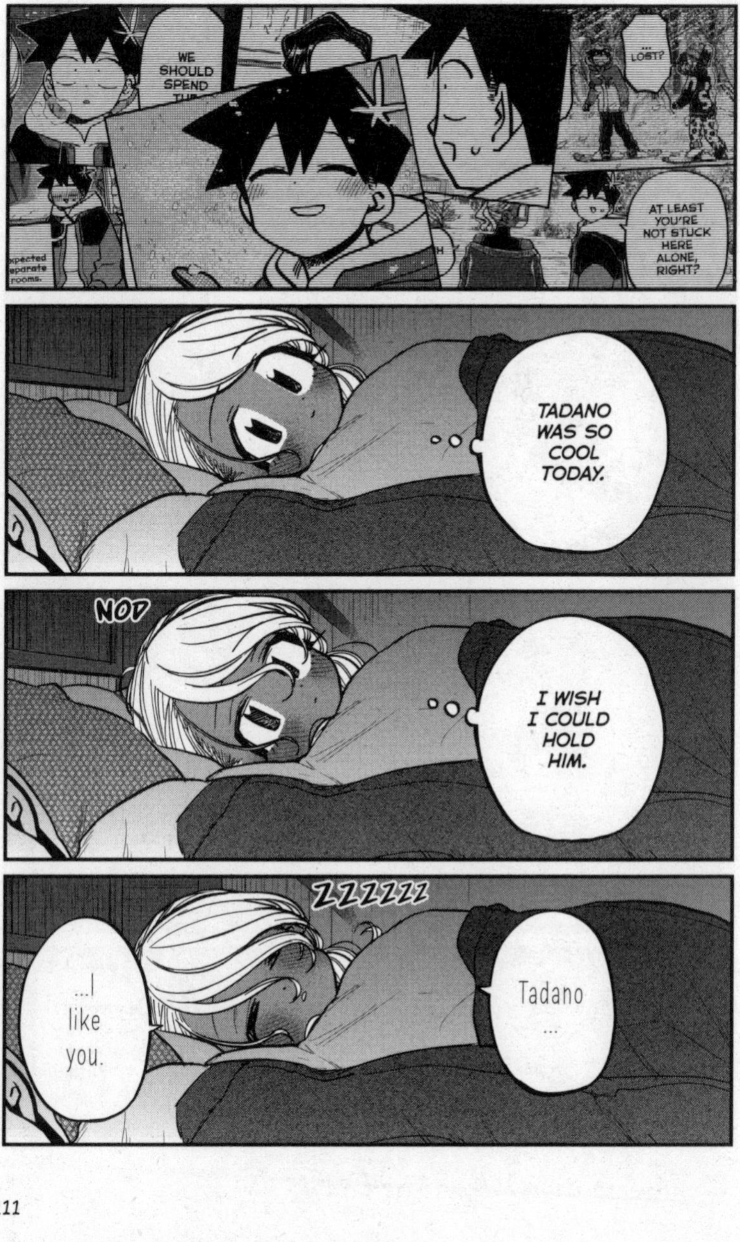
...LOST?
AT LEAST YOU'RE NOT STUCK HERE ALONE, RIGHT?
WE SHOULD SPEND
TADANO WAS SO COOL TODAY.
NOD
I WISH I COULD HOLD HIM.
ZZZZZZ
Tadano...
...I like you.

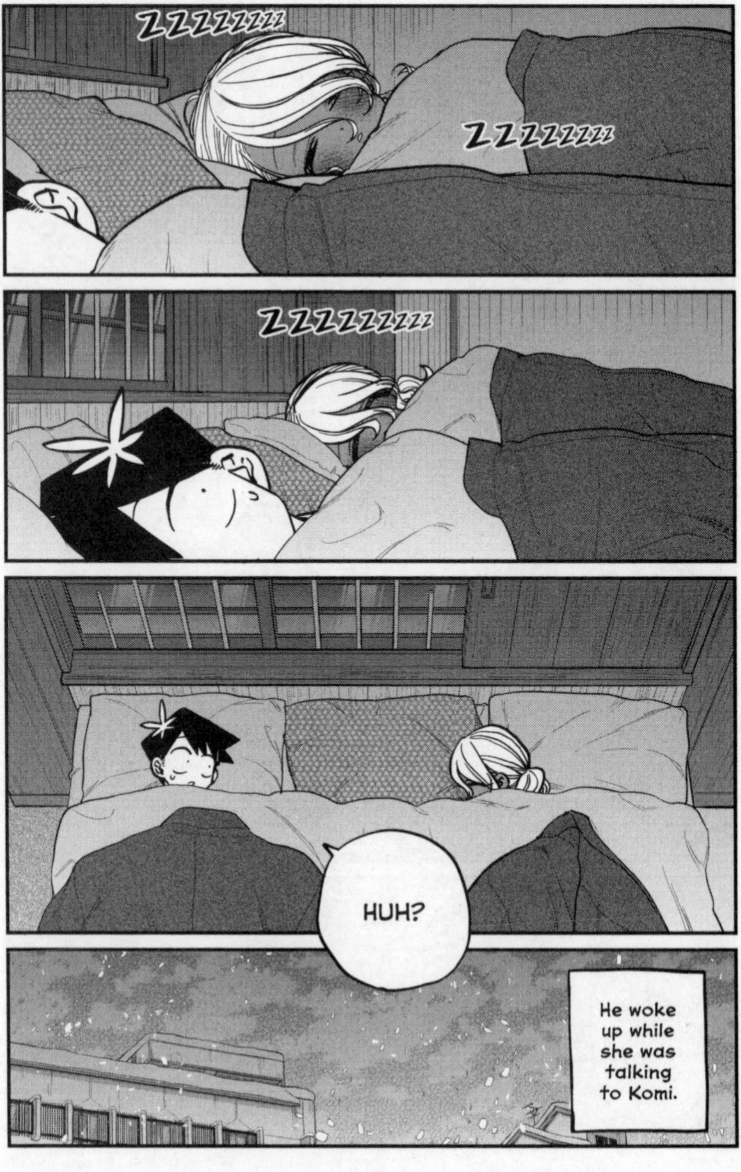
ZZZZZZZZ
ZZZZZZZZ
ZZZZZZZZZ
HUH?
He woke up while she was talking to Komi.

Communication 264 — The End

Komi Can't Communicate

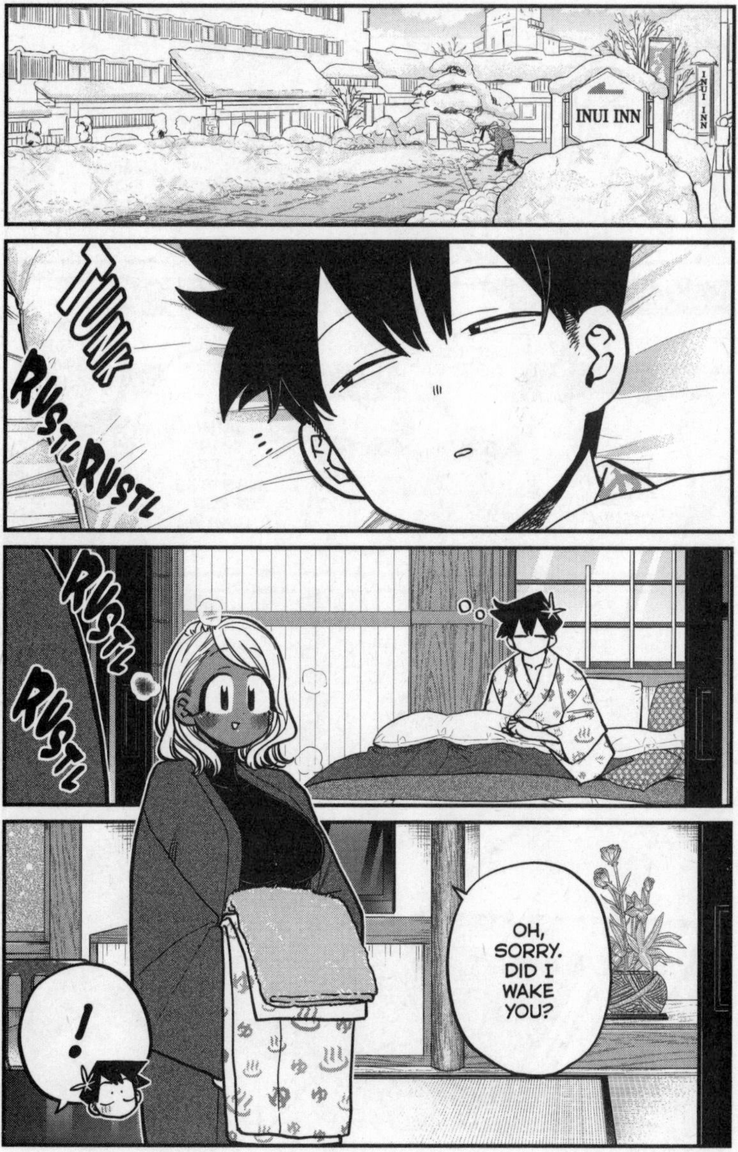
INUI INN
INUI INN
TUNK
RUSTL
RUSTL
RUSTL
RUSTL
RUSTL
OH, SORRY. DID I WAKE YOU?
!

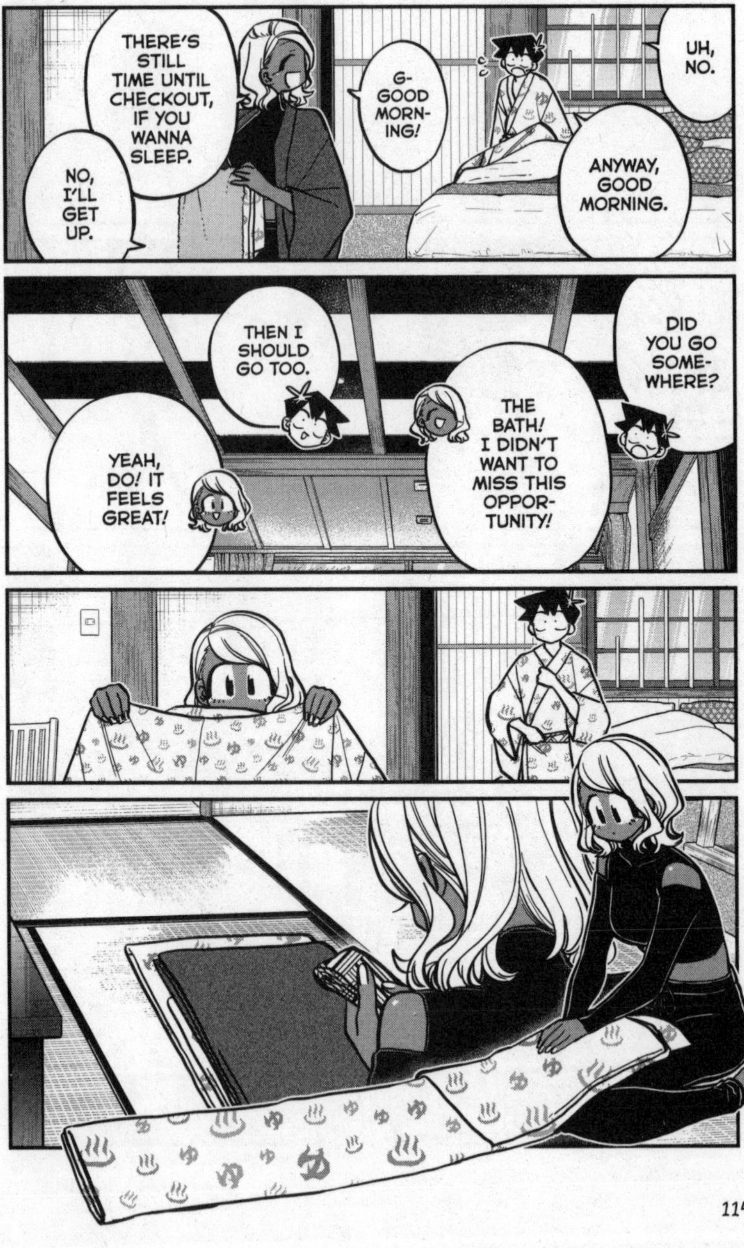
UH, NO.
G-GOOD MORNING!
ANYWAY, GOOD MORNING.
THERE'S STILL TIME UNTIL CHECKOUT, IF YOU WANNA SLEEP.
NO, I'LL GET UP.
DID YOU GO SOMEWHERE?
THE BATH! I DIDN'T WANT TO MISS THIS OPPORTUNITY!
THEN I SHOULD GO TOO.
YEAH, DO! IT FEELS GREAT!

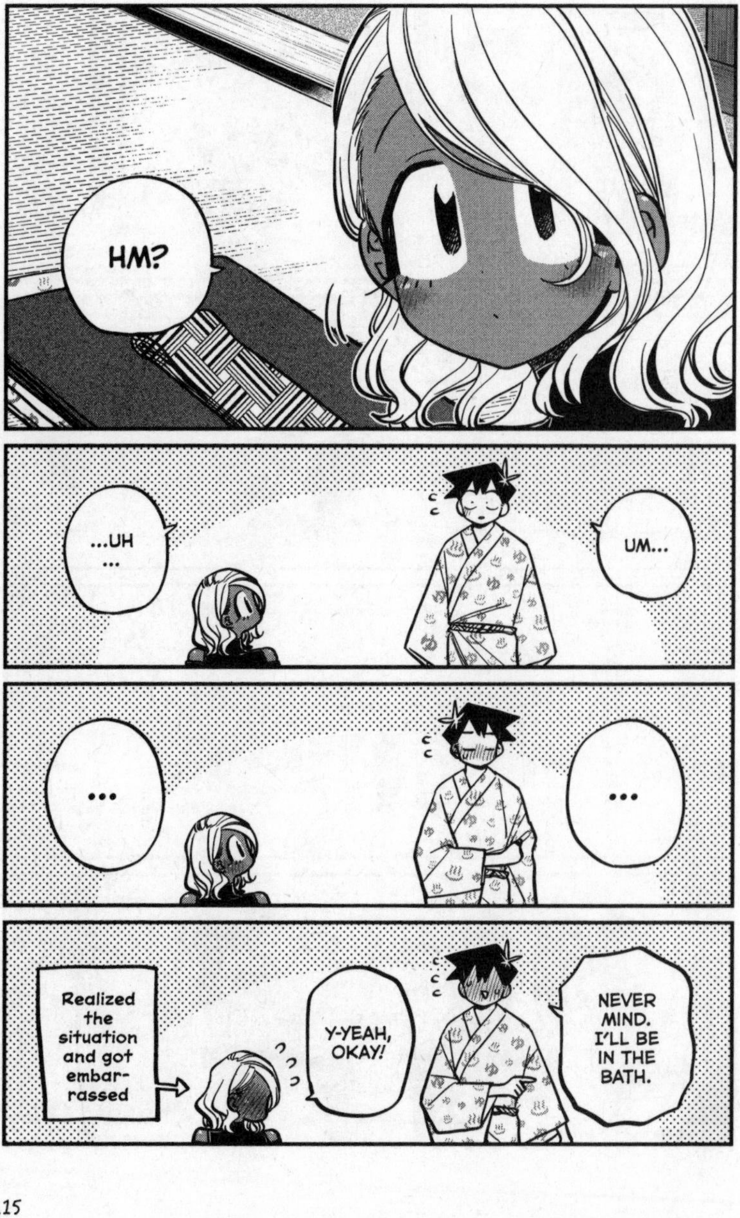
HM?
UM...
...UH ...
...
...
NEVER MIND. I'LL BE IN THE BATH.
Y-YEAH, OKAY!
Realized the situation and got embarrassed

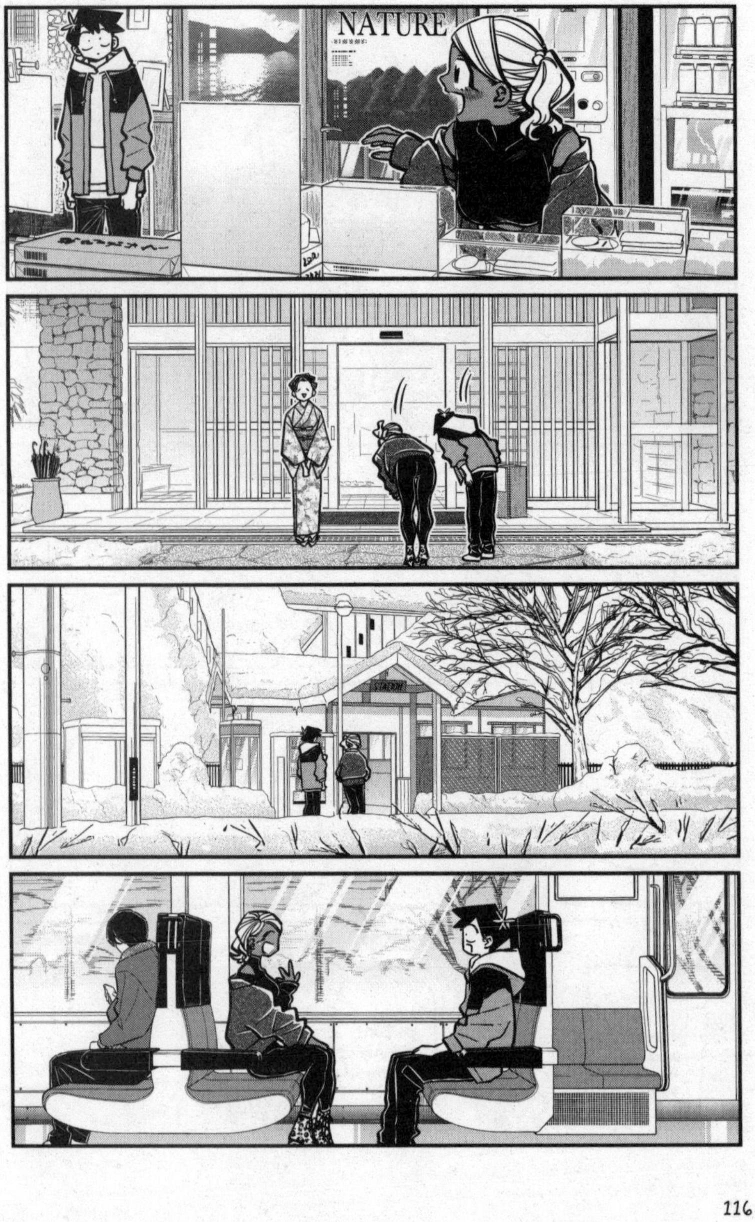
NATURE

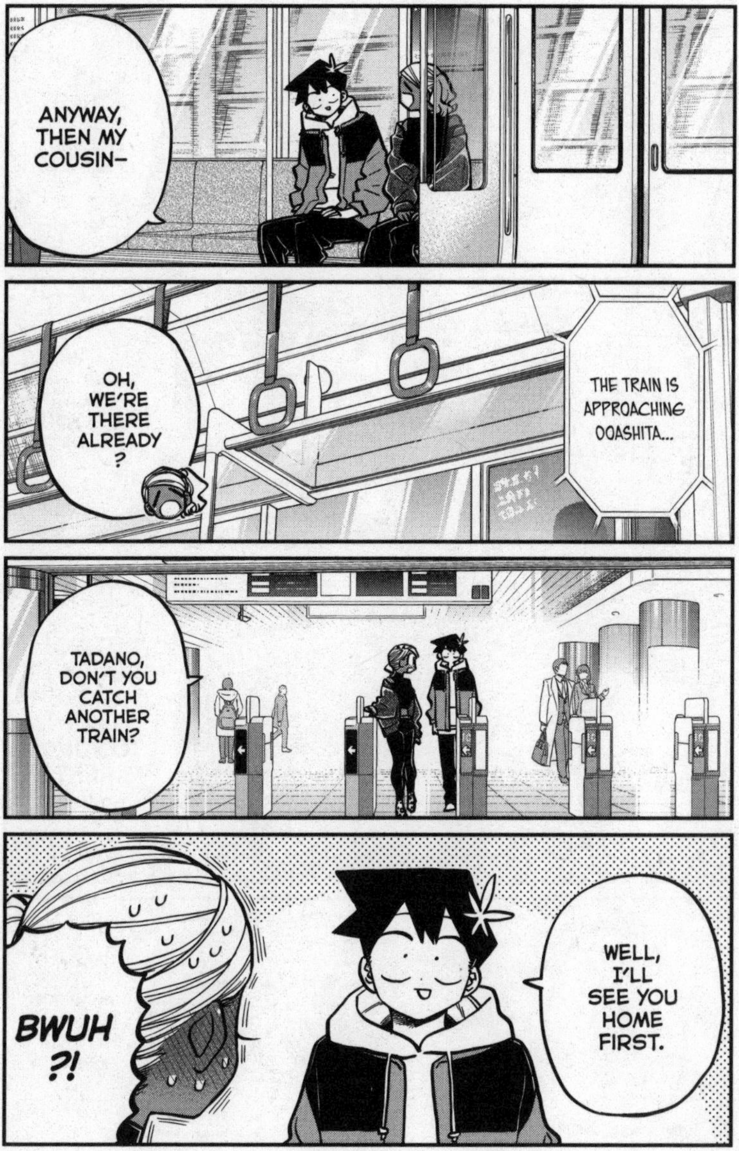
ANYWAY, THEN MY COUSIN—
THE TRAIN IS APPROACHING OOASHITA...
OH, WE'RE THERE ALREADY?
TADANO, DON'T YOU CATCH ANOTHER TRAIN?
WELL, I'LL SEE YOU HOME FIRST.
BWUH ?!

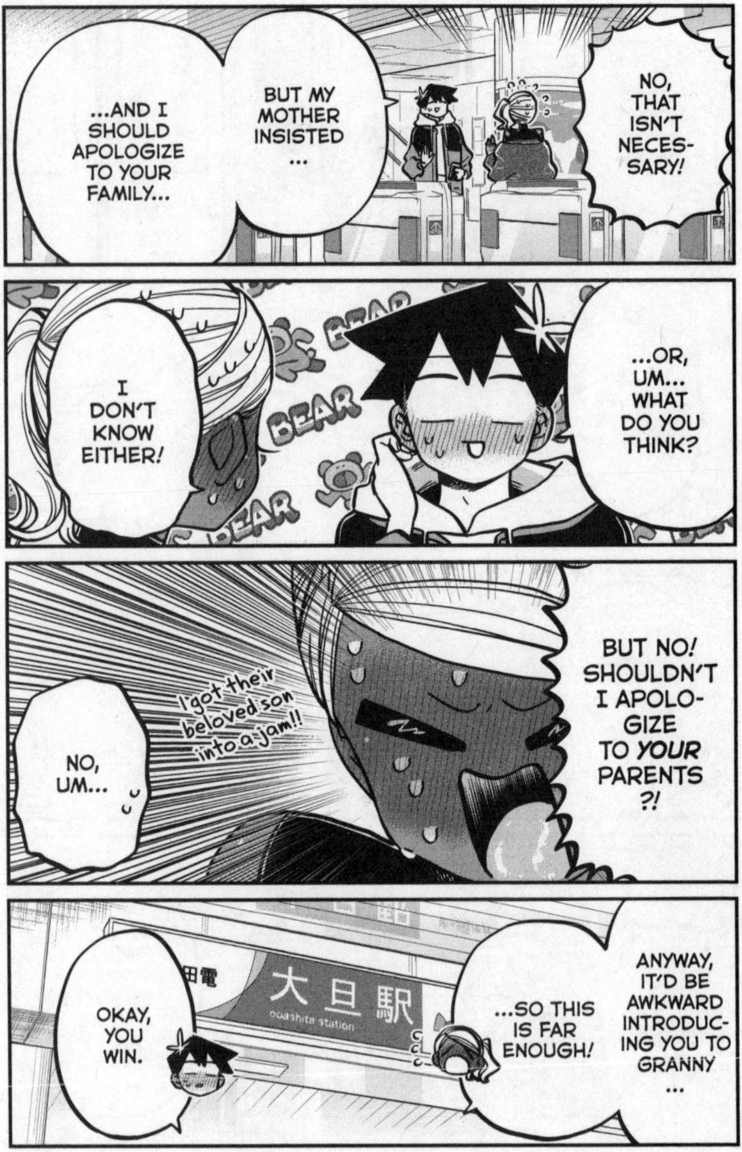
NO, THAT ISN'T NECES-SARY!
BUT MY MOTHER INSISTED ...
...AND I SHOULD APOLOGIZE TO YOUR FAMILY...
...OR, UM... WHAT DO YOU THINK?
BEAR
BEAR
I DON'T KNOW EITHER!
BUT NO! SHOULDN'T I APOLOGIZE TO *YOUR* PARENTS ?!
I got their beloved son into a jam!!
NO, UM...
ANYWAY, IT'D BE AWKWARD INTRODUCING YOU TO GRANNY ...
...SO THIS IS FAR ENOUGH!
大旦駅
ooashita station
OKAY, YOU WIN.

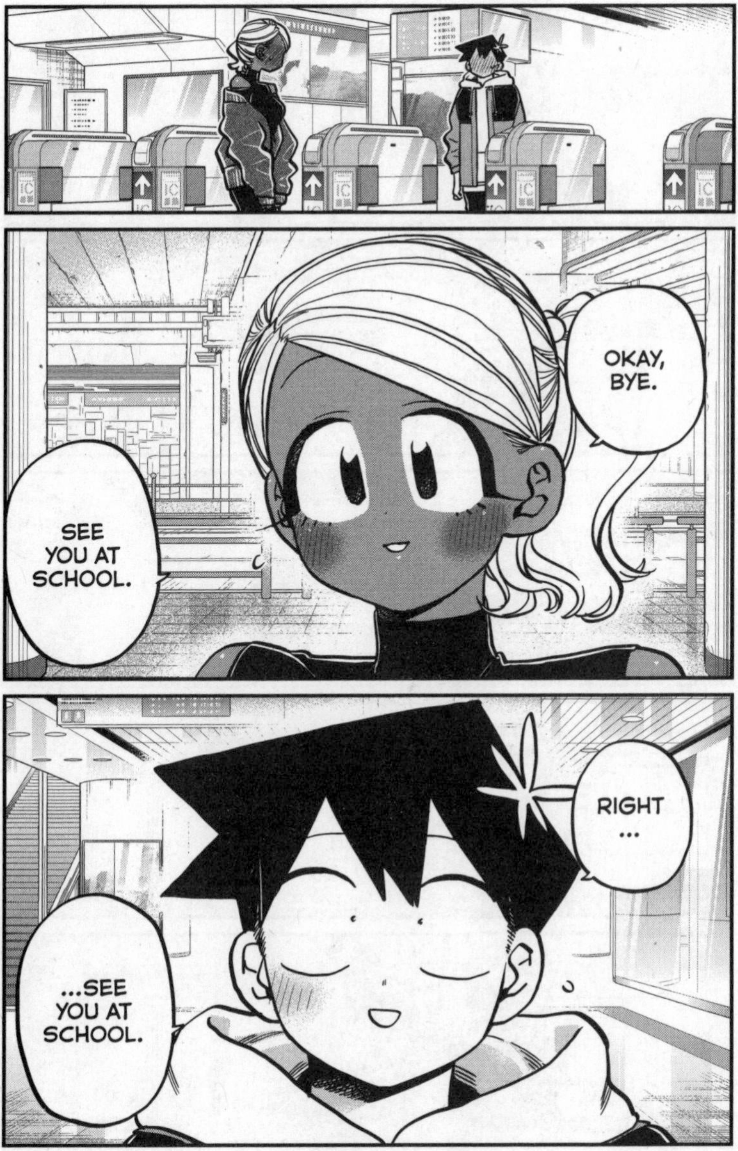
OKAY, BYE.
SEE YOU AT SCHOOL.
RIGHT ...
...SEE YOU AT SCHOOL.

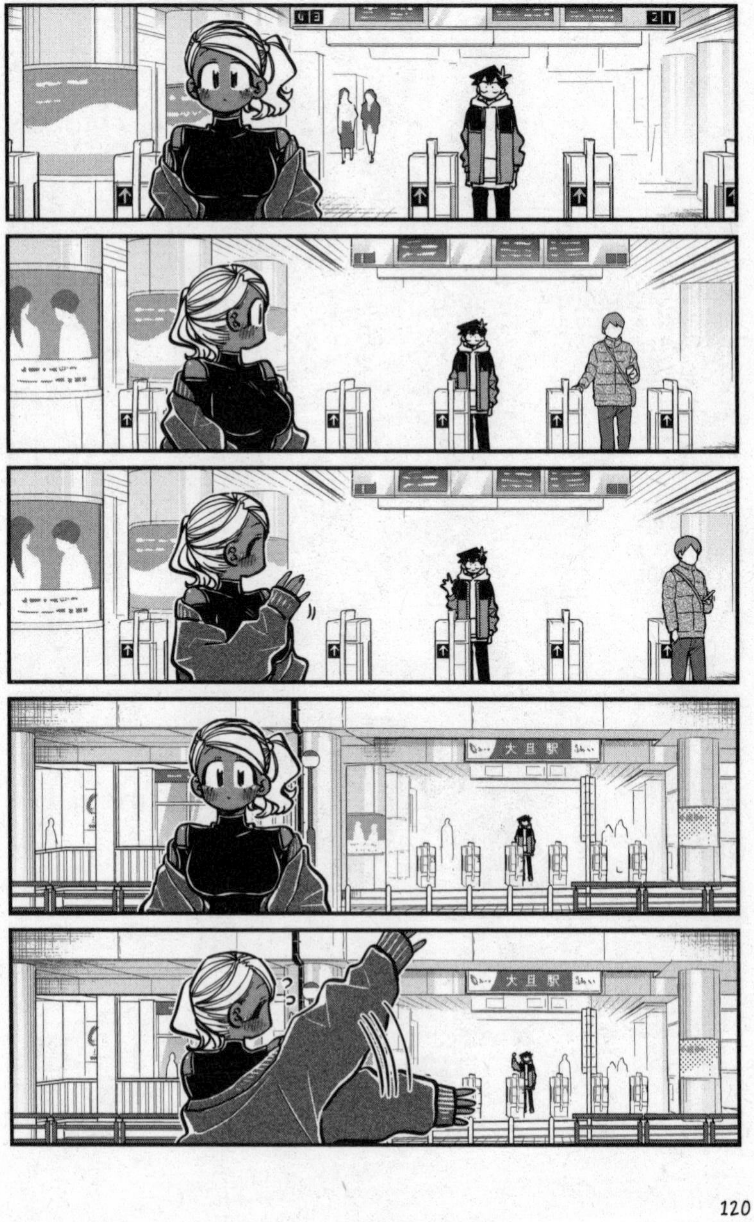
大旦駅
大旦駅

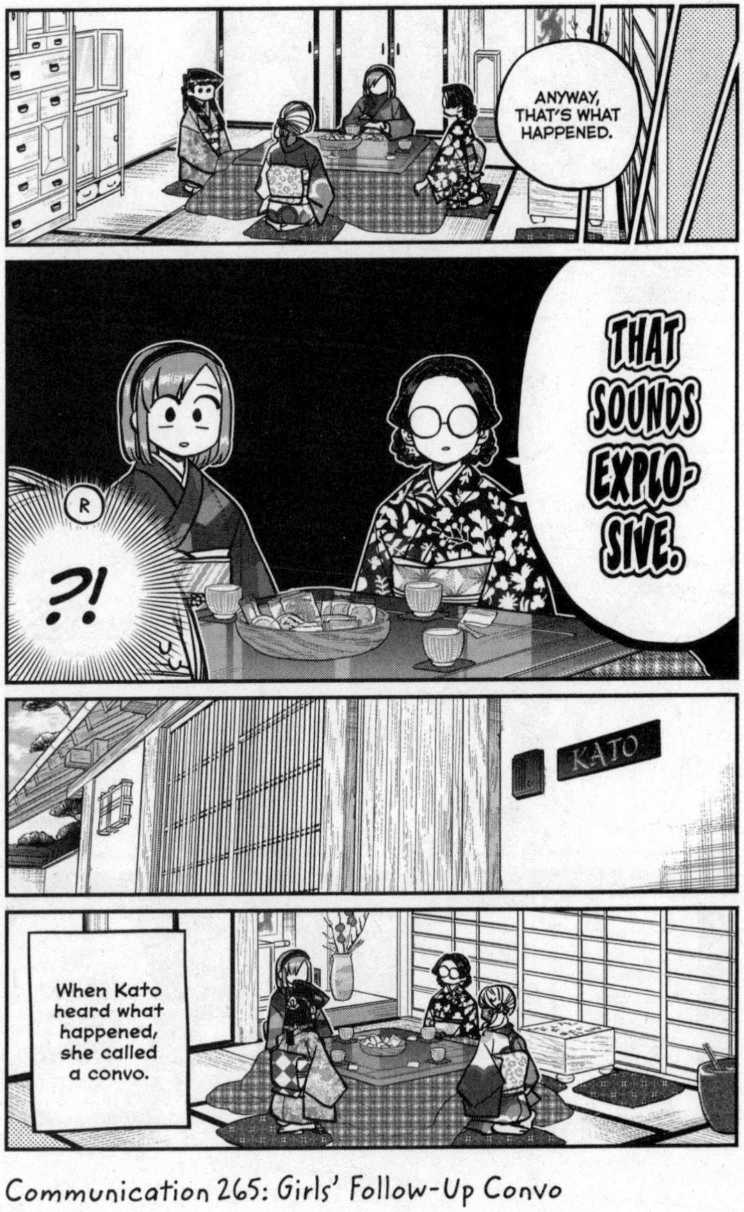
ANYWAY, THAT'S WHAT HAPPENED.
THAT SOUNDS EXPLO-SIVE.
R
?!
KATO
When Kato heard what happened, she called a convo.

Communication 265: Girls' Follow-Up Convo

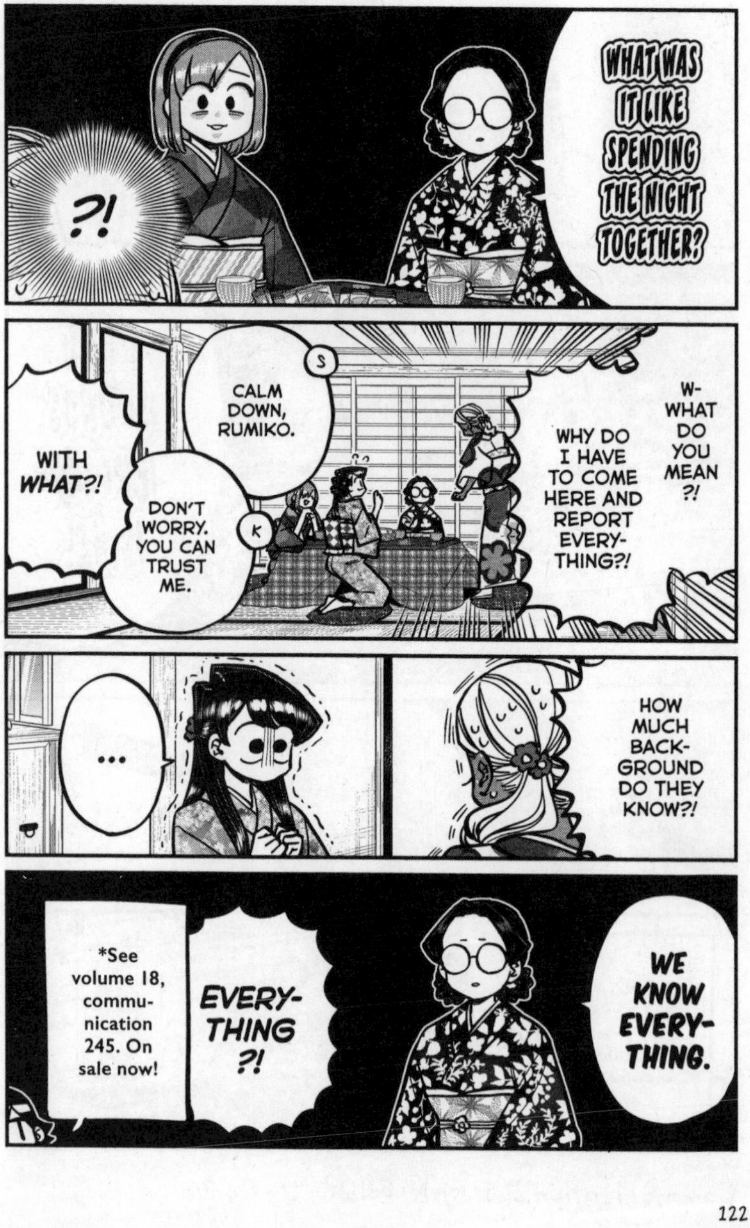
WHAT WAS IT LIKE SPENDING THE NIGHT TOGETHER?
?!
W-WHAT DO YOU MEAN?!
WHY DO I HAVE TO COME HERE AND REPORT EVERYTHING?!
CALM DOWN, RUMIKO.
DON'T WORRY. YOU CAN TRUST ME.
WITH WHAT?!
HOW MUCH BACKGROUND DO THEY KNOW?!
...
WE KNOW EVERYTHING.
EVERYTHING?!
*See volume 18, communication 245. On sale now!

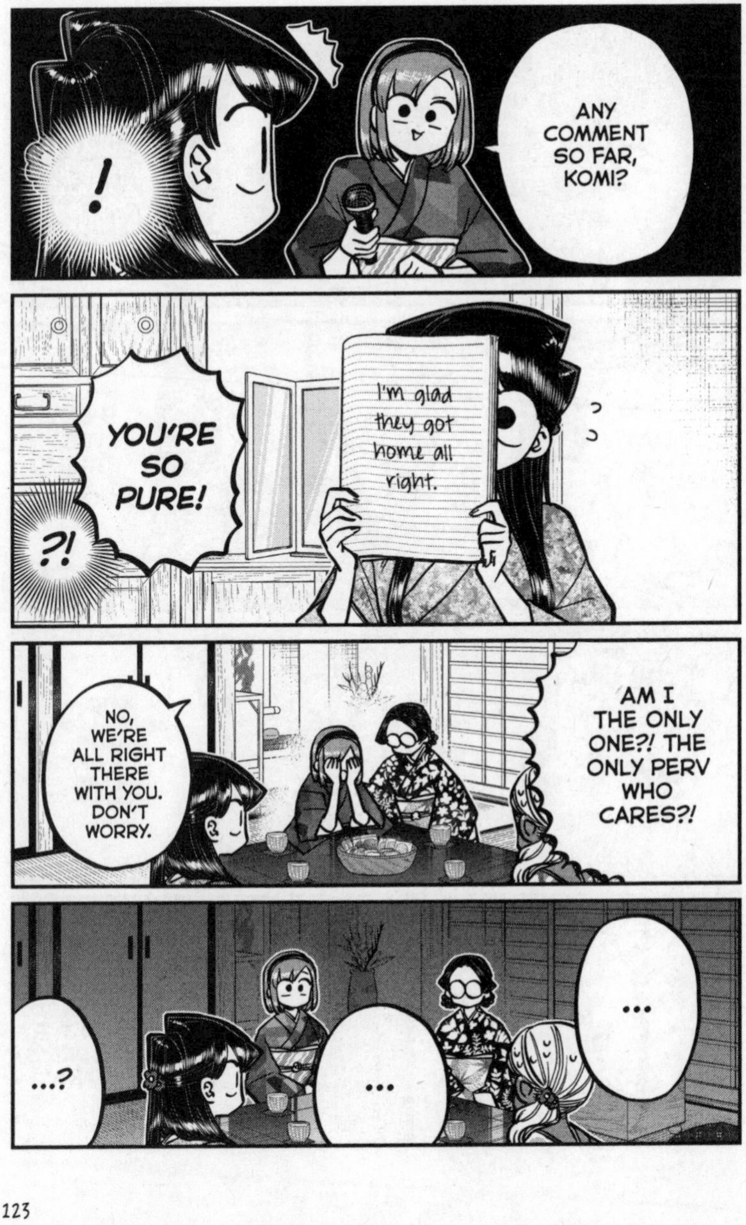
ANY COMMENT SO FAR, KOMI?
!
I'm glad they got home all right.
YOU'RE SO PURE!
?!
AM I THE ONLY ONE?! THE ONLY PERV WHO CARES?!
NO, WE'RE ALL RIGHT THERE WITH YOU. DON'T WORRY.
...
...
...?

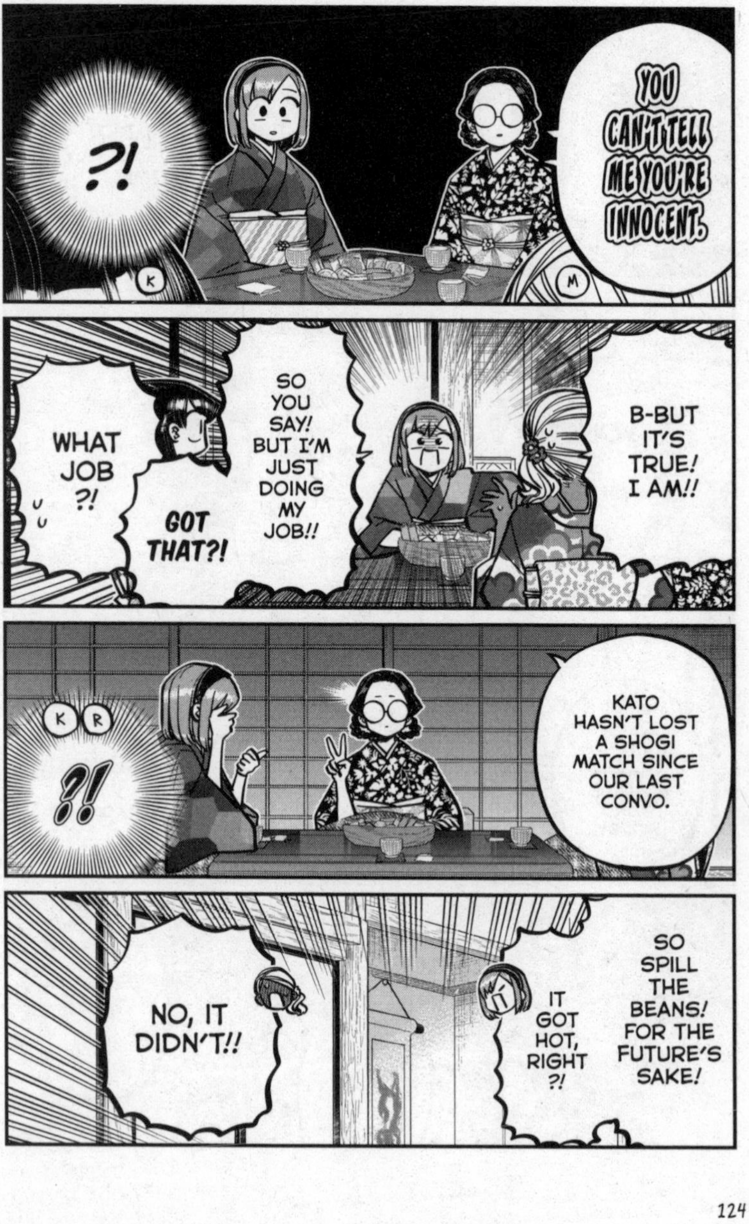
YOU CAN'T TELL ME YOU'RE INNOCENT.
?!
B-BUT IT'S TRUE! I AM!!
SO YOU SAY! BUT I'M JUST DOING MY JOB!!
GOT THAT?!
WHAT JOB ?!
KATO HASN'T LOST A SHOGI MATCH SINCE OUR LAST CONVO.
?!
SO SPILL THE BEANS! FOR THE FUTURE'S SAKE!
IT GOT HOT, RIGHT ?!
NO, IT DIDN'T!!

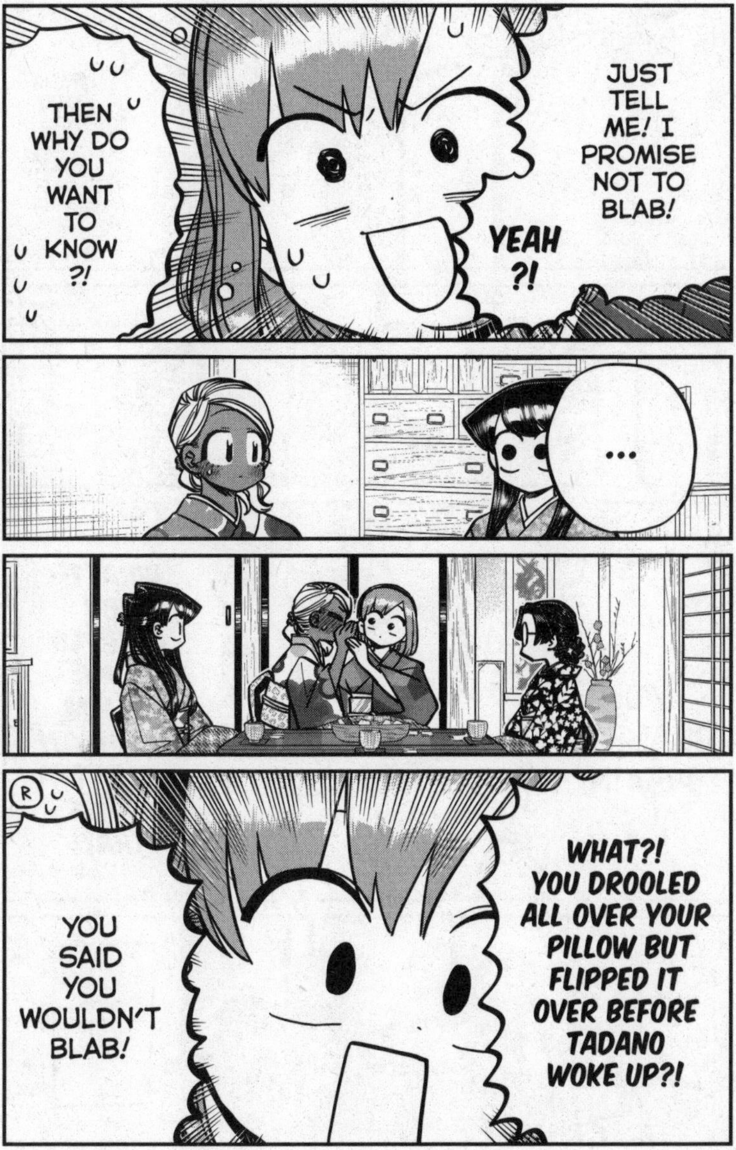
JUST TELL ME! I PROMISE NOT TO BLAB!
YEAH ?!
THEN WHY DO YOU WANT TO KNOW ?!
...
WHAT?! YOU DROOLED ALL OVER YOUR PILLOW BUT FLIPPED IT OVER BEFORE TADANO WOKE UP?!
YOU SAID YOU WOULDN'T BLAB!

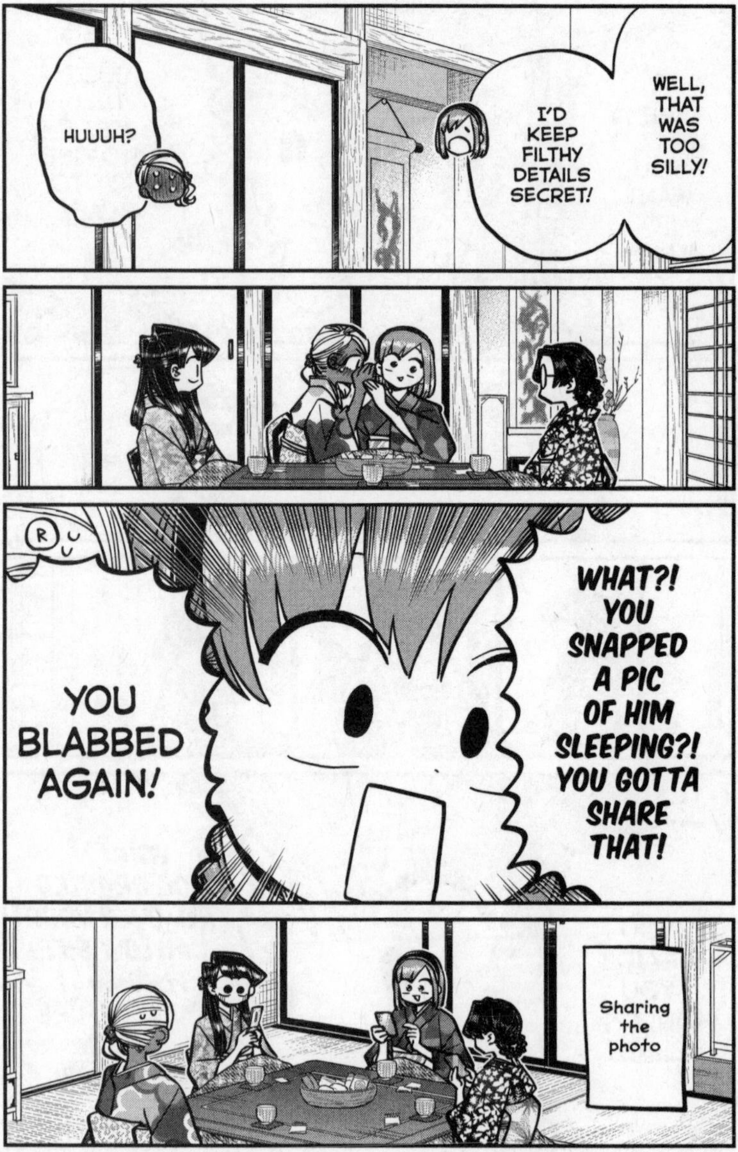
WELL, THAT WAS TOO SILLY!
I'D KEEP FILTHY DETAILS SECRET!
HUUUH?
WHAT?! YOU SNAPPED A PIC OF HIM SLEEPING?! YOU GOTTA SHARE THAT!
YOU BLABBED AGAIN!
Sharing the photo

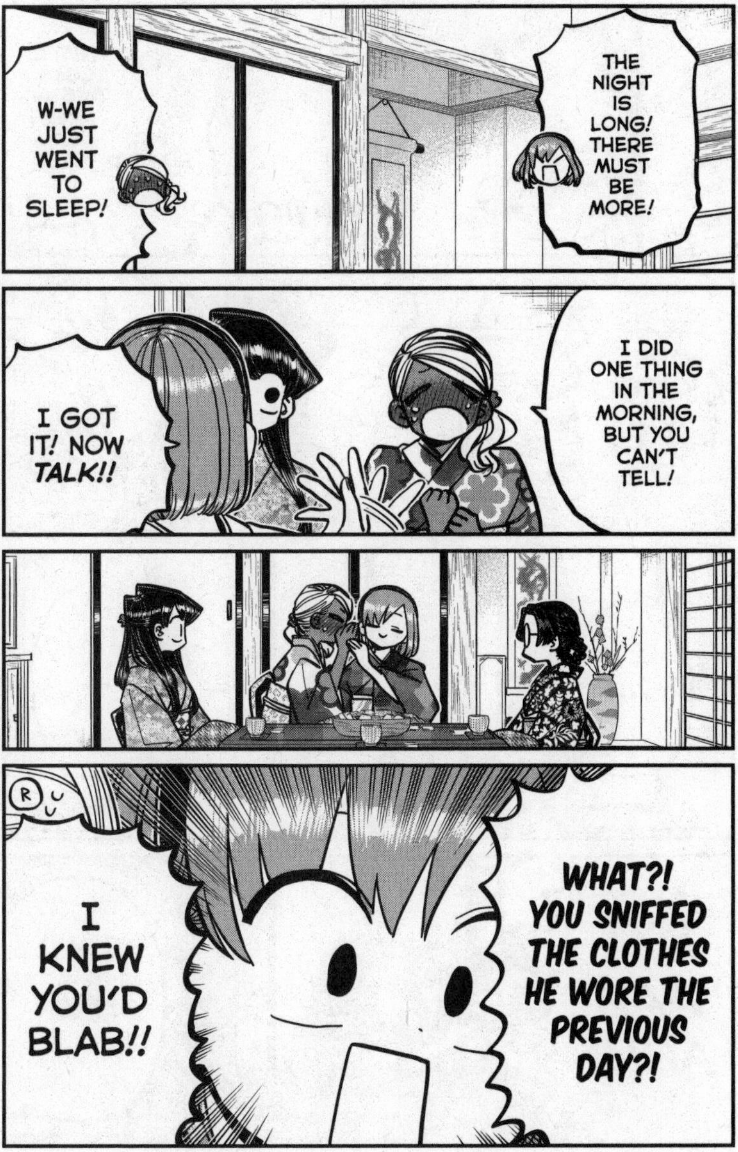
THE NIGHT IS LONG! THERE MUST BE MORE!
W-WE JUST WENT TO SLEEP!
I DID ONE THING IN THE MORNING, BUT YOU CAN'T TELL!
I GOT IT! NOW *TALK!!*
WHAT?! YOU SNIFFED THE CLOTHES HE WORE THE PREVIOUS DAY?!
I KNEW YOU'D BLAB!!

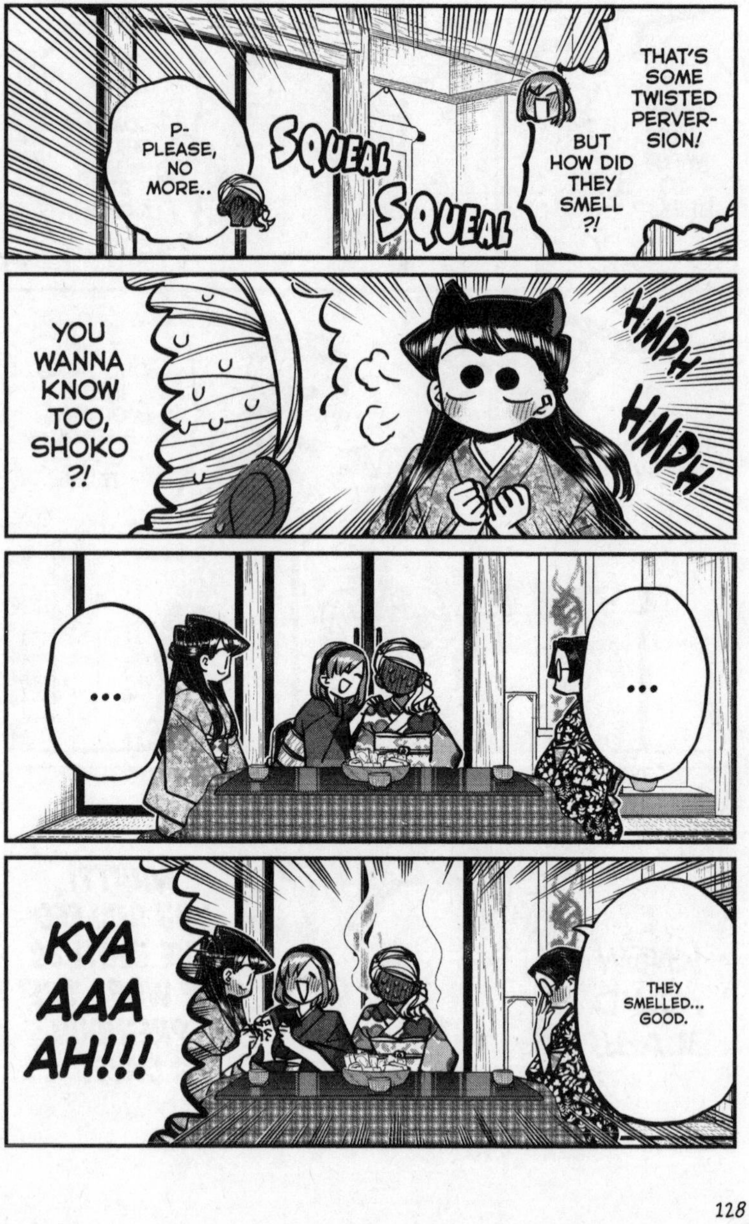
THAT'S SOME TWISTED PERVERSION!
BUT HOW DID THEY SMELL?!
SQUEAL
SQUEAL
P-PLEASE, NO MORE..
HMPH
HMPH
YOU WANNA KNOW TOO, SHOKO?!
...
...
THEY SMELLED... GOOD.
KYAAAAAH!!!

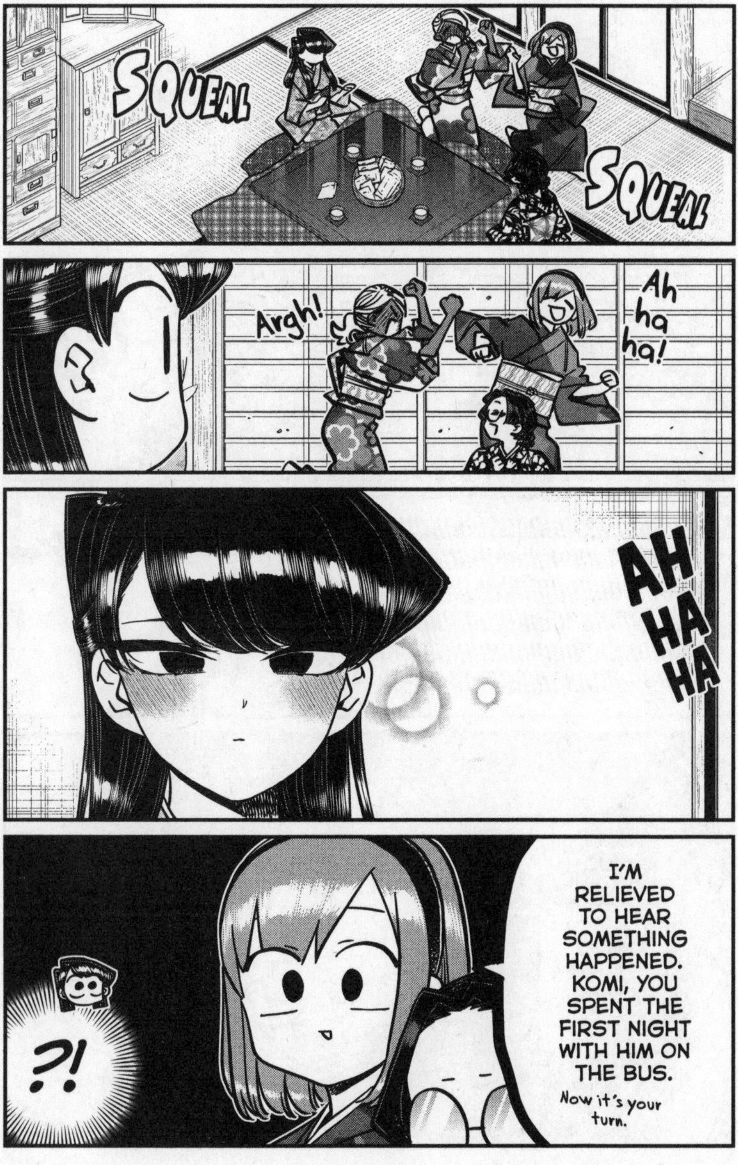
SQUEAL
SQUEAL
Ah ha ha!
Argh!
AH HA HA
I'M RELIEVED TO HEAR SOMETHING HAPPENED. KOMI, YOU SPENT THE FIRST NIGHT WITH HIM ON THE BUS.
Now it's your turn.
?!

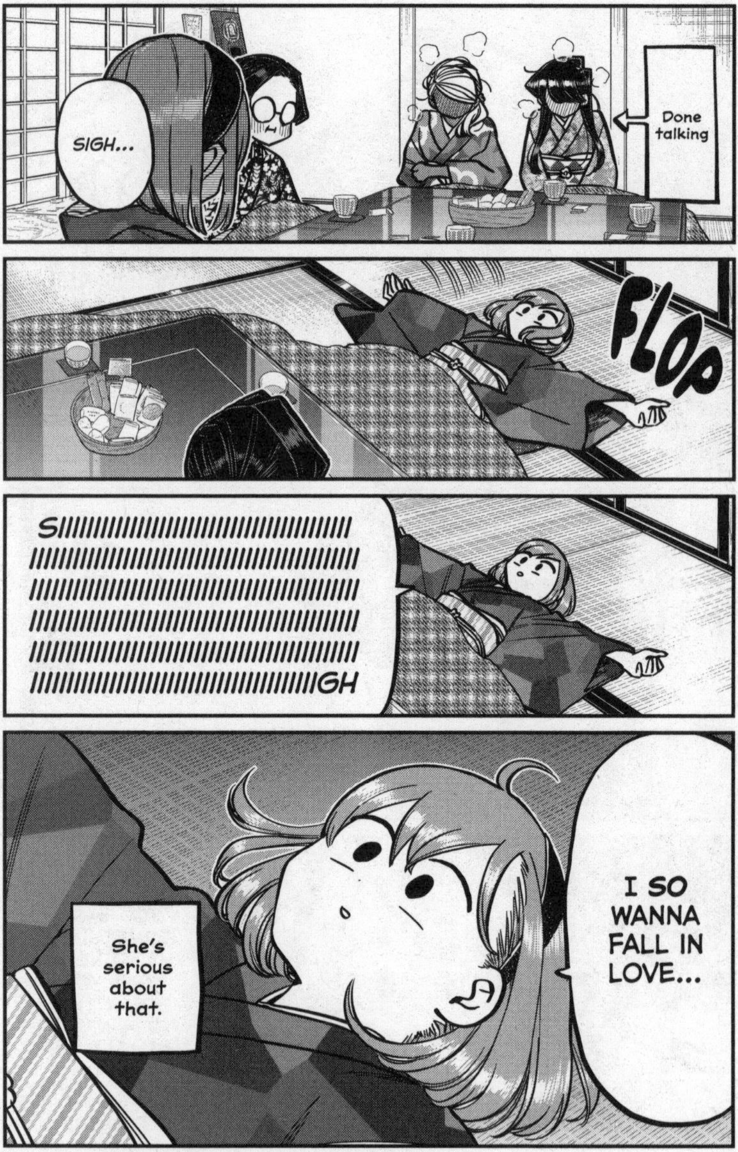
Done talking
SIGH...
FLOP
SIIIIIIIIIIIIIIIIIIIIIIIIIIIIIIIIIIIIIIIIIIIIIIIIIIIIIIIIIIIIIIIIIIIIIIIIIIIIIIIIIIIIIIIIIIIIIIIIIIIIIIIIIIIIIIIIIIIIIIIIIIIIIIIIIIIIIIIIIIIIIIIIIIIIIIIIIIIIIIIIIIIIIIIIIIIGH
I SO WANNA FALL IN LOVE...
She's serious about that.

Communication 265 — The End

Komi Can't Communicate

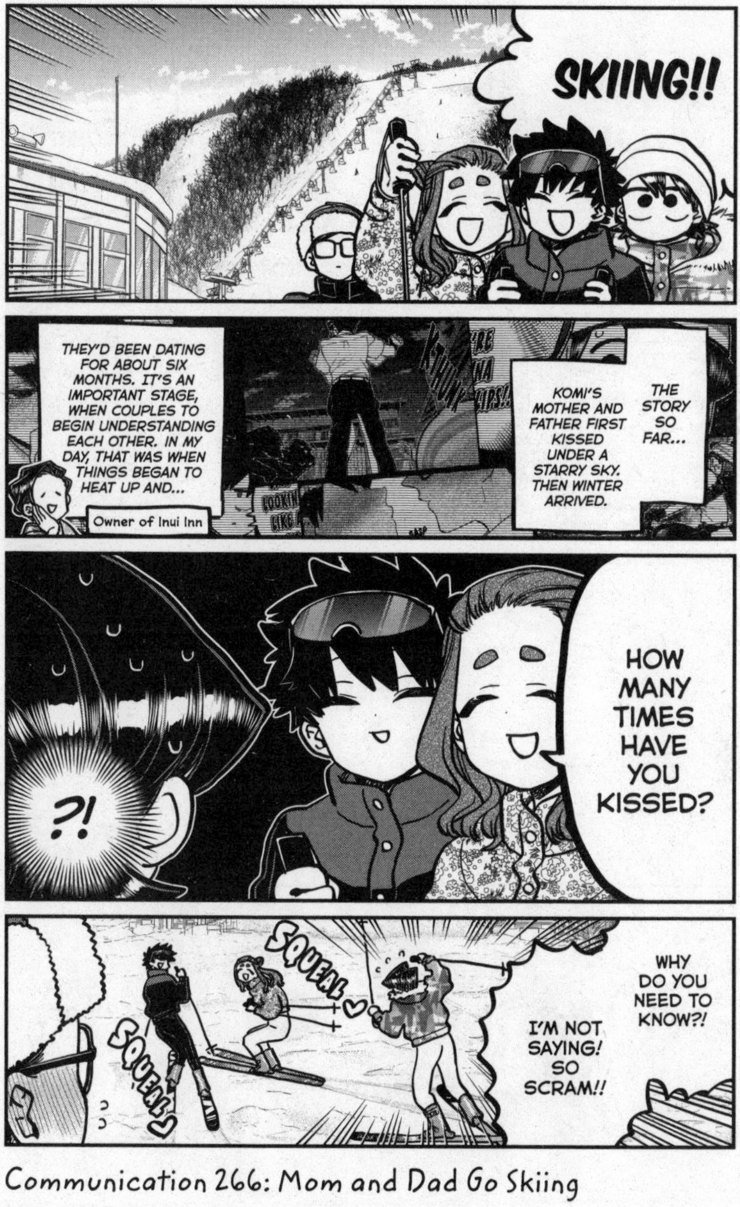
SKIING!!
THE STORY SO FAR...
KOMI'S MOTHER AND FATHER FIRST KISSED UNDER A STARRY SKY. THEN WINTER ARRIVED.
THEY'D BEEN DATING FOR ABOUT SIX MONTHS. IT'S AN IMPORTANT STAGE, WHEN COUPLES TO BEGIN UNDERSTANDING EACH OTHER. IN MY DAY, THAT WAS WHEN THINGS BEGAN TO HEAT UP AND...
Owner of Inui Inn
HOW MANY TIMES HAVE YOU KISSED?
?!
WHY DO YOU NEED TO KNOW?!
I'M NOT SAYING! SO SCRAM!!
SQUEAL ♥
SQUEAL ♥

Communication 266: Mom and Dad Go Skiing

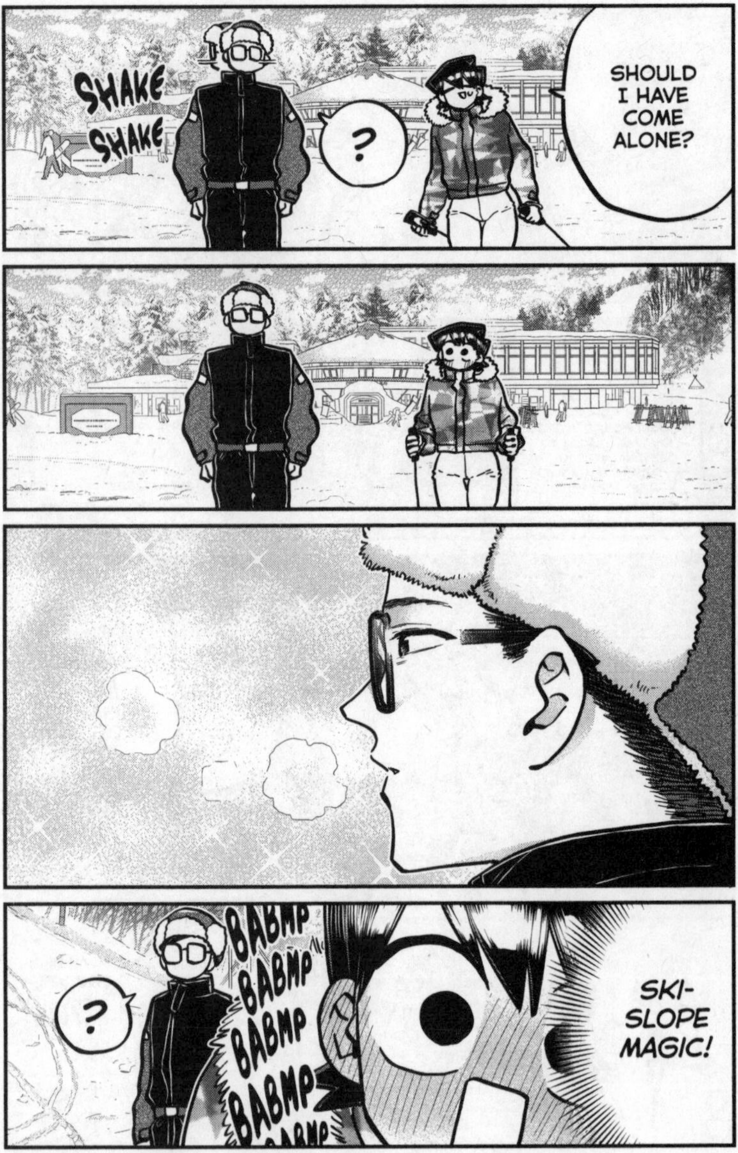
SHOULD I HAVE COME ALONE?
?
SHAKE
SHAKE
SKI-SLOPE MAGIC!
BABMP
BABMP
BABMP
BABMP
?

ARE Y-YOU GOOD AT S-SKIING, MASA?

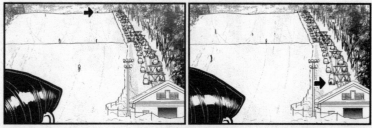

FOOSH

?!

Im-pressed

OOO-OOH-OOO-OOH!

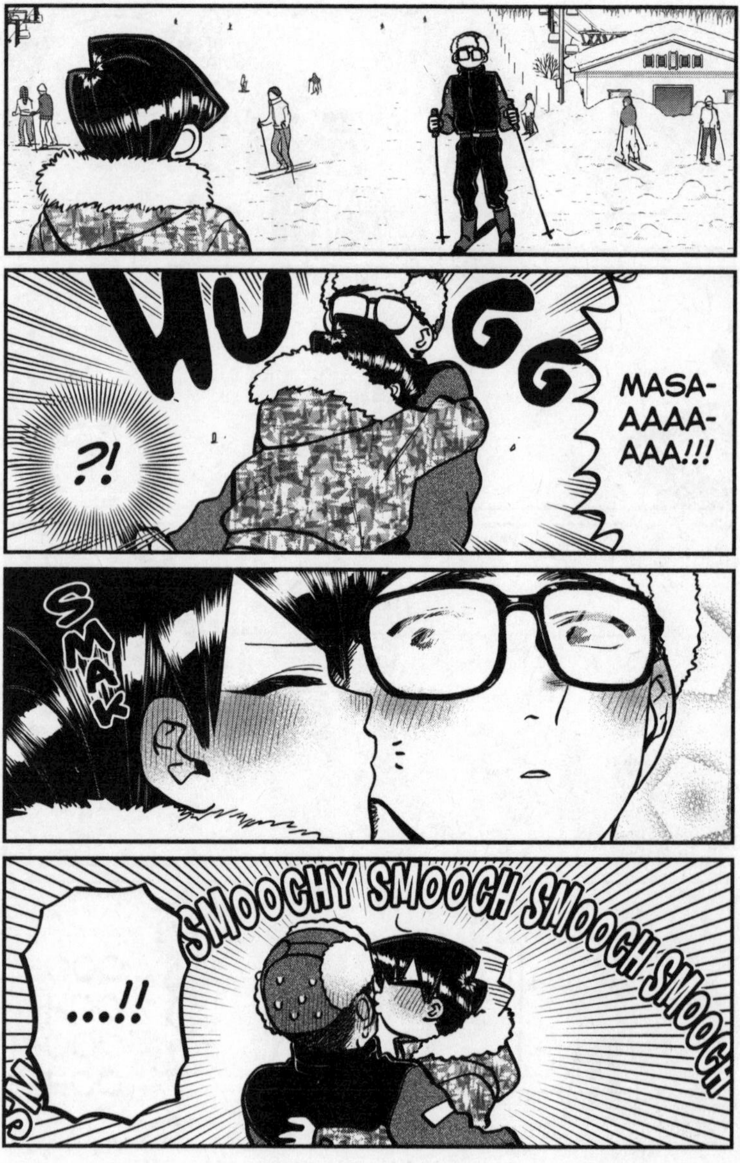
MASA-AAAA-AAA!!!
HUGG
?!
SMAK
SMOOCHY SMOOCH SMOOCH SMOOCH SMOOCH
...!!

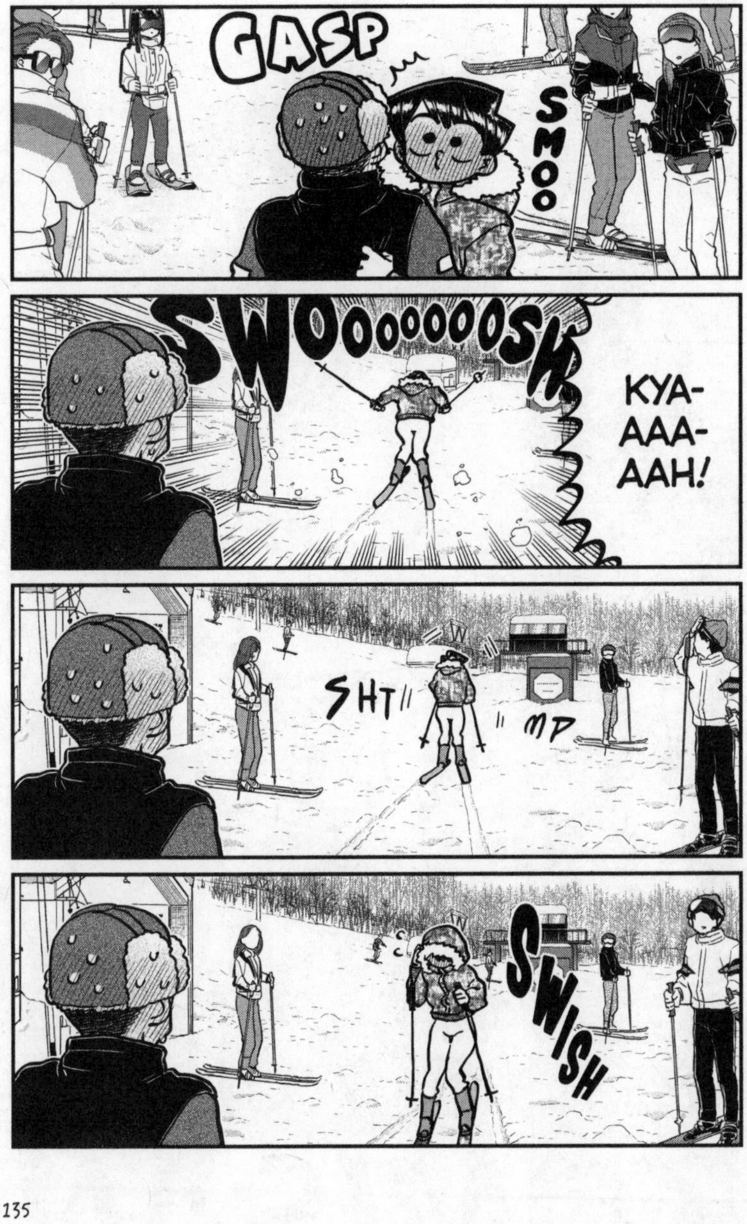
GASP
SMOO
SWOOOOOOSH
KYA-AAA-AAH!
SHT
MP
SWISH

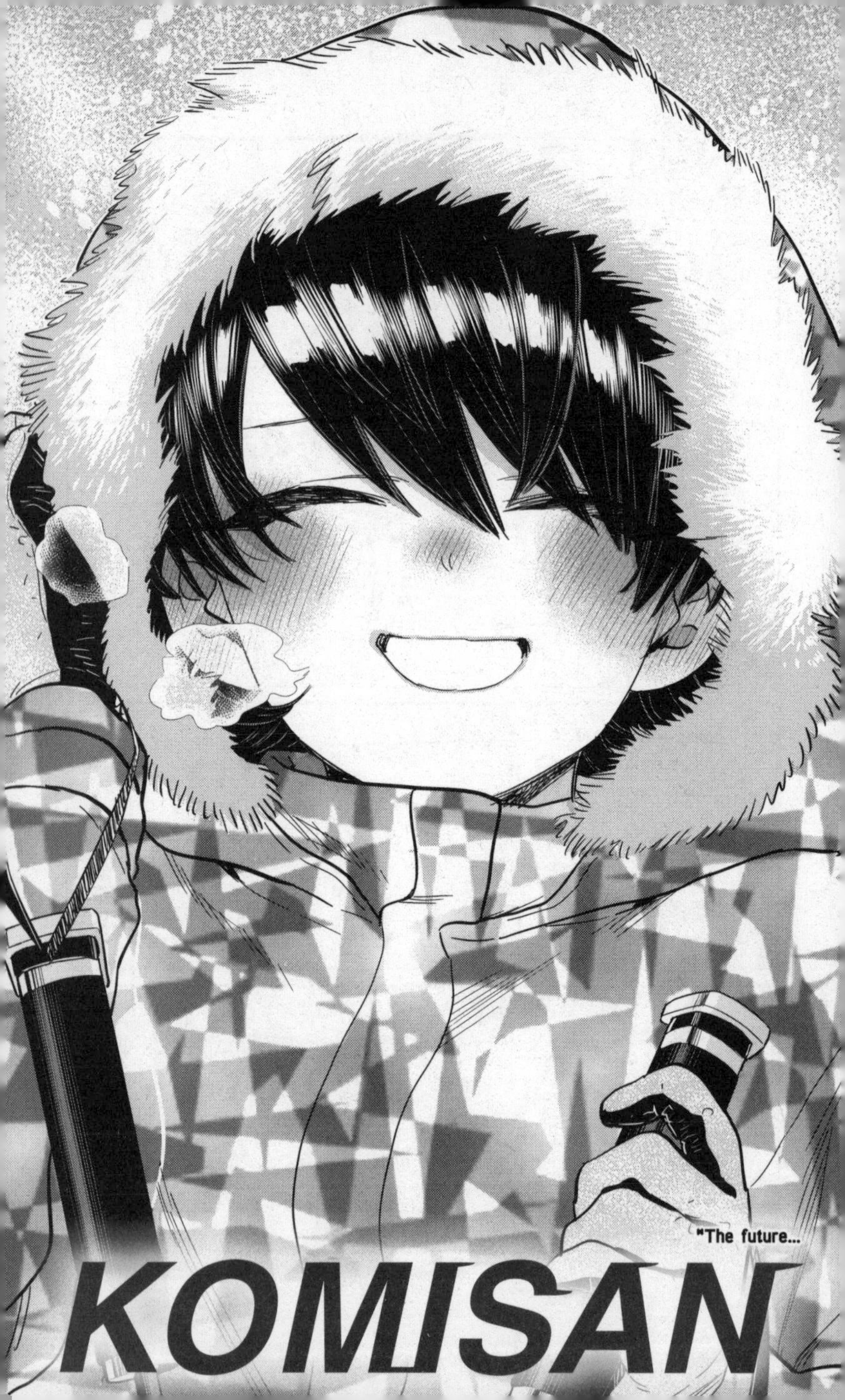
"The future...
KOMISAN

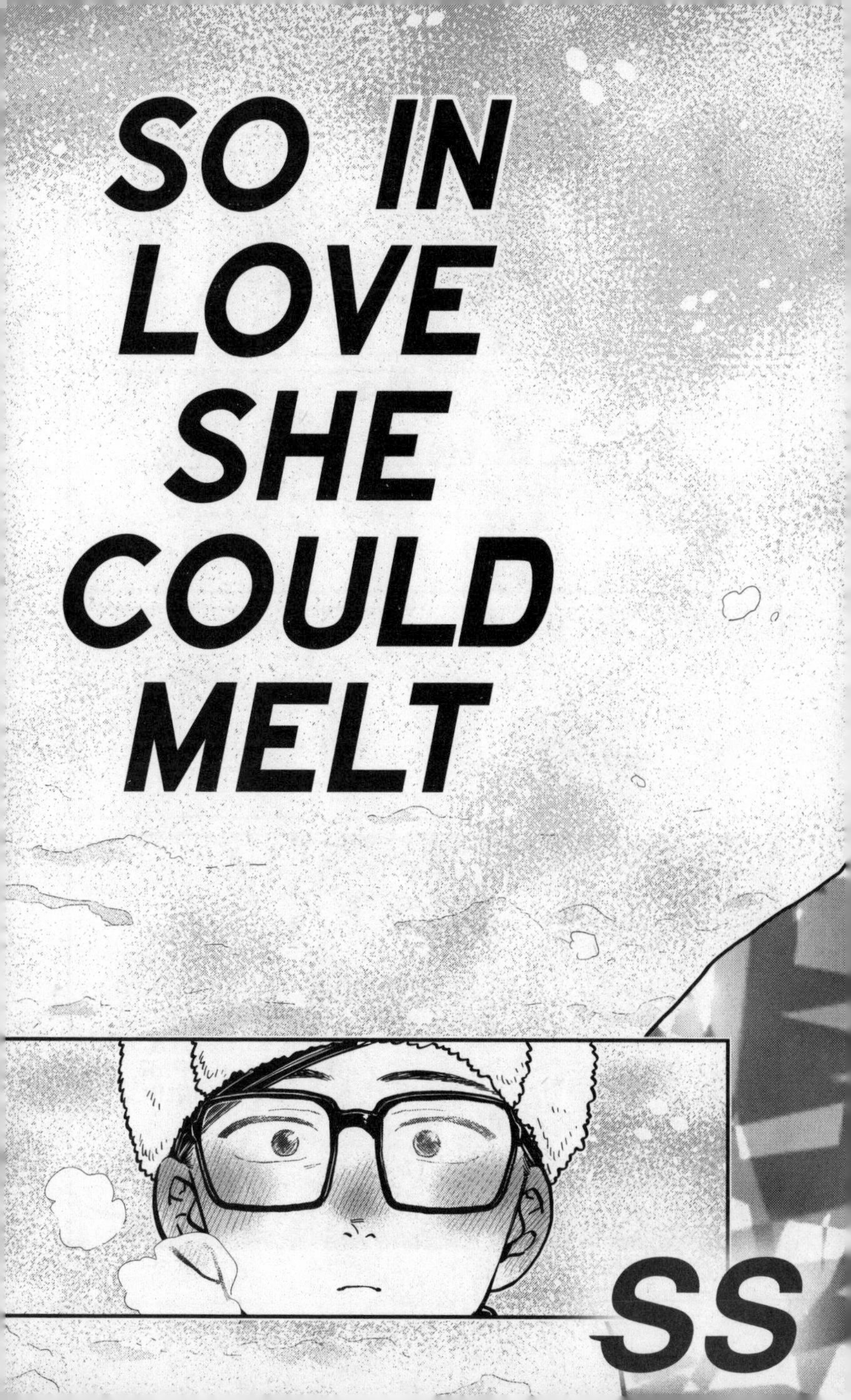
SO IN LOVE SHE COULD MELT
SS

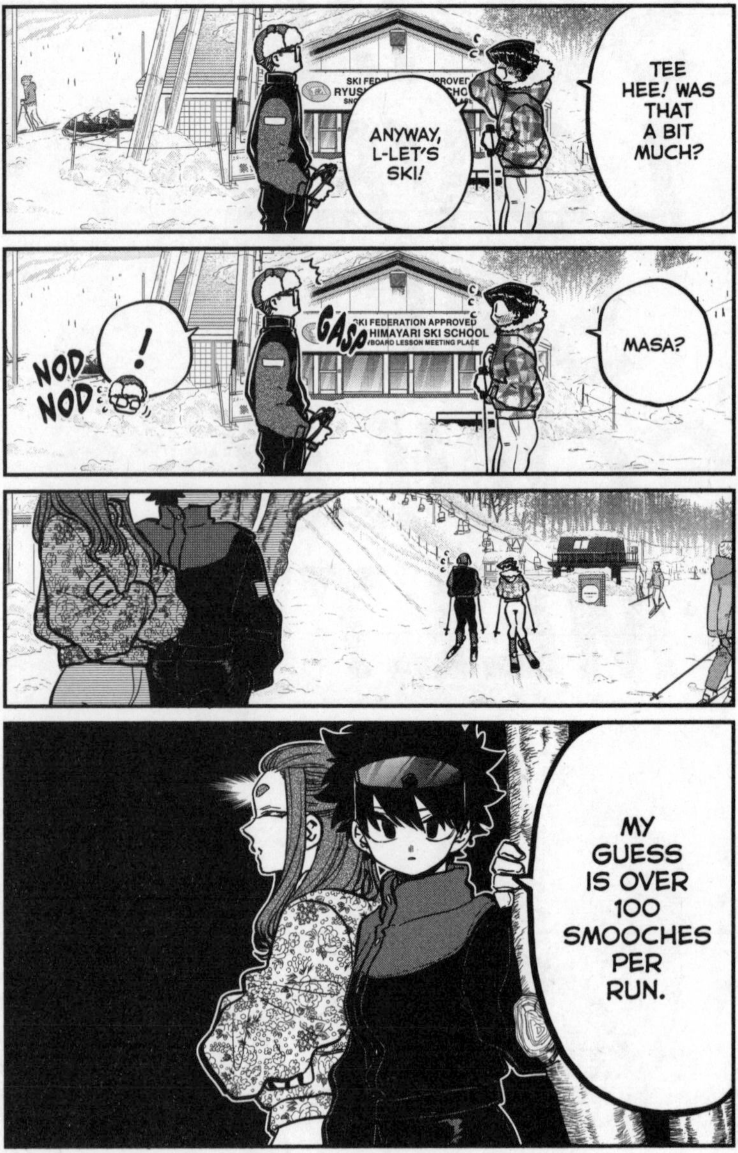
TEE HEE! WAS THAT A BIT MUCH?
ANYWAY, L-LET'S SKI!
MASA?
GASP
!
NOD NOD
MY GUESS IS OVER 100 SMOOCHES PER RUN.

Communication 266 — The End

For once, no teasing!!
They're too embarrassed.

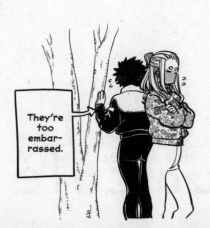

Komi Can't
Communicate

Komi Can't Communicate

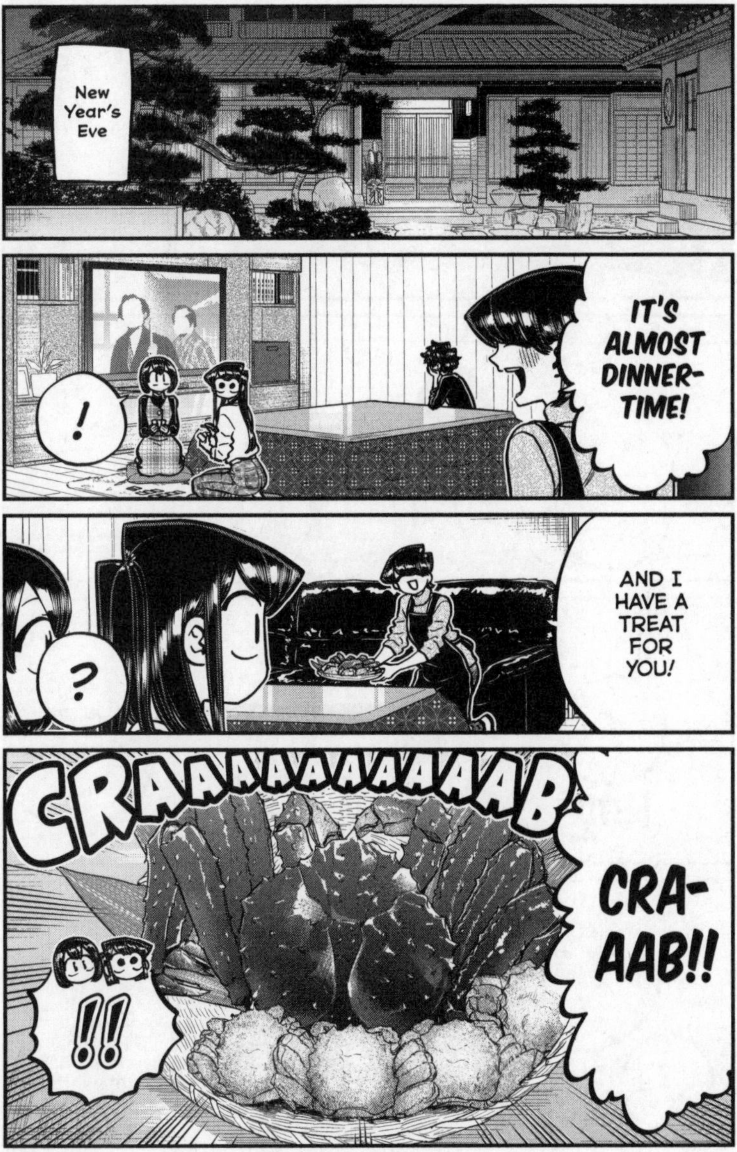
New Year's Eve
IT'S ALMOST DINNER-TIME!
!
AND I HAVE A TREAT FOR YOU!
?
CRAAAAAAAAAAB
CRA-AAB!!
!!

Communication 267: Crab

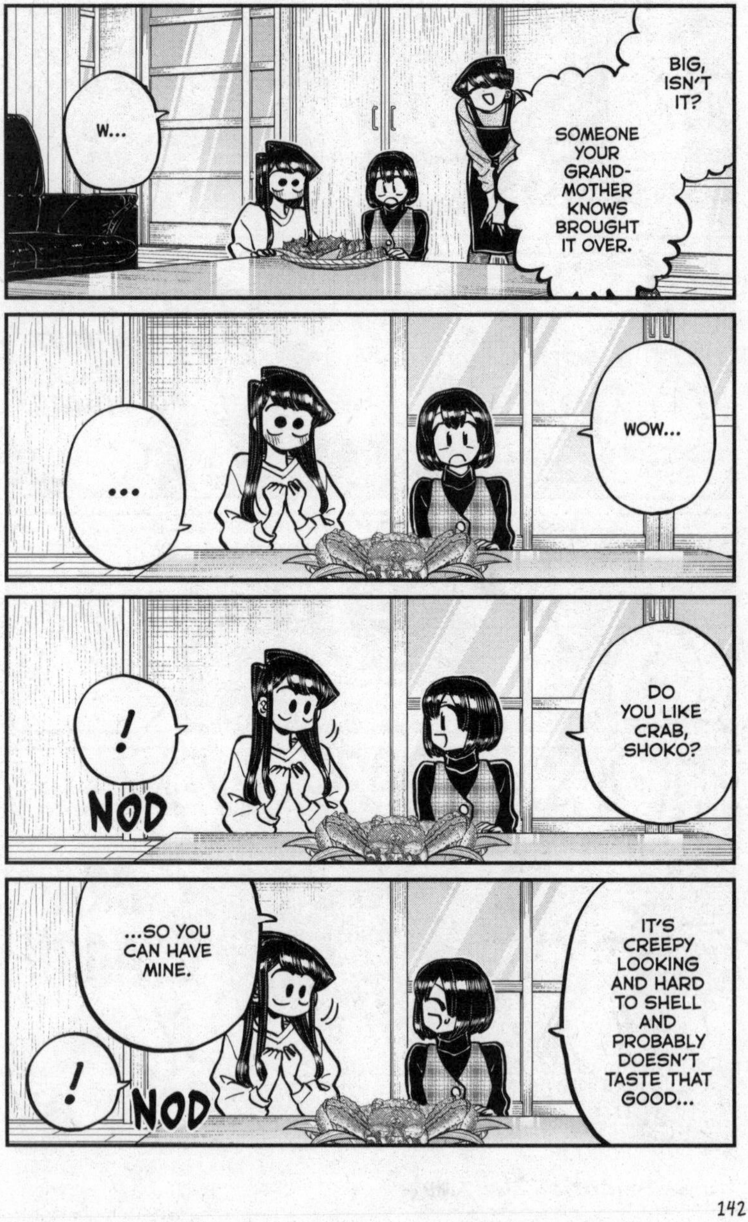
BIG, ISN'T IT?
SOMEONE YOUR GRAND-MOTHER KNOWS BROUGHT IT OVER.
W...
WOW...
...
DO YOU LIKE CRAB, SHOKO?
!
NOD
IT'S CREEPY LOOKING AND HARD TO SHELL AND PROBABLY DOESN'T TASTE THAT GOOD...
...SO YOU CAN HAVE MINE.
!
NOD

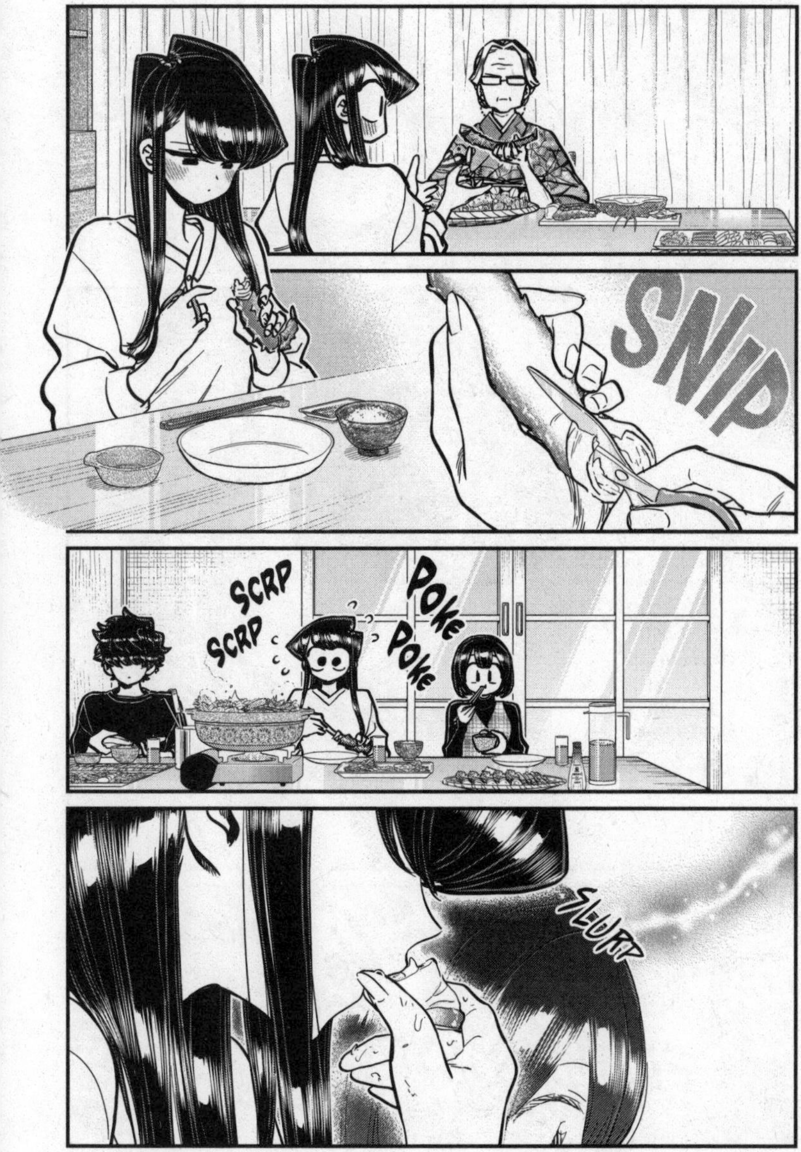
SNIP
POKE POKE
SCRP SCRP
SLURP

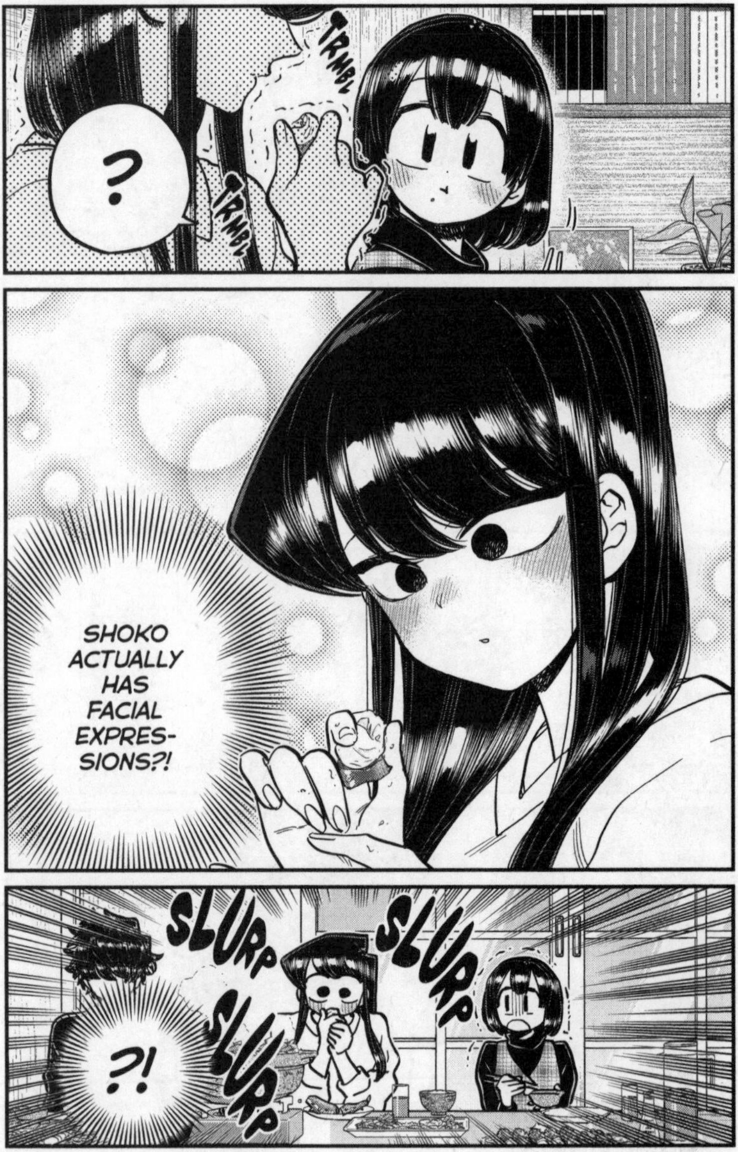
TRMBL
TRMBL
?
SHOKO ACTUALLY HAS FACIAL EXPRES-SIONS?!
SLURP
SLURP
SLURP
SLURP
?!

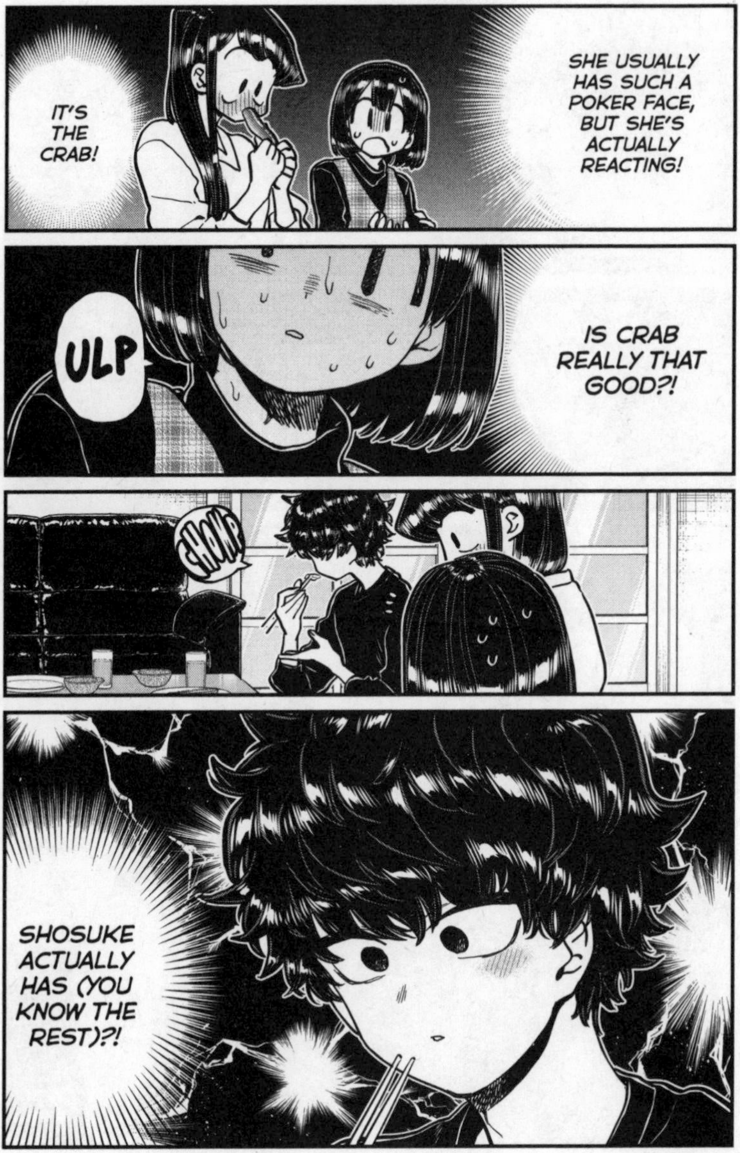
SHE USUALLY HAS SUCH A POKER FACE, BUT SHE'S ACTUALLY REACTING!
IT'S THE CRAB!
IS CRAB REALLY THAT GOOD?!
ULP
CHOMP
SHOSUKE ACTUALLY HAS (YOU KNOW THE REST)?!

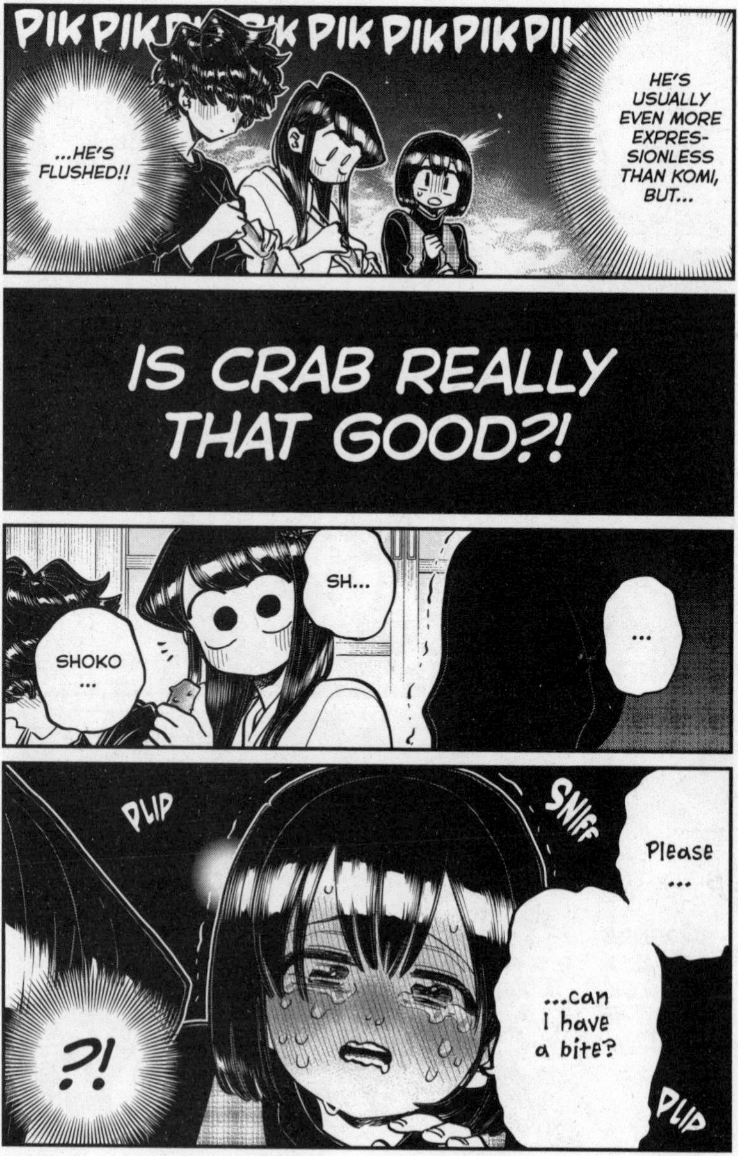
PIK PIK PIK PIK PIK PIK PIK
HE'S USUALLY EVEN MORE EXPRES-SIONLESS THAN KOMI, BUT...
...HE'S FLUSHED!!
IS CRAB REALLY THAT GOOD?!
...
SH...
SHOKO ...
SNIFF
Please ...
...can I have a bite?
PLIP
PLIP
?!

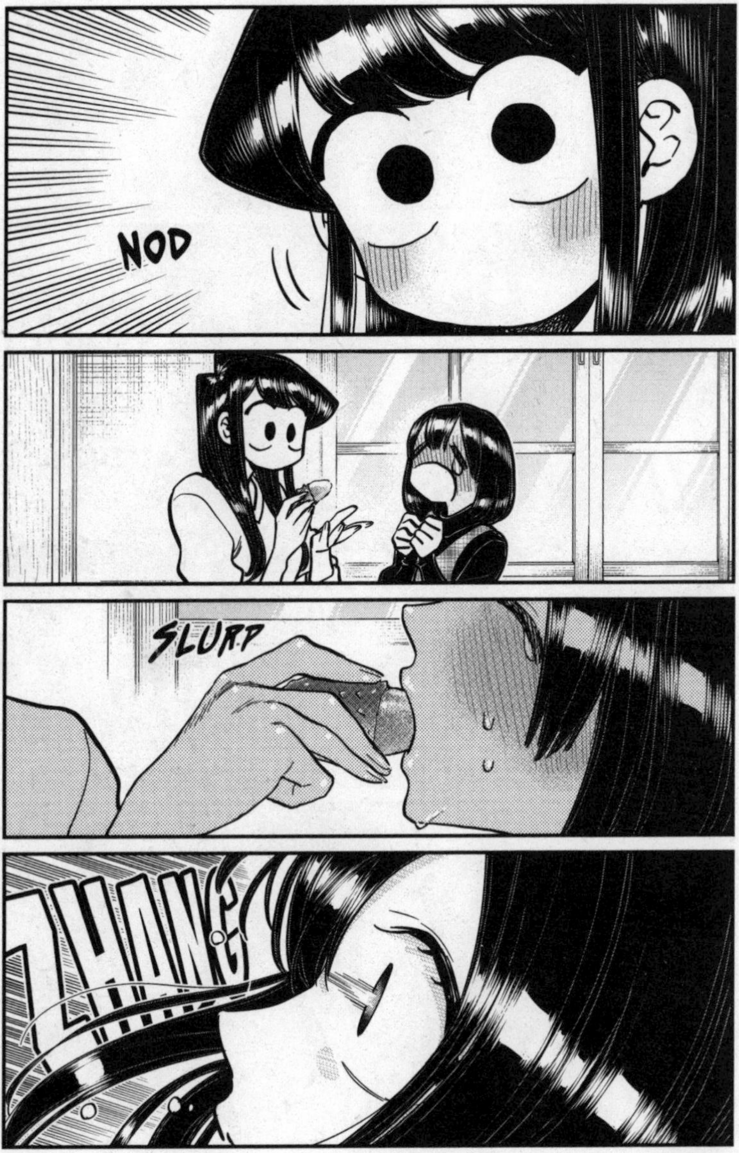
NOD
SLURP

GRANDMA ...
... TEACH ME HOW TO SHELL THAT THING.
!!
HWAH
CHOMP CHOMP
CHOMP
SLURP
SLURP
CHOMP
PIK PIK
HWAH
WAOOO
WAOOO
WE CAME, WE SAW ...
They con-quered.

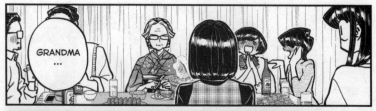

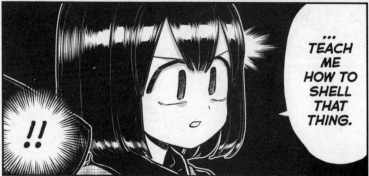

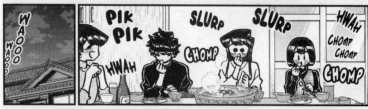

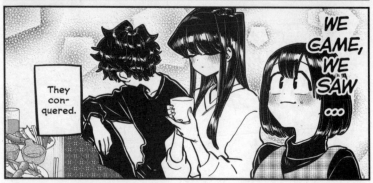

Communication 267 — The End

Komi Can't Communicate

Isagi on the Way There

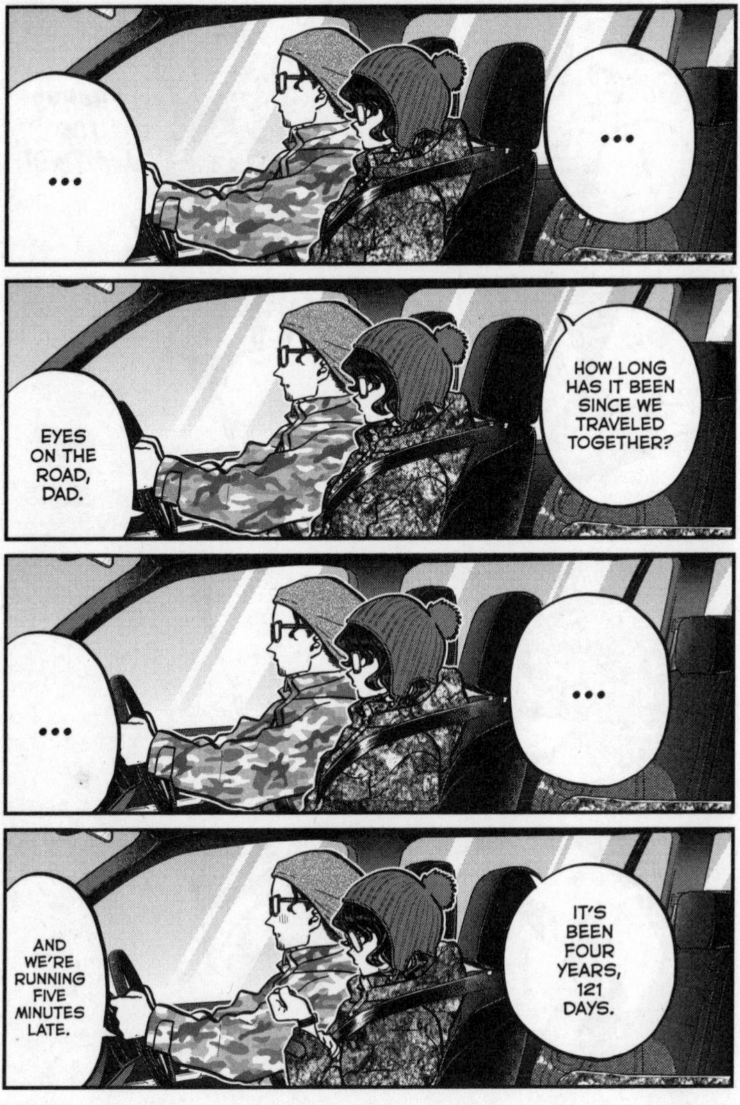
...
...
HOW LONG HAS IT BEEN SINCE WE TRAVELED TOGETHER?
EYES ON THE ROAD, DAD.
...
...
IT'S BEEN FOUR YEARS, 121 DAYS.
AND WE'RE RUNNING FIVE MINUTES LATE.

Communication 268: Ski Conversations

Ski-Slope Magic All Around

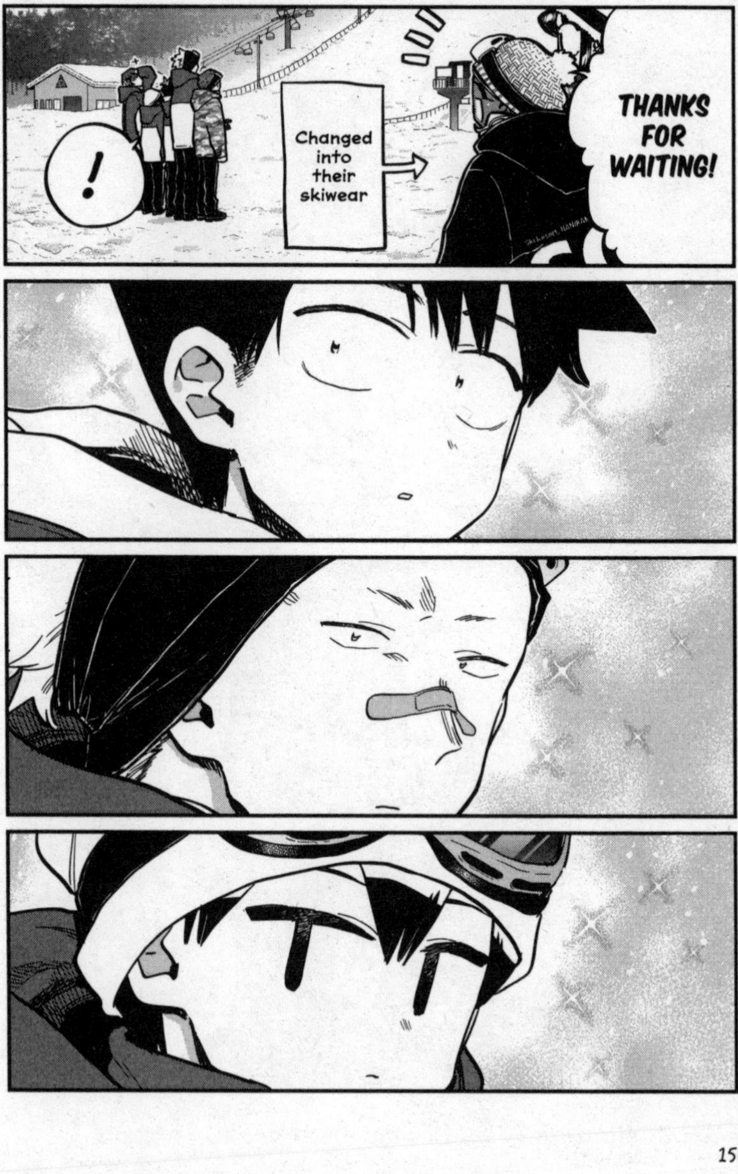
THANKS FOR WAITING!
Changed into their skiwear
!

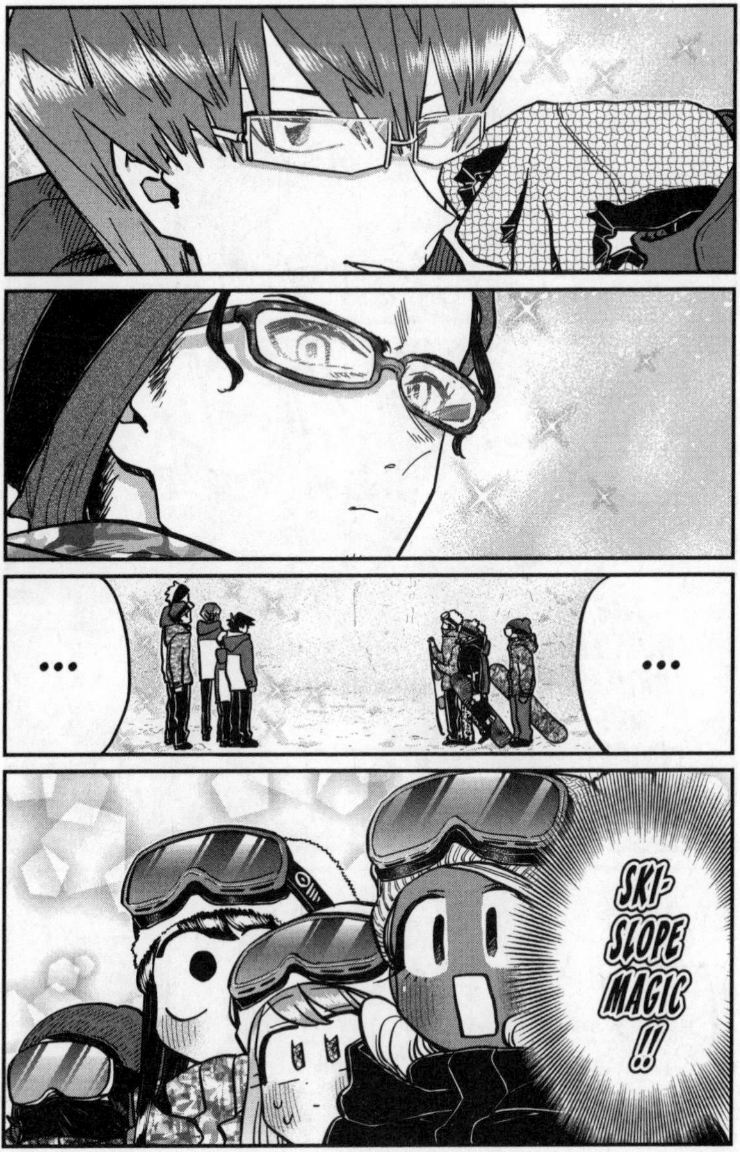
...
...
SKI-SLOPE MAGIC!!

Winter of the Pickup Artists

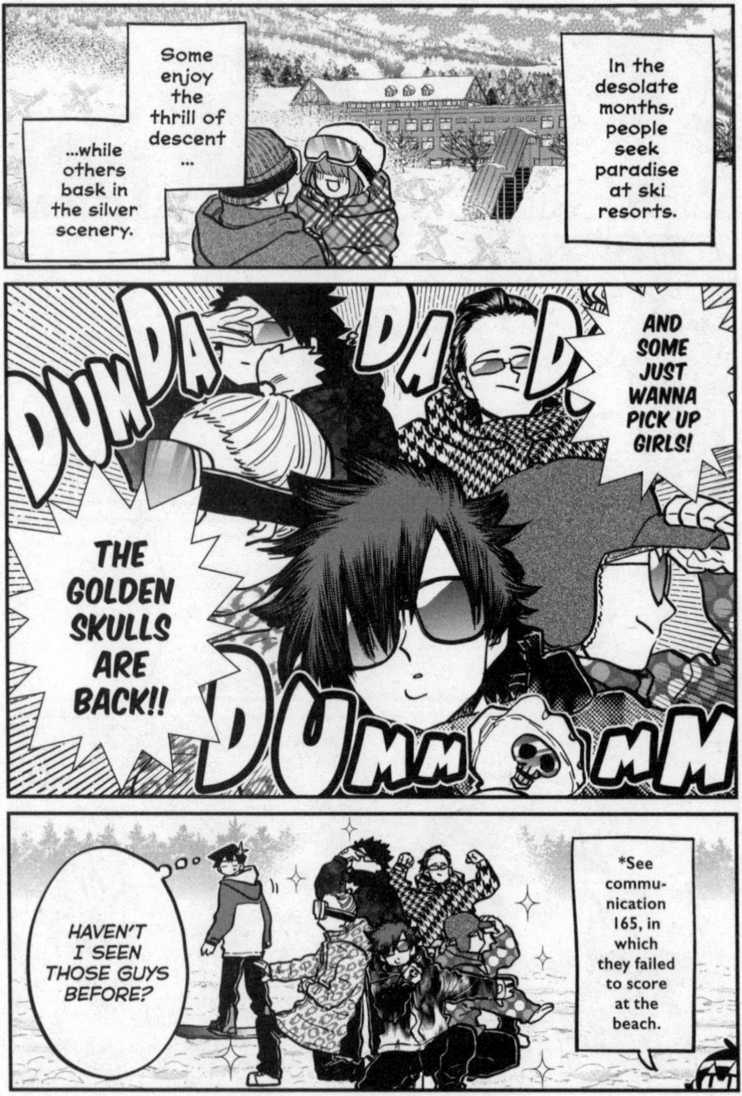
In the desolate months, people seek paradise at ski resorts.
Some enjoy the thrill of descent...
...while others bask in the silver scenery.
AND SOME JUST WANNA PICK UP GIRLS!
DUM DA DA D
THE GOLDEN SKULLS ARE BACK!!
DUMM MM
*See communication 165, in which they failed to score at the beach.
HAVEN'T I SEEN THOSE GUYS BEFORE?

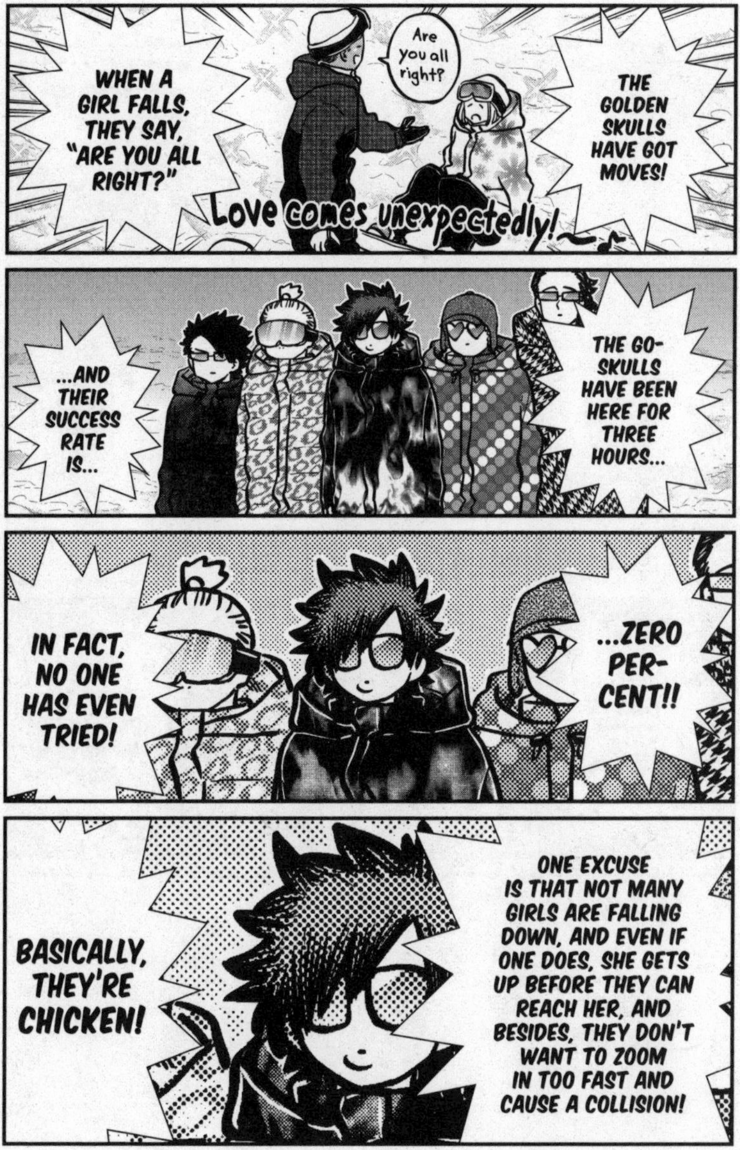
THE GOLDEN SKULLS HAVE GOT MOVES!
Are you all right?
WHEN A GIRL FALLS, THEY SAY, "ARE YOU ALL RIGHT?"
Love comes unexpectedly!
THE GO-SKULLS HAVE BEEN HERE FOR THREE HOURS...
...AND THEIR SUCCESS RATE IS...
...ZERO PER-CENT!!
IN FACT, NO ONE HAS EVEN TRIED!
ONE EXCUSE IS THAT NOT MANY GIRLS ARE FALLING DOWN, AND EVEN IF ONE DOES, SHE GETS UP BEFORE THEY CAN REACH HER, AND BESIDES, THEY DON'T WANT TO ZOOM IN TOO FAST AND CAUSE A COLLISION!
BASICALLY, THEY'RE CHICKEN!

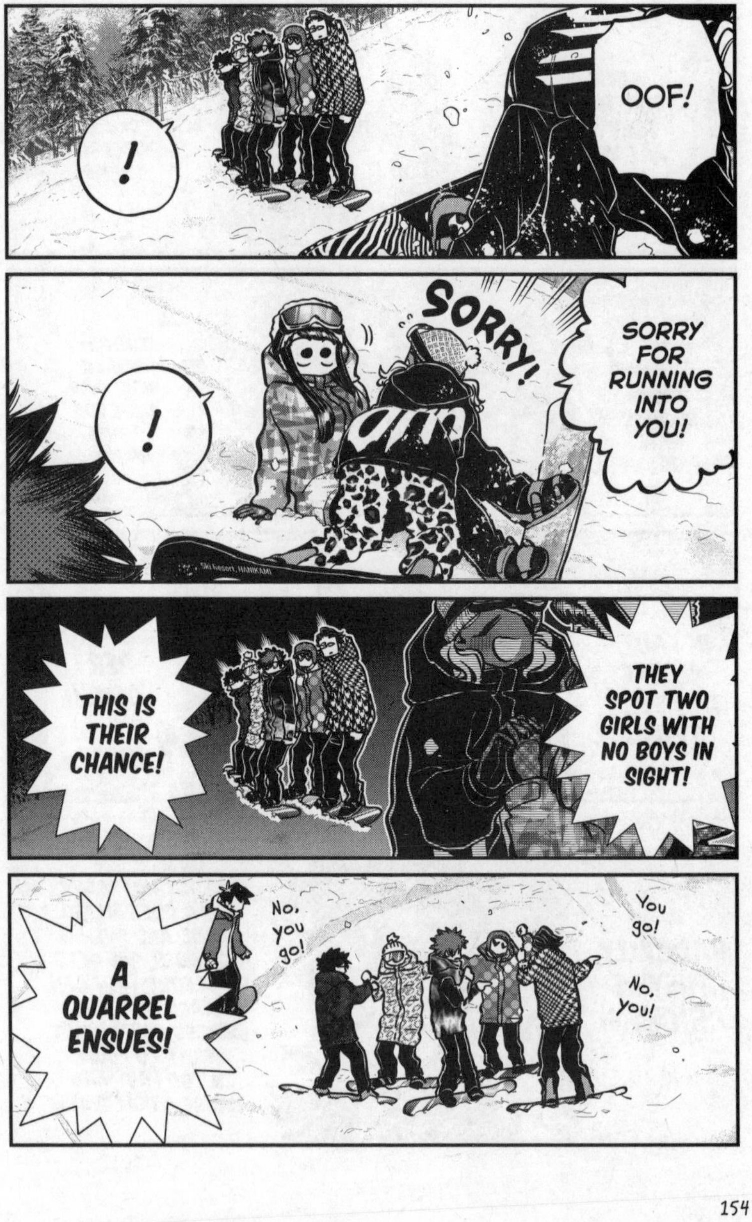
OOF!
!
SORRY FOR RUNNING INTO YOU!
SORRY!
!
THEY SPOT TWO GIRLS WITH NO BOYS IN SIGHT!
THIS IS THEIR CHANCE!
You go!
No, you!
No, you go!
A QUARREL ENSUES!

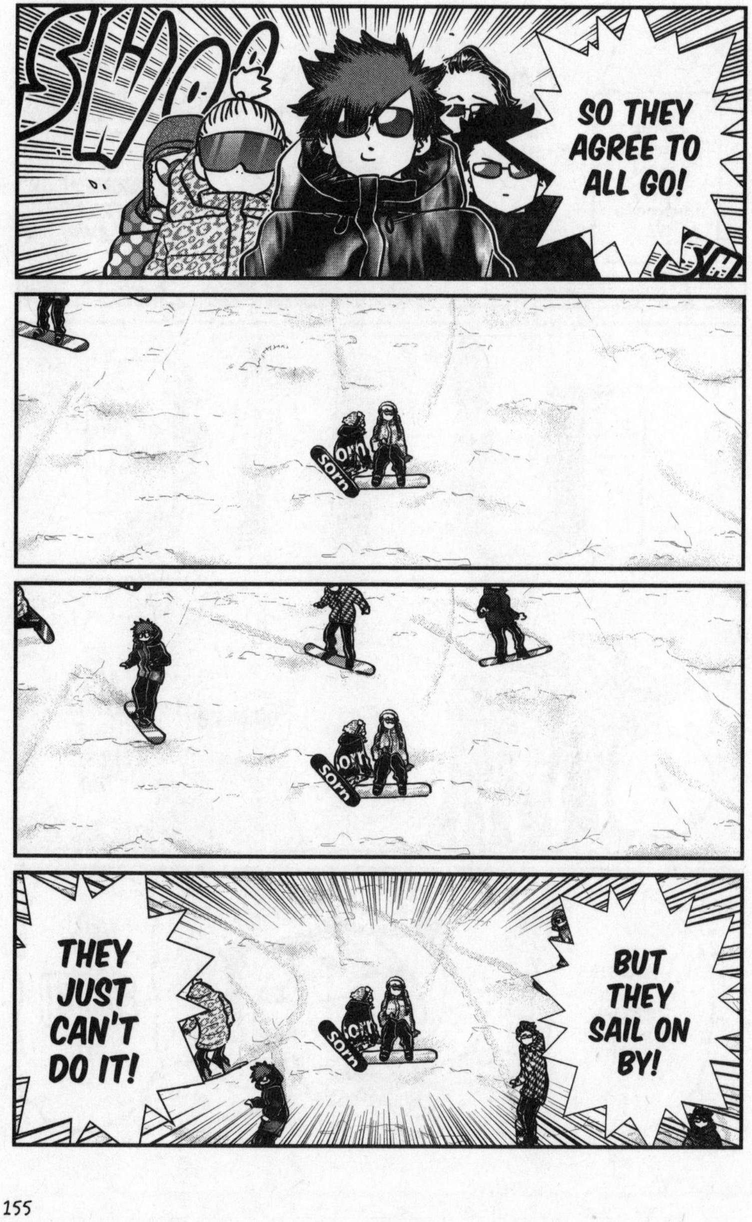
SO THEY AGREE TO ALL GO!
SH
SHOO
BUT THEY SAIL ON BY!
THEY JUST CAN'T DO IT!

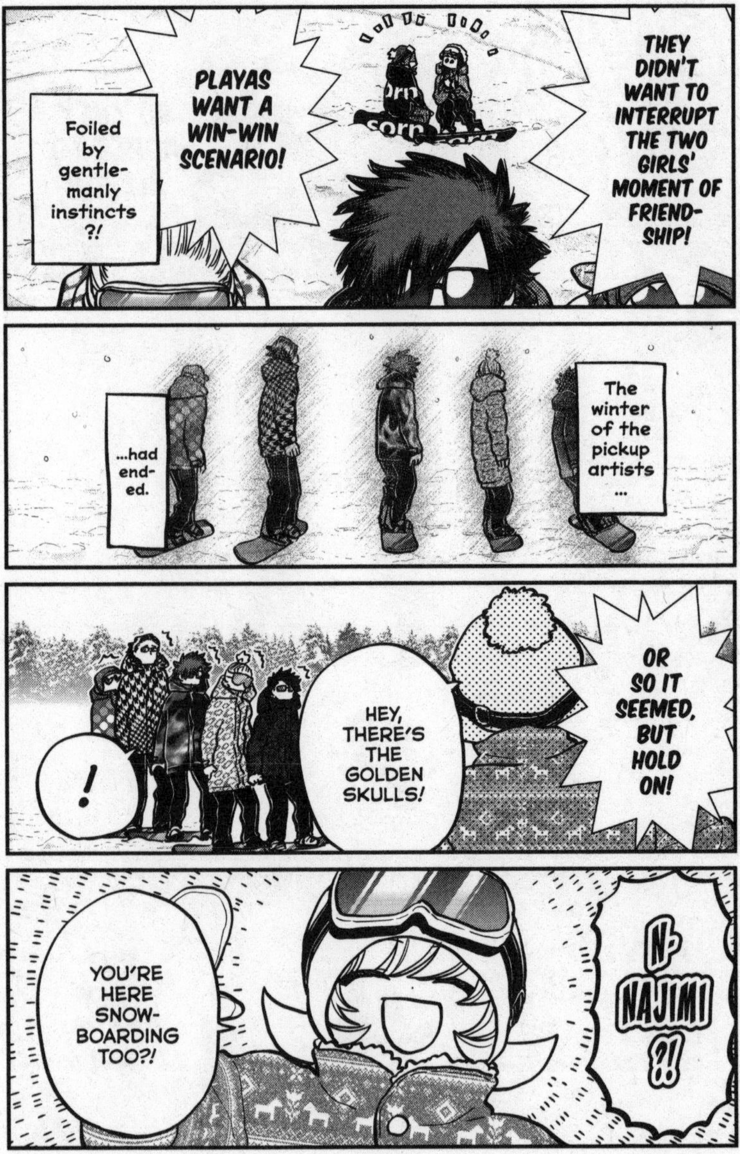
THEY DIDN'T WANT TO INTERRUPT THE TWO GIRLS' MOMENT OF FRIEND-SHIP!
PLAYAS WANT A WIN-WIN SCENARIO!
Foiled by gentle-manly instincts ?!
The winter of the pickup artists ...
...had end-ed.
OR SO IT SEEMED, BUT HOLD ON!
HEY, THERE'S THE GOLDEN SKULLS!
!
N-NAJIMI ?!
YOU'RE HERE SNOW-BOARDING TOO?!

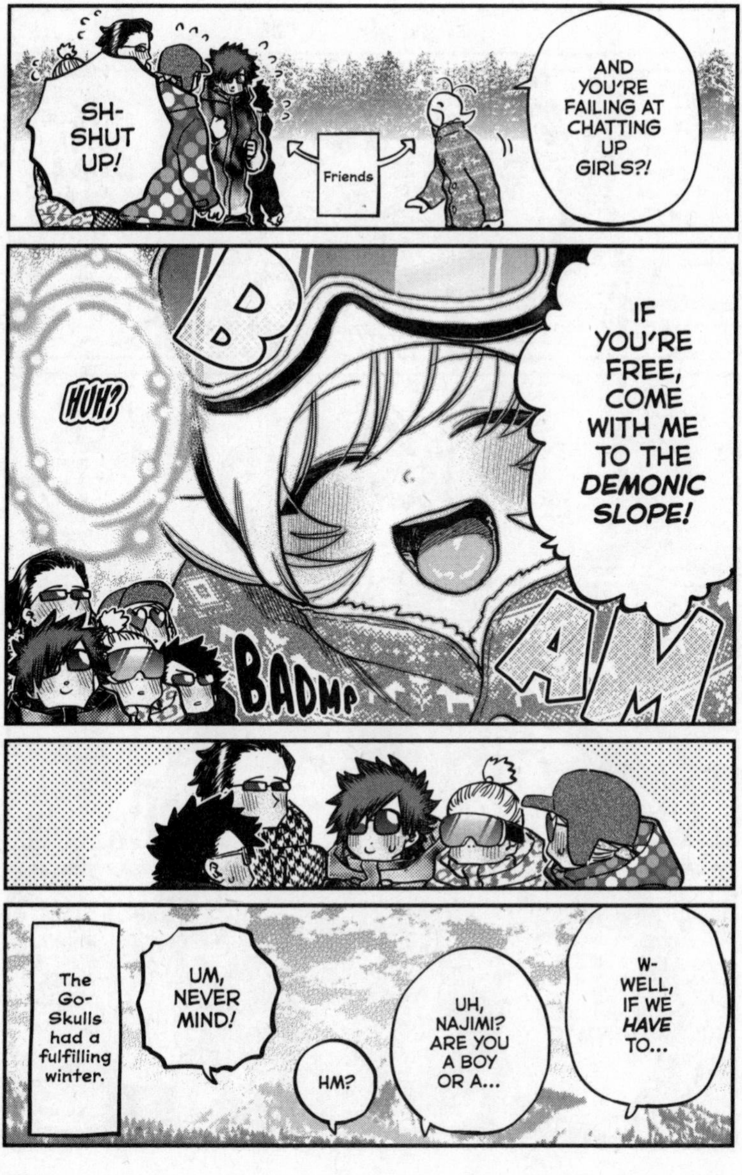
AND YOU'RE FAILING AT CHATTING UP GIRLS?!
Friends
SH-SHUT UP!
IF YOU'RE FREE, COME WITH ME TO THE DEMONIC SLOPE!
BAM
BADMP
HUH?
W-WELL, IF WE HAVE TO...
UH, NAJIMI? ARE YOU A BOY OR A...
HM?
UM, NEVER MIND!
The Go-Skulls had a fulfilling winter.

Snow, Ski Lift, Love Talk

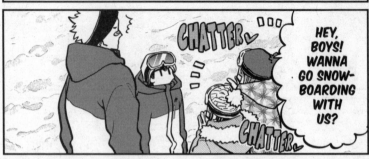

HEY, BOYS! WANNA GO SNOW-BOARDING WITH US?
CHATTER
CHATTER
AH, BUTTER-FLIES ATTRACTED BY MY COMELY FORM!
BUT MY HONEY IS NOT SO EASILY—
ON SECOND THOUGHT, WE'RE GOOD.
?!
...
WANNA SHARE A LIFT, ASE?
S-SURE, TADANO.

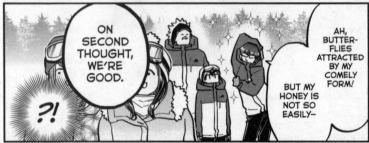

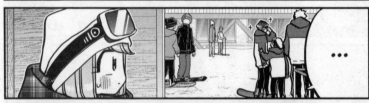

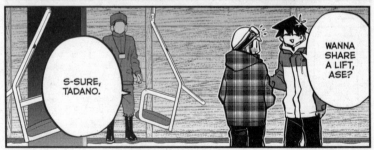

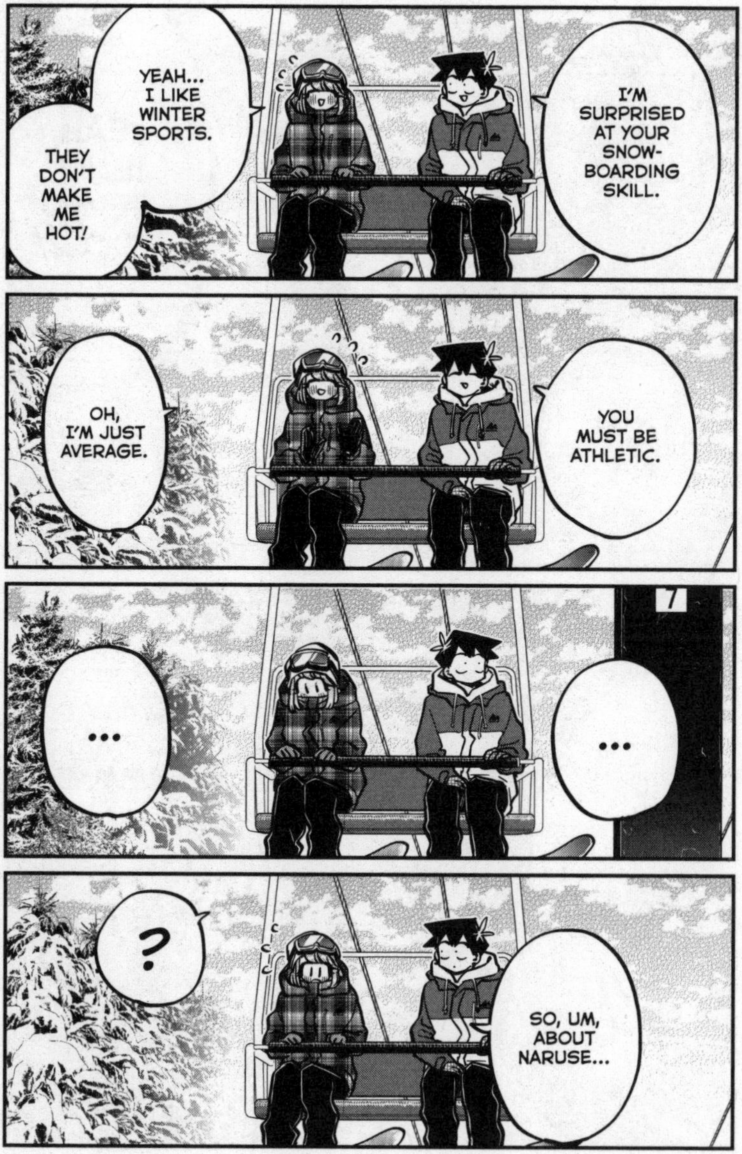
I'M SURPRISED AT YOUR SNOW-BOARDING SKILL.
YEAH... I LIKE WINTER SPORTS.
THEY DON'T MAKE ME HOT!
YOU MUST BE ATHLETIC.
OH, I'M JUST AVERAGE.
7
...
...
SO, UM, ABOUT NARUSE...
?

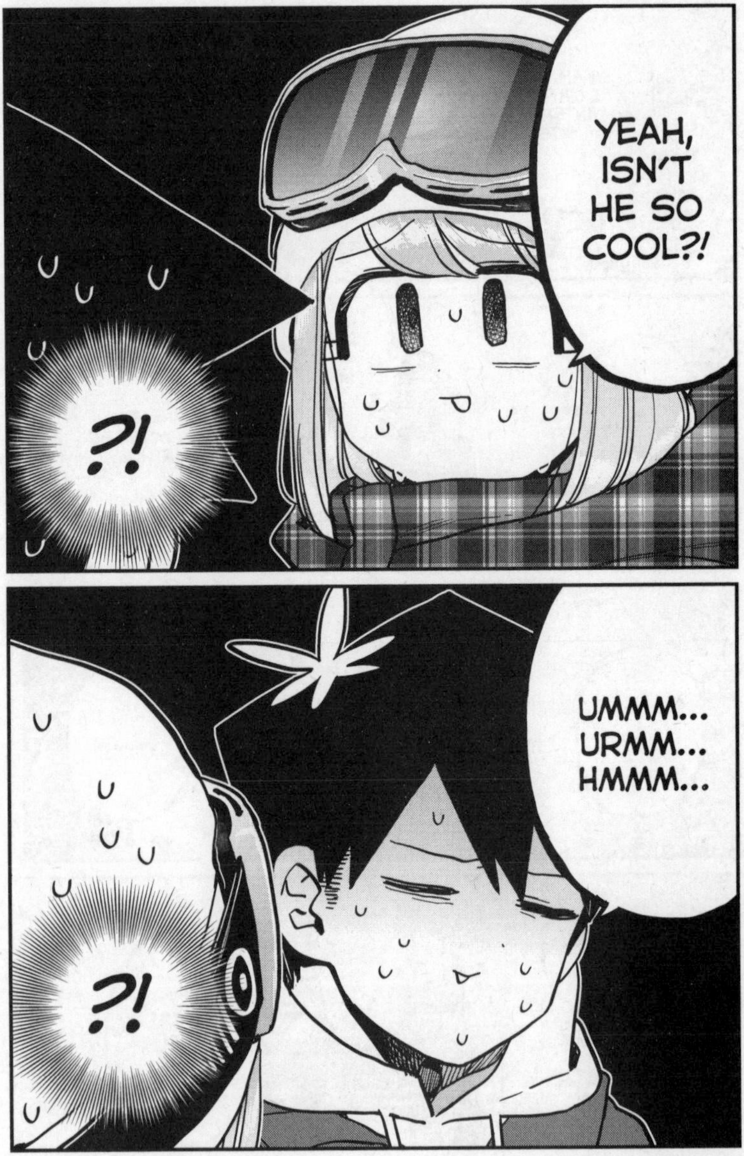
YEAH, ISN'T HE SO COOL?!
?!
UMMM... URMM... HMMM...
?!

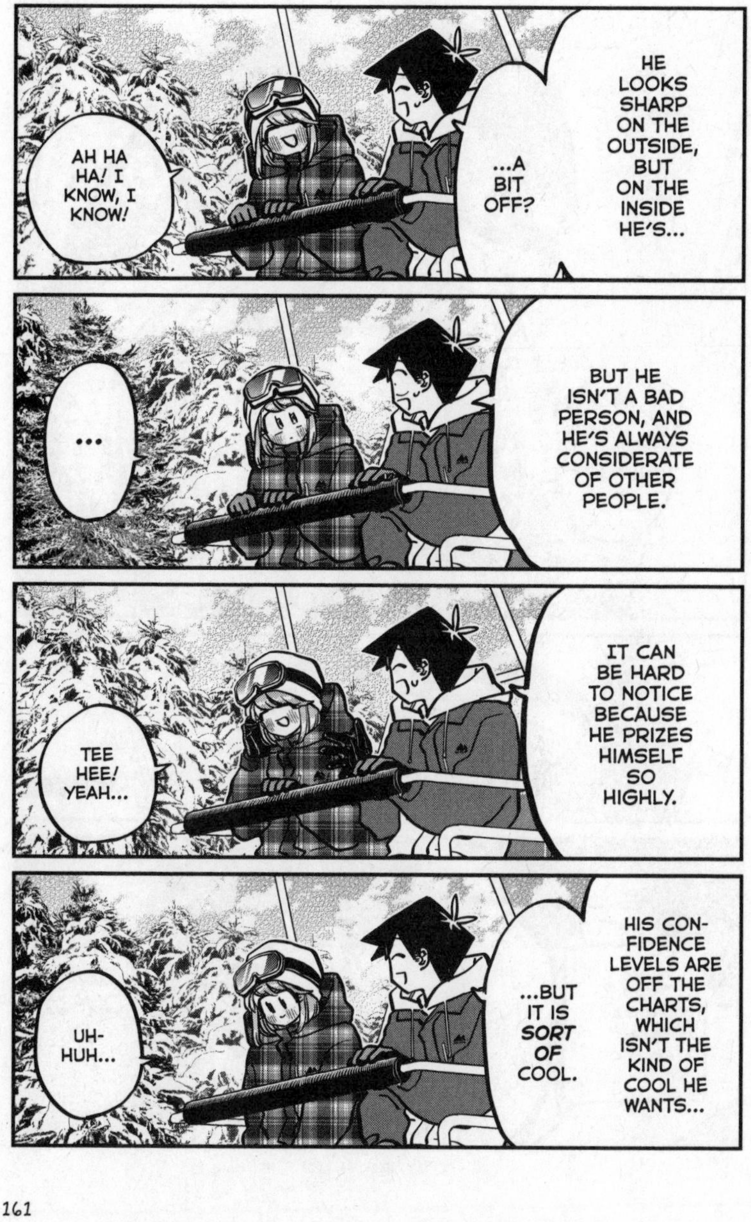

HE LOOKS SHARP ON THE OUTSIDE, BUT ON THE INSIDE HE'S...
...A BIT OFF?
AH HA HA! I KNOW, I KNOW!
BUT HE ISN'T A BAD PERSON, AND HE'S ALWAYS CONSIDERATE OF OTHER PEOPLE.
...
IT CAN BE HARD TO NOTICE BECAUSE HE PRIZES HIMSELF SO HIGHLY.
TEE HEE! YEAH...
HIS CONFIDENCE LEVELS ARE OFF THE CHARTS, WHICH ISN'T THE KIND OF COOL HE WANTS...
...BUT IT IS *SORT OF* COOL.
UH-HUH...

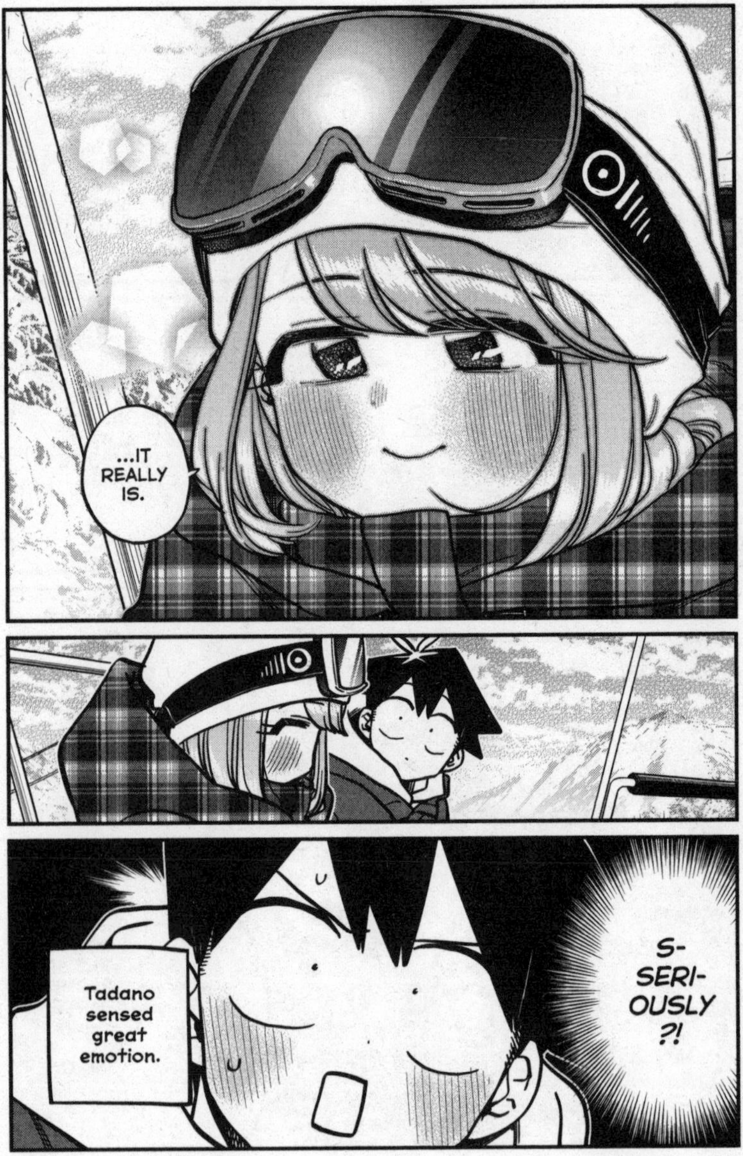
...IT REALLY IS.
S-SERI-OUSLY?!
Tadano sensed great emotion.

Snow, Ski Lift, Love Talk, Part 2

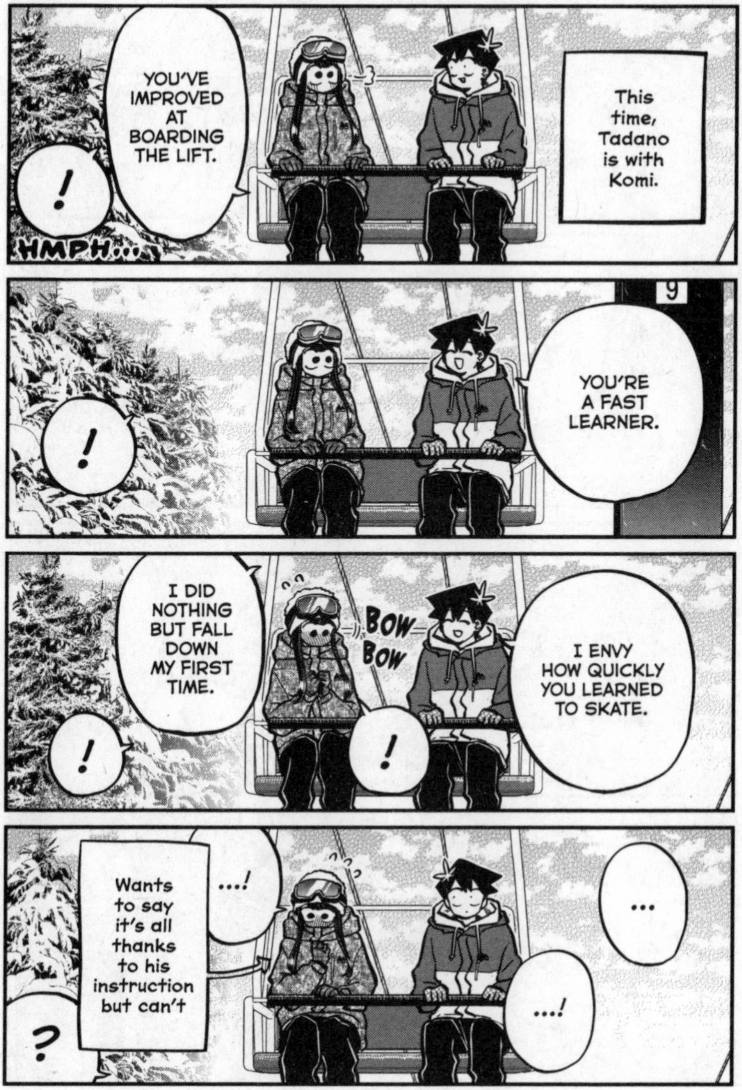
This time, Tadano is with Komi.
YOU'VE IMPROVED AT BOARDING THE LIFT.
!
HMPH...
9
YOU'RE A FAST LEARNER.
!
I ENVY HOW QUICKLY YOU LEARNED TO SKATE.
!
BOW BOW
I DID NOTHING BUT FALL DOWN MY FIRST TIME.
!
...
...!
...!
Wants to say it's all thanks to his instruction but can't
?

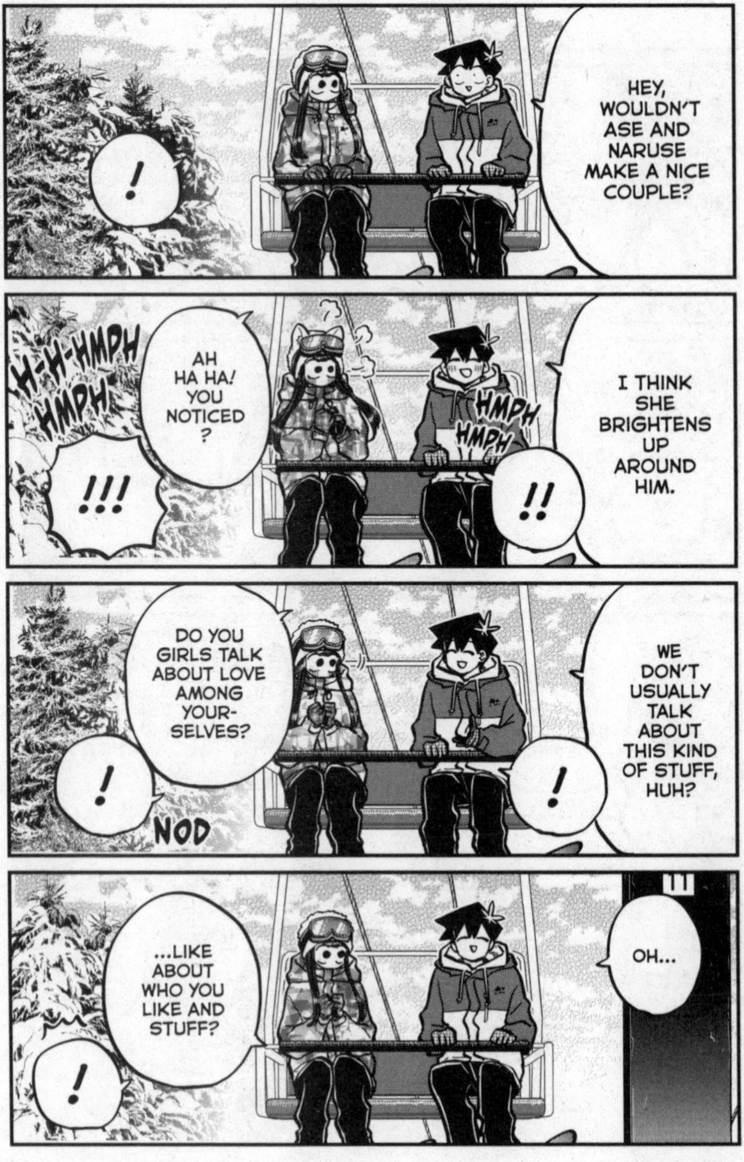
HEY, WOULDN'T ASE AND NARUSE MAKE A NICE COUPLE?
!
I THINK SHE BRIGHTENS UP AROUND HIM.
HMPH HMPH
!!
AH HA HA! YOU NOTICED?
H-H-HMPH HMPH
!!!
WE DON'T USUALLY TALK ABOUT THIS KIND OF STUFF, HUH?
!
DO YOU GIRLS TALK ABOUT LOVE AMONG YOUR-SELVES?
!
NOD
OH...
...LIKE ABOUT WHO YOU LIKE AND STUFF?
!

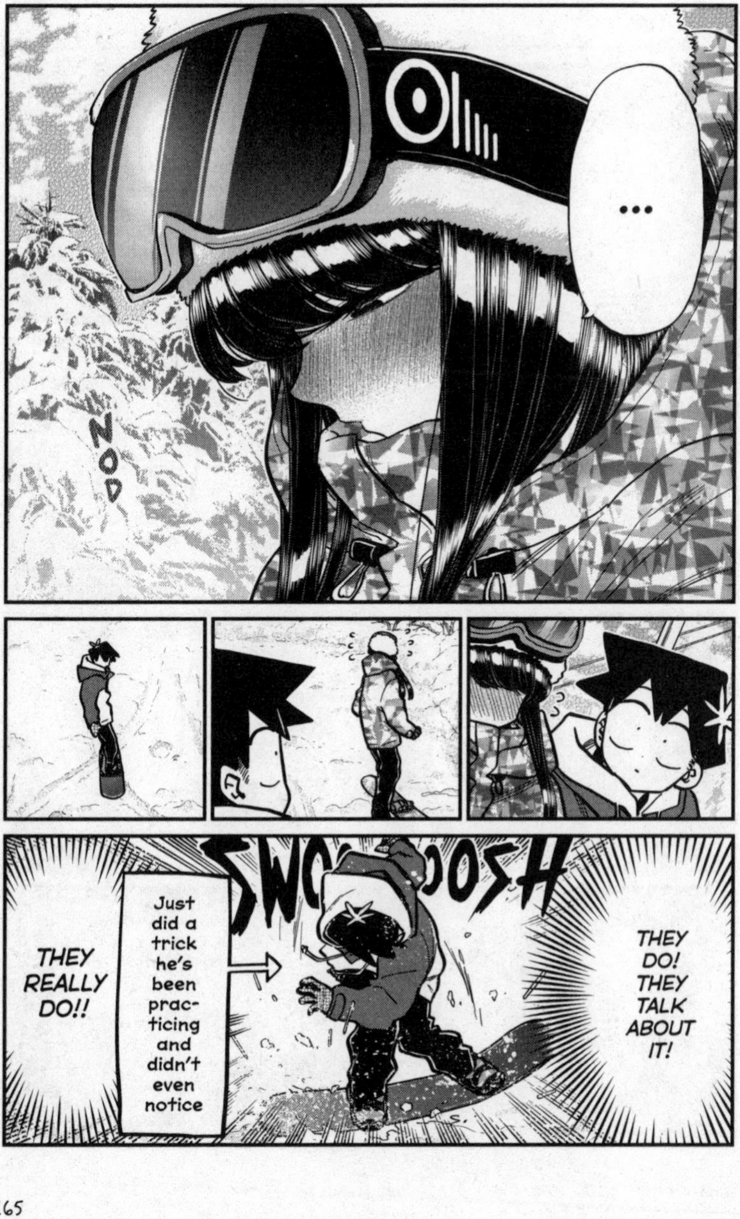
...
NOD
THEY DO! THEY TALK ABOUT IT!
Just did a trick he's been prac-ticing and didn't even notice
THEY REALLY DO!!

Isagi on the Way Home

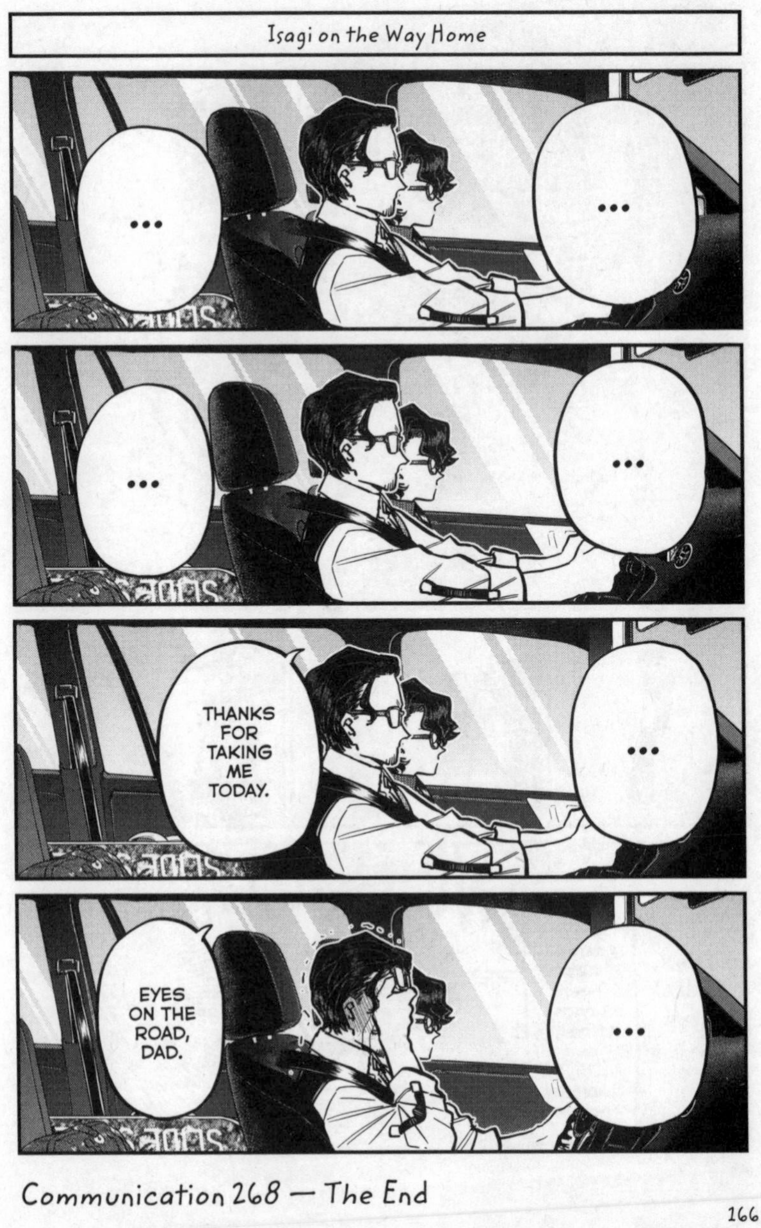
...
...
...
...
...
THANKS FOR TAKING ME TODAY.
...
EYES ON THE ROAD, DAD.

Communication 268 — The End

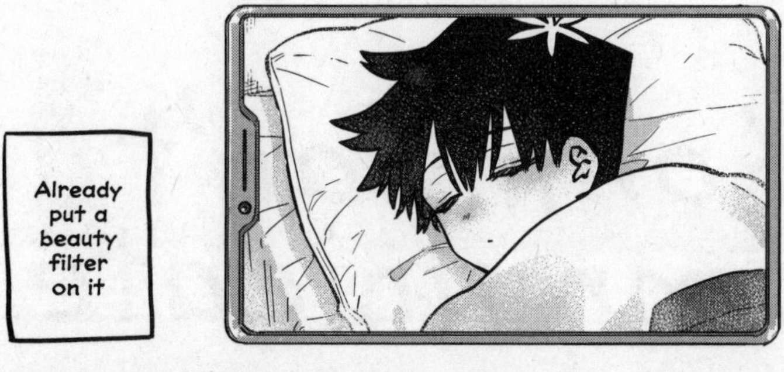
Already put a beauty filter on it

Komi Can't
Communicate

Komi Can't Communicate

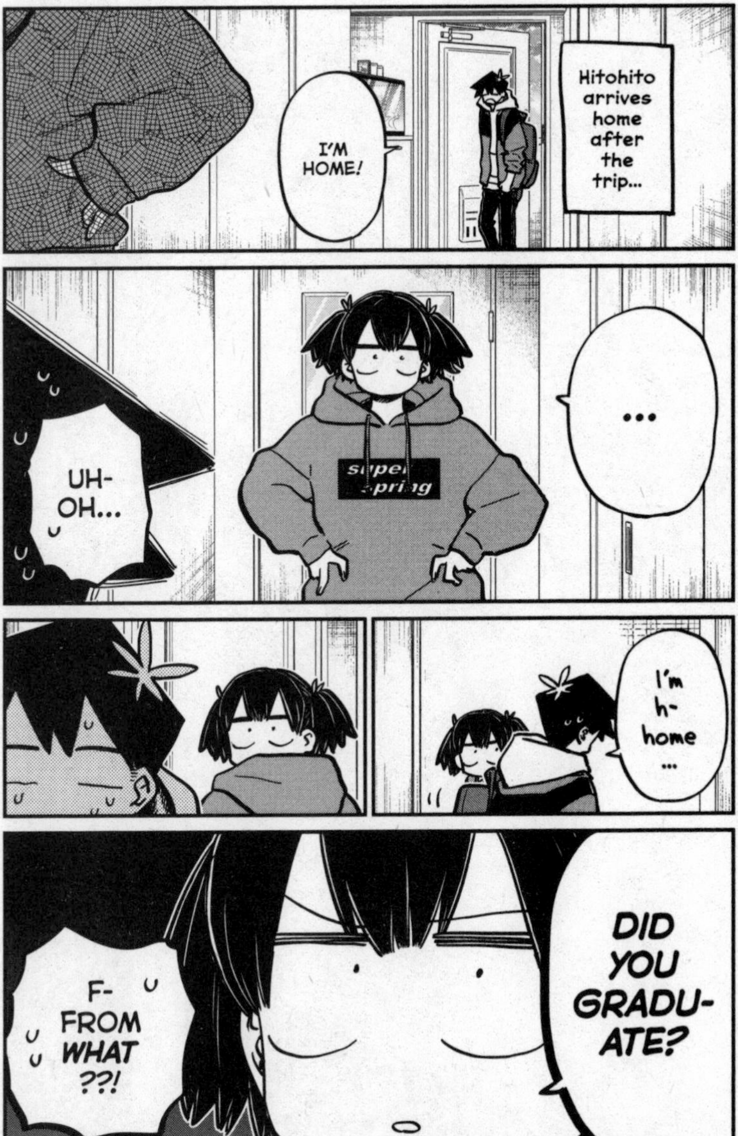
Hitohito arrives home after the trip...
I'M HOME!
...
UH-OH...
I'm h-home ...
DID YOU GRADUATE?
F-FROM WHAT??!

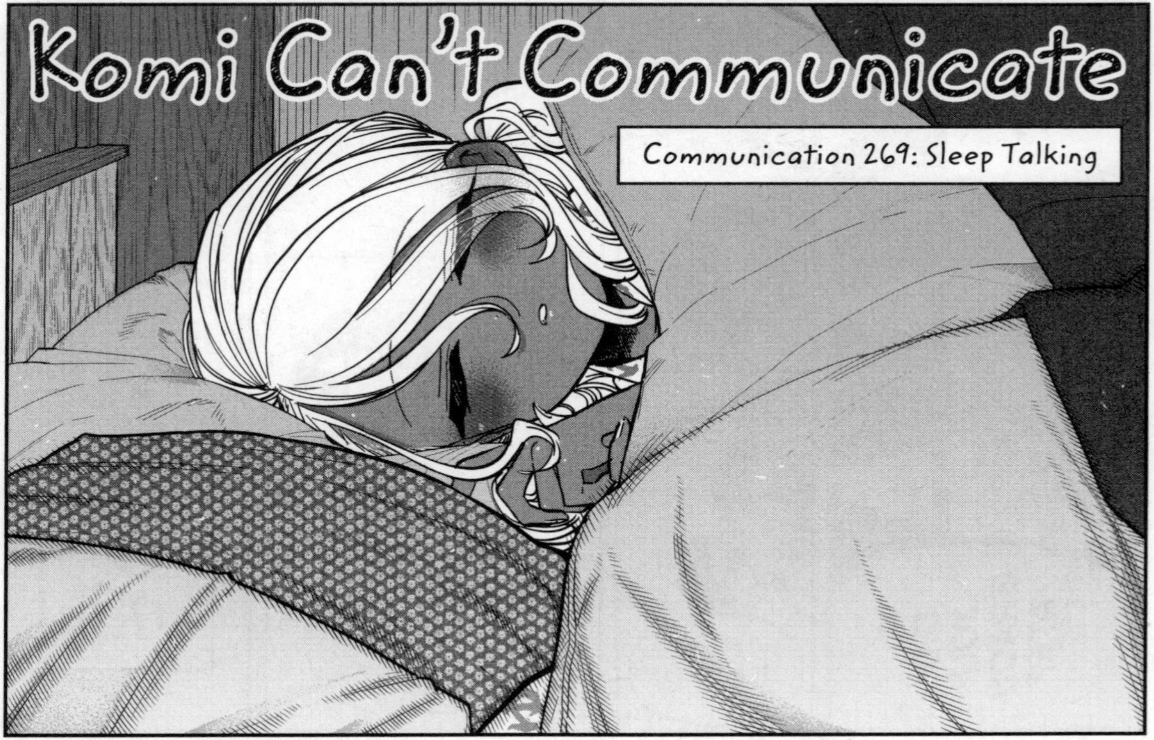
Komi Can't Communicate
Communication 269: Sleep Talking

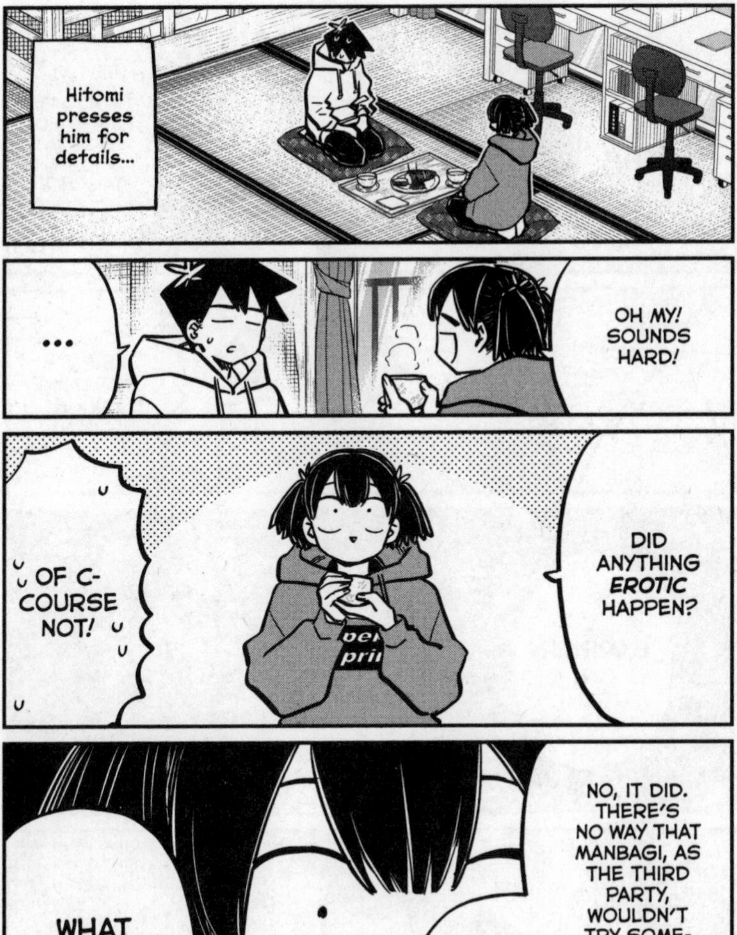
Hitomi presses him for details...
OH MY! SOUNDS HARD!
...
DID ANYTHING *EROTIC* HAPPEN?
OF C-COURSE NOT!
NO, IT DID. THERE'S NO WAY THAT MANBAGI, AS THE THIRD PARTY, WOULDN'T TRY SOME-THING!
SHE'S A GYARU, RIGHT? AND THEY GO HARD!
WHAT KIND OF STEREO-TYPE IS THAT?!

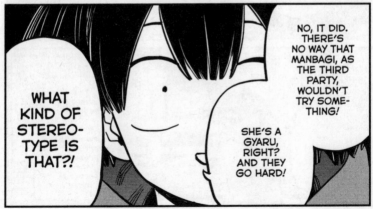

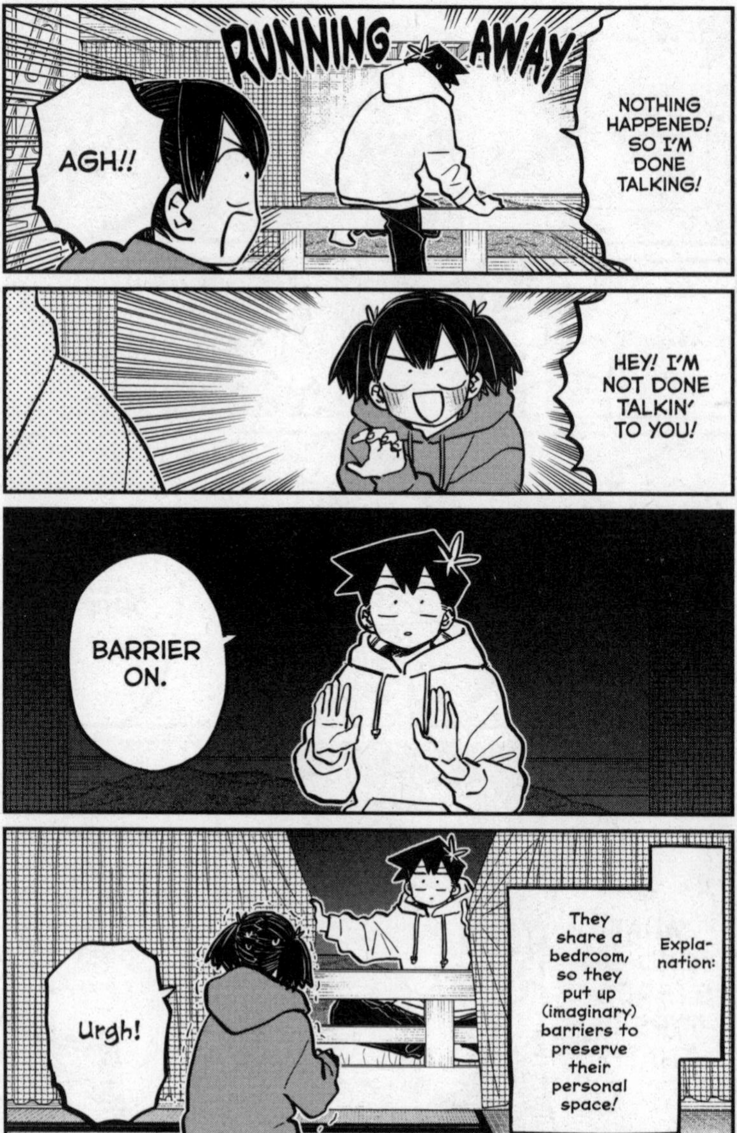
RUNNING AWAY
NOTHING HAPPENED! SO I'M DONE TALKING!
AGH!!
HEY! I'M NOT DONE TALKIN' TO YOU!
BARRIER ON.
Explanation:
They share a bedroom, so they put up (imaginary) barriers to preserve their personal space!
Urgh!

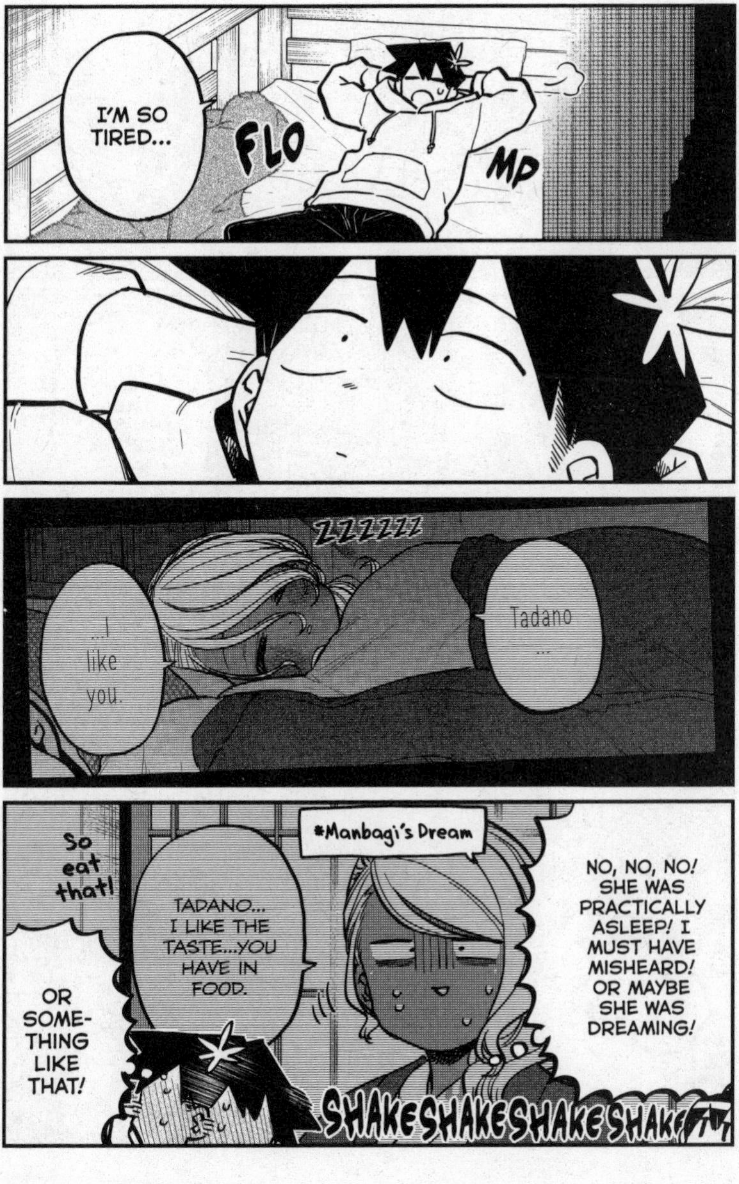
I'M SO TIRED...
FLOMP
ZZZZZZ
Tadano...
...I like you.
NO, NO, NO! SHE WAS PRACTICALLY ASLEEP! I MUST HAVE MISHEARD! OR MAYBE SHE WAS DREAMING!
#Manbagi's Dream
TADANO... I LIKE THE TASTE...YOU HAVE IN FOOD.
So eat that!
OR SOME-THING LIKE THAT!
SHAKE SHAKE SHAKE SHAKE

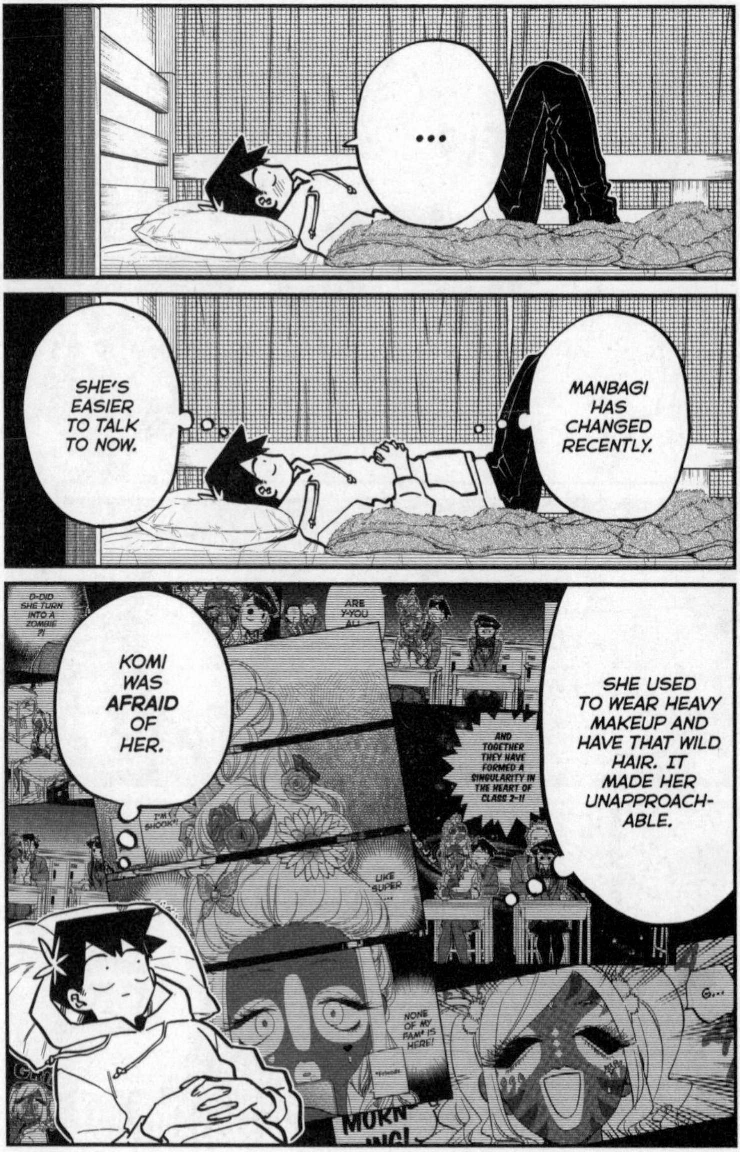
...
MANBAGI HAS CHANGED RECENTLY.
SHE'S EASIER TO TALK TO NOW.
SHE USED TO WEAR HEAVY MAKEUP AND HAVE THAT WILD HAIR. IT MADE HER UNAPPROACHABLE.
G...
AND TOGETHER THEY HAVE FORMED A SINGULARITY IN THE HEART OF CLASS 2-1!
KOMI WAS AFRAID OF HER.
D-DID SHE TURN INTO A ZOMBIE ?!
LIKE SUPER ...
NONE OF MY FAM* IS HERE!

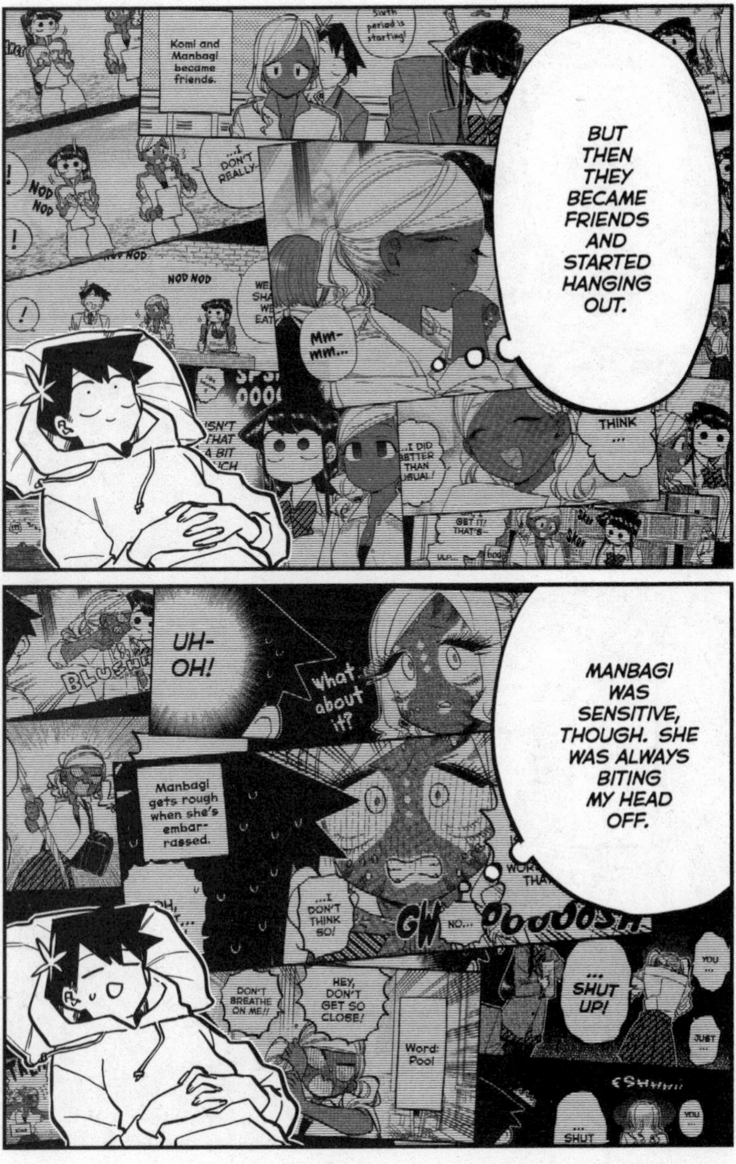
BUT THEN THEY BECAME FRIENDS AND STARTED HANGING OUT.
Sixth period is starting!
Komi and Manbagi became friends.
...I DON'T REALLY...
NOD NOD
NOD NOD
Mm-mm...
THINK ...
...I DID BETTER THAN USUAL!
GET IT! THAT'S-
MANBAGI WAS SENSITIVE, THOUGH. SHE WAS ALWAYS BITING MY HEAD OFF.
what about it?
UH-OH!
Manbagi gets rough when she's embar-rassed.
NO...
...I DON'T THINK SO!
YOU ...
... SHUT UP!
JUST ...
HEY, DON'T GET SO CLOSE!
DON'T BREATHE ON ME!!
Word: Pool
YOU ...
... SHUT

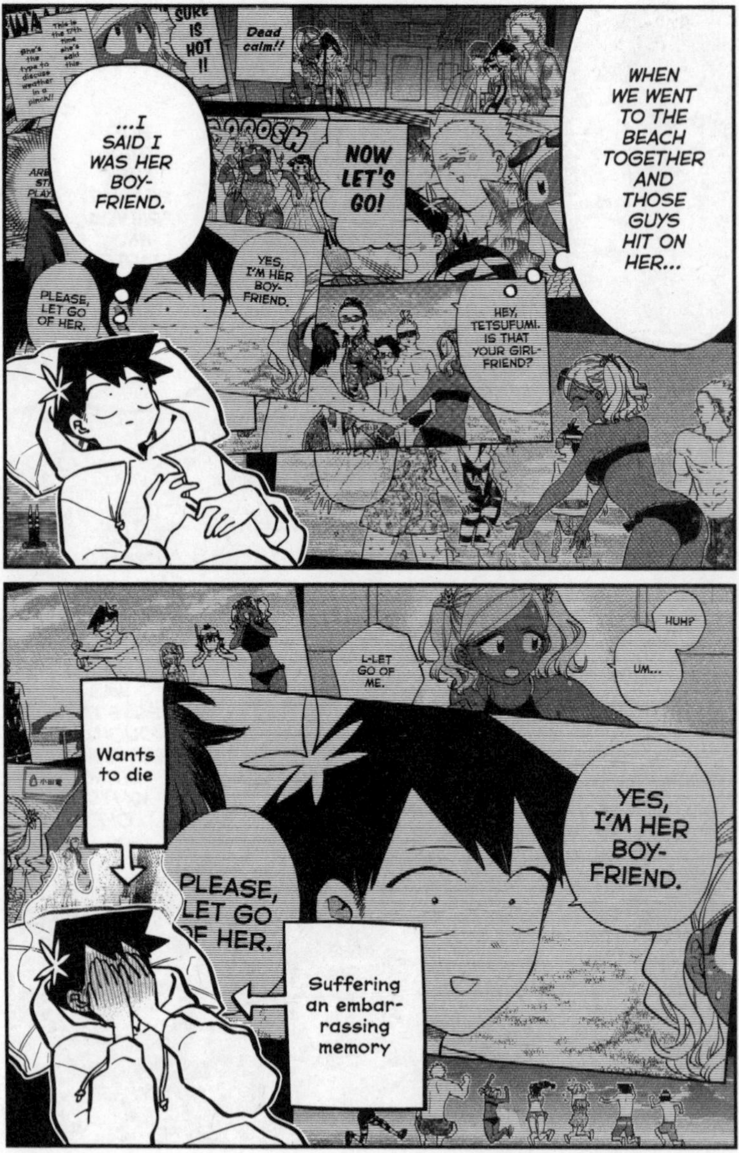
WHEN WE WENT TO THE BEACH TOGETHER AND THOSE GUYS HIT ON HER...
SURE IS HOT!!
Dead calm!!
HEY, TETSUFUMI. IS THAT YOUR GIRLFRIEND?
NOW LET'S GO!
YES, I'M HER BOYFRIEND.
...I SAID I WAS HER BOYFRIEND.
PLEASE, LET GO OF HER.
HUH?
UM...
L-LET GO OF ME.
YES, I'M HER BOYFRIEND.
PLEASE, LET GO OF HER.
Wants to die
Suffering an embarrassing memory

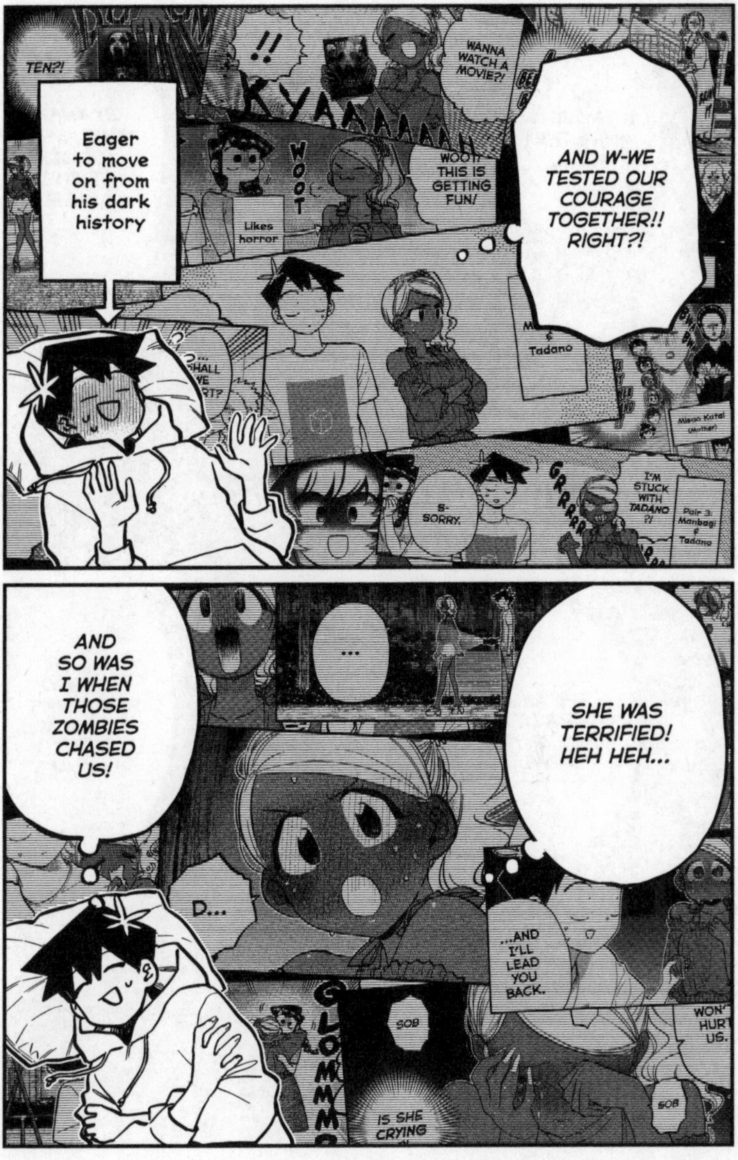
AND W-WE TESTED OUR COURAGE TOGETHER!! RIGHT?!
WANNA WATCH A MOVIE?!
!!
KYAAAAAAAH
TEN?!
WOOT! THIS IS GETTING FUN!
WOOT
Likes horror
Eager to move on from his dark history
Tadano
Misao Katai (Mother)
I'M STUCK WITH TADANO ?!
Pair 3: Manbagi & Tadano
S-SORRY.
SHE WAS TERRIFIED! HEH HEH...
...
AND SO WAS I WHEN THOSE ZOMBIES CHASED US!
...AND I'LL LEAD YOU BACK.
D...
SOB
SOB
IS SHE CRYING

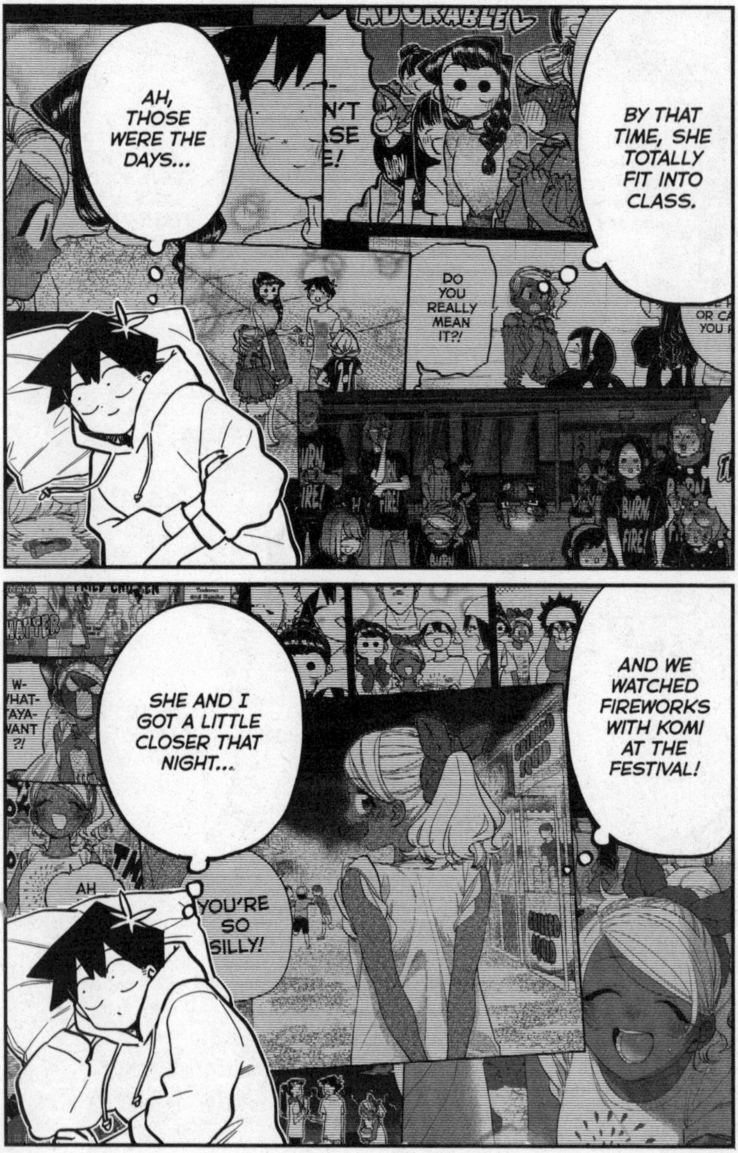
ADORABLE
BY THAT TIME, SHE TOTALLY FIT INTO CLASS.
AH, THOSE WERE THE DAYS...
DO YOU REALLY MEAN IT?!
AND WE WATCHED FIREWORKS WITH KOMI AT THE FESTIVAL!
SHE AND I GOT A LITTLE CLOSER THAT NIGHT...
YOU'RE SO SILLY!
AH
W-WHAT-TAYA-WANT?!

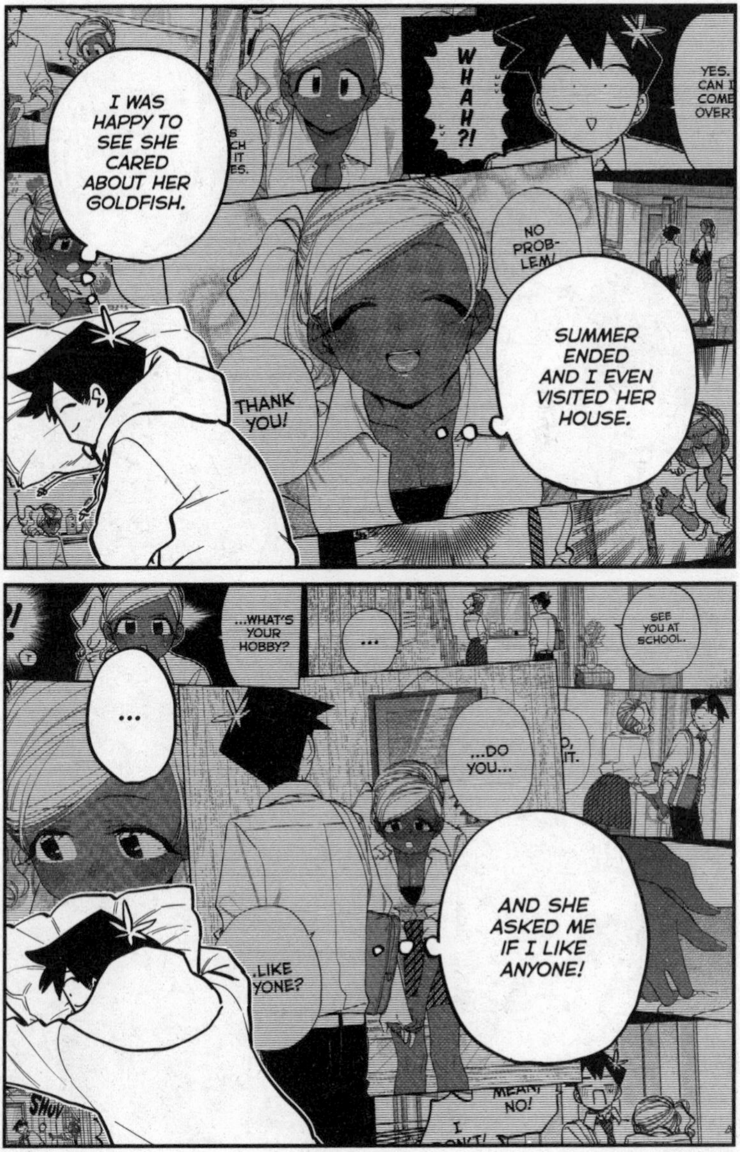
YES. CAN I COME OVER?
WHAH?!
NO PROBLEM!
SUMMER ENDED AND I EVEN VISITED HER HOUSE.
THANK YOU!
I WAS HAPPY TO SEE SHE CARED ABOUT HER GOLDFISH.
SEE YOU AT SCHOOL.
...
...WHAT'S YOUR HOBBY?
...DO YOU...
...
AND SHE ASKED ME IF I LIKE ANYONE!
NO!

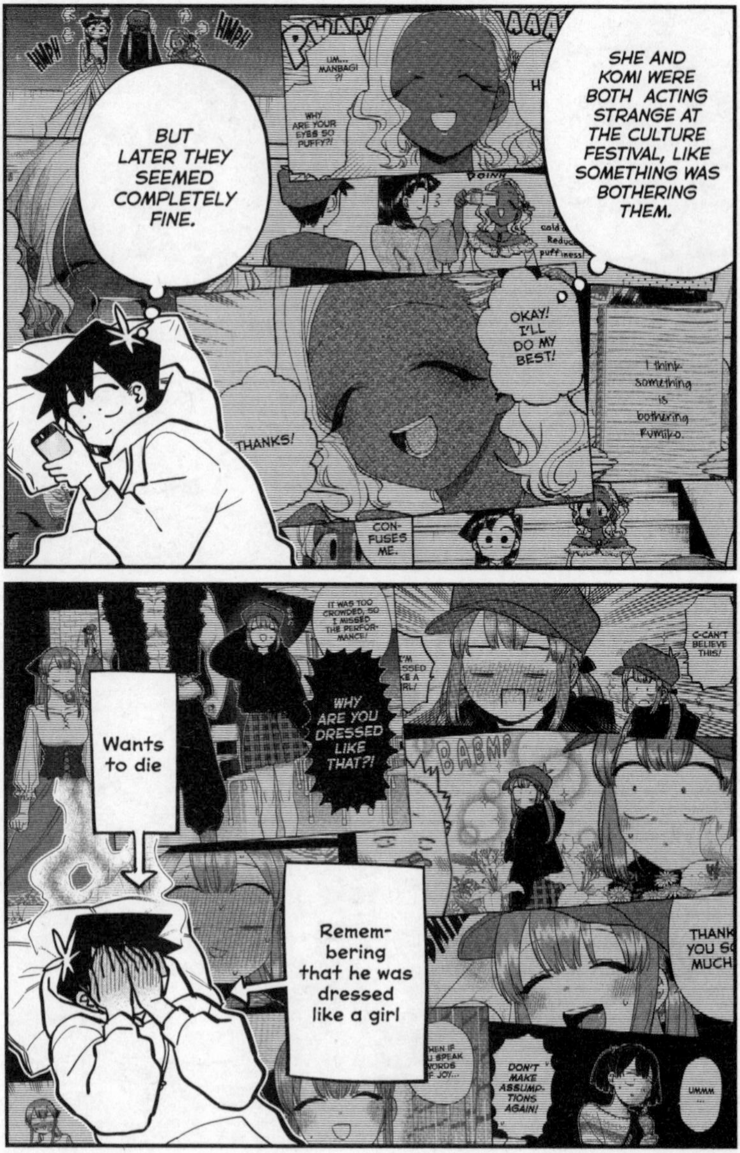
SHE AND KOMI WERE BOTH ACTING STRANGE AT THE CULTURE FESTIVAL, LIKE SOMETHING WAS BOTHERING THEM.
UM... MANBAGI ?!
WHY ARE YOUR EYES SO PUFFY?!
DOINK
BUT LATER THEY SEEMED COMPLETELY FINE.
I think something is bothering Rumiko.
OKAY! I'LL DO MY BEST!
THANKS!
CON-FUSES ME.
I C-CAN'T BELIEVE THIS!
IT WAS TOO CROWDED, SO I MISSED THE PERFOR-MANCE!
WHY ARE YOU DRESSED LIKE THAT?!
Wants to die
BABMP
UMMM ...
DON'T MAKE ASSUMP-TIONS AGAIN!
Remem-bering that he was dressed like a girl

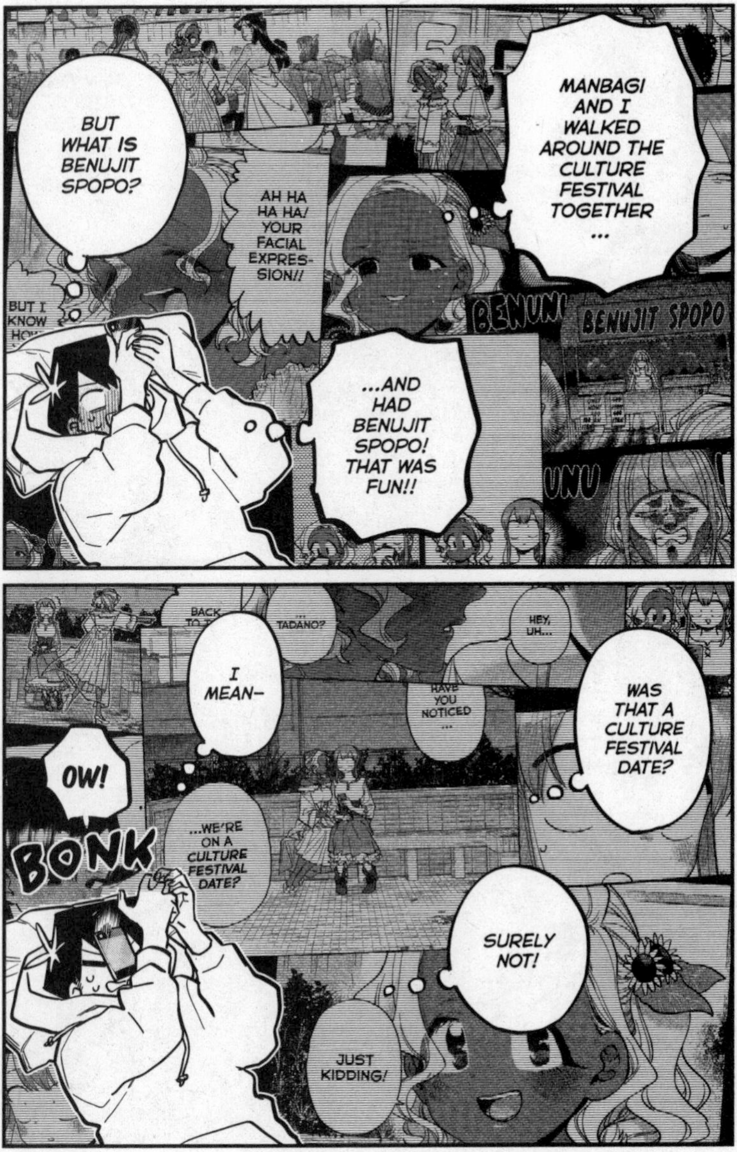
MANBAGI AND I WALKED AROUND THE CULTURE FESTIVAL TOGETHER ...
BENUJIT SPOPO
BENUNU
UNU
...AND HAD BENUJIT SPOPO! THAT WAS FUN!!
AH HA HA HA! YOUR FACIAL EXPRES-SION!!
BUT WHAT IS BENUJIT SPOPO?
BUT I KNOW
HEY, UH...
WAS THAT A CULTURE FESTIVAL DATE?
HAVE YOU NOTICED ...
...TADANO?
BACK TO
I MEAN—
...WE'RE ON A CULTURE FESTIVAL DATE?
SURELY NOT!
JUST KIDDING!
OW!
BONK

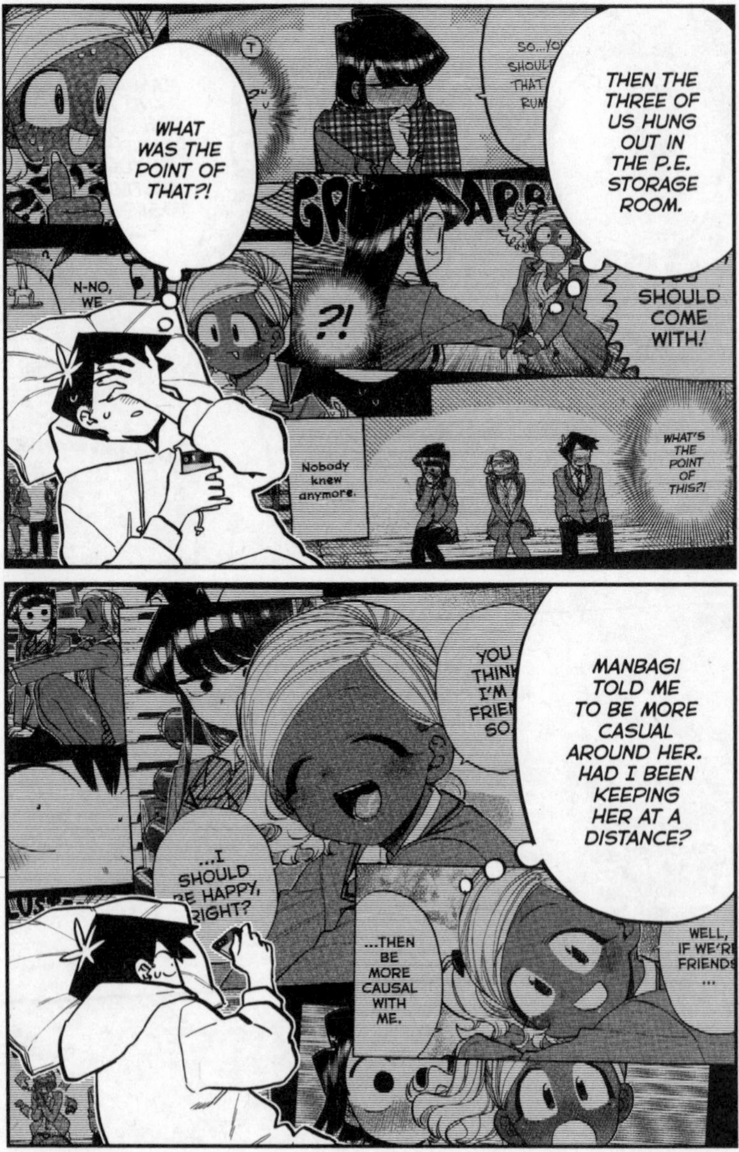
THEN THE THREE OF US HUNG OUT IN THE P.E. STORAGE ROOM.
SO...YOU
SHOULD COME WITH!
?!
WHAT'S THE POINT OF THIS?!
Nobody knew anymore.
WHAT WAS THE POINT OF THAT?!
N-NO, WE
MANBAGI TOLD ME TO BE MORE CASUAL AROUND HER. HAD I BEEN KEEPING HER AT A DISTANCE?
YOU
...THEN BE MORE CAUSAL WITH ME.
...I SHOULD BE HAPPY, RIGHT?

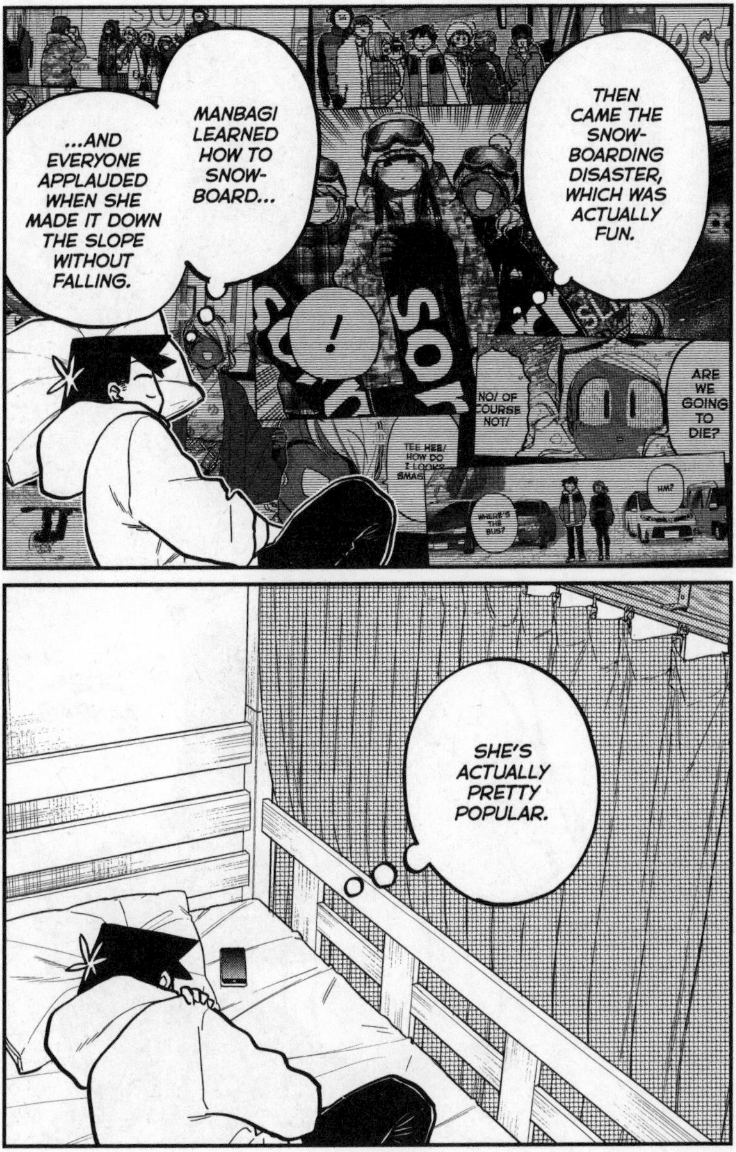
THEN CAME THE SNOW-BOARDING DISASTER, WHICH WAS ACTUALLY FUN.
MANBAGI LEARNED HOW TO SNOW-BOARD...
...AND EVERYONE APPLAUDED WHEN SHE MADE IT DOWN THE SLOPE WITHOUT FALLING.
!
ARE WE GOING TO DIE?
NO! OF COURSE NOT!
TEE HEE! HOW DO I LOOK?
HM?
WHERE'S THE BUS?
SHE'S ACTUALLY PRETTY POPULAR.

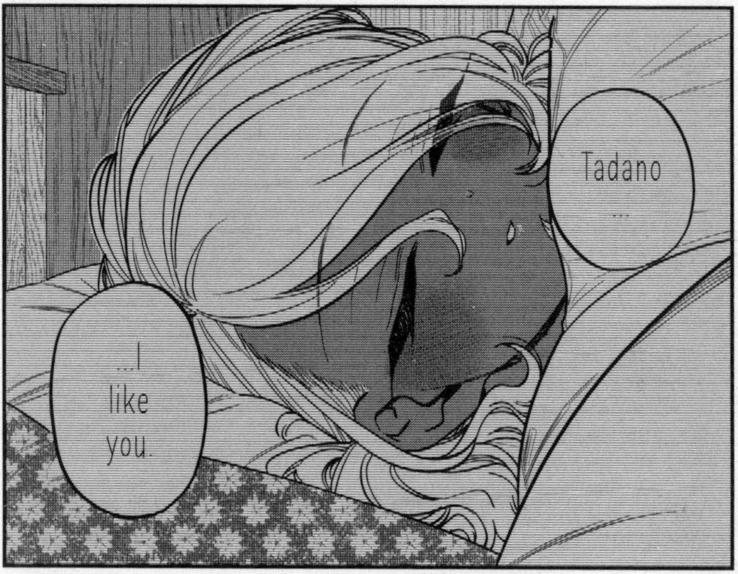
Tadano ...
...I like you.
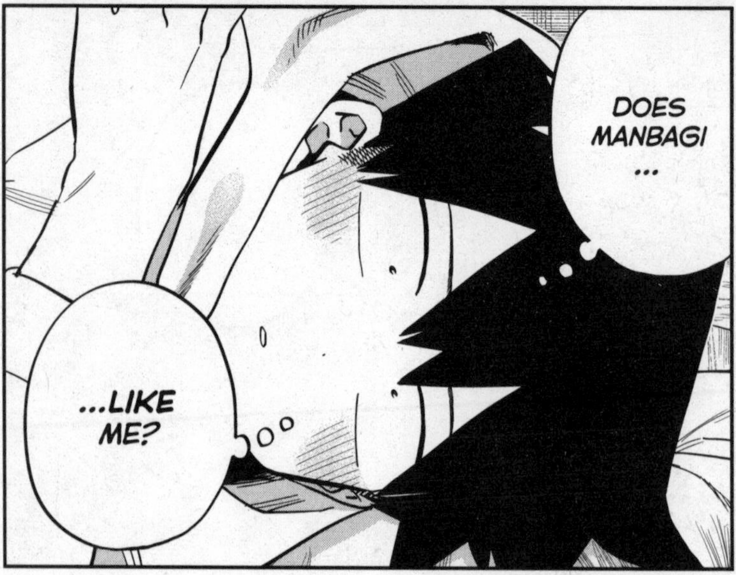
DOES MANBAGI ...
...LIKE ME?

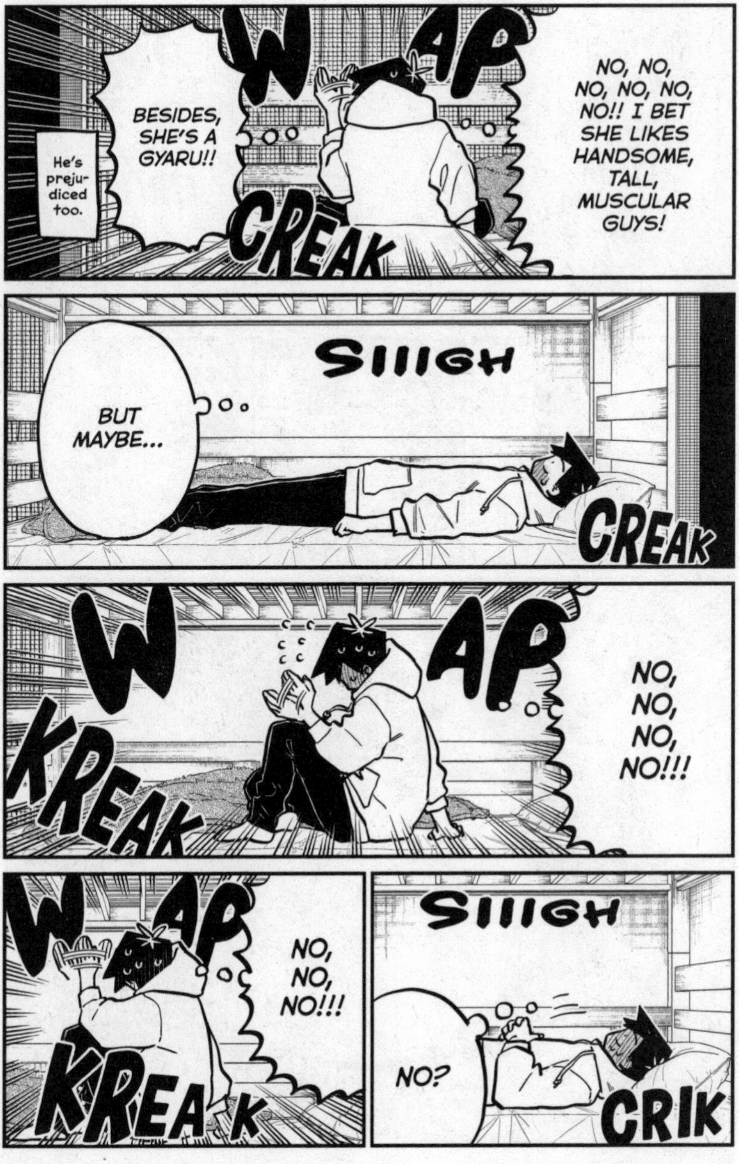
NO, NO, NO, NO, NO, NO!! I BET SHE LIKES HANDSOME, TALL, MUSCULAR GUYS!
WAP
BESIDES, SHE'S A GYARU!!
He's preju-diced too.
CREAK
SIIIGH
BUT MAYBE...
CREAK
NO, NO, NO, NO!!!
WAP
KREAK
SIIIGH
NO?
CRIK
NO, NO, NO!!!
WAP
KREAK

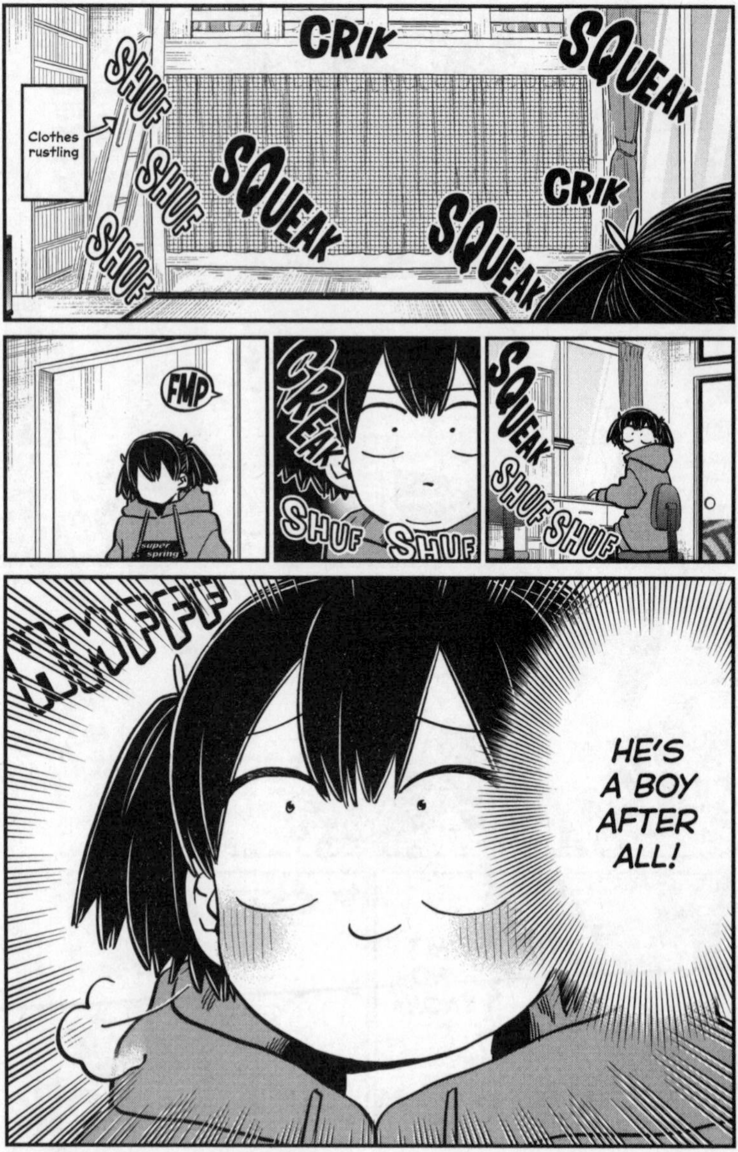
SQUEAK
CRIK
CRIK
SQUEAK
SQUEAK
SHUF
SHUF
SHUF
Clothes rustling
SQUEAK
SHUF SHUF
CREAK
SHUF
SHUF
FMP
HE'S A BOY AFTER ALL!

Communication 269 — The End

Komi Can't Communicate

Komi Can't Communicate Bonus

Apparently People Born in July Are Considerate

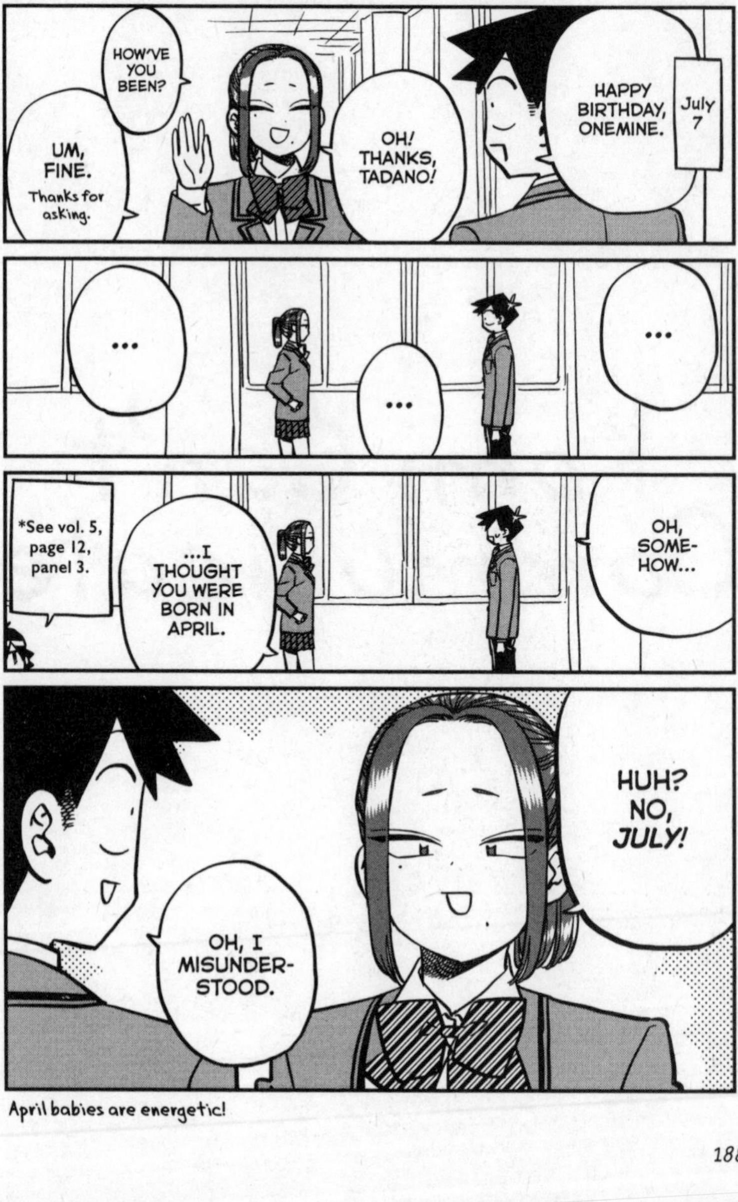
July 7
HAPPY BIRTHDAY, ONEMINE.
OH! THANKS, TADANO!
HOW'VE YOU BEEN?
UM, FINE.
Thanks for asking.
...
...
...
OH, SOME-HOW...
...I THOUGHT YOU WERE BORN IN APRIL.
*See vol. 5, page 12, panel 3.
HUH? NO, JULY!
OH, I MISUNDER-STOOD.

April babies are energetic!

Komi Can't Communicate Bonus

Birthday Return Gift

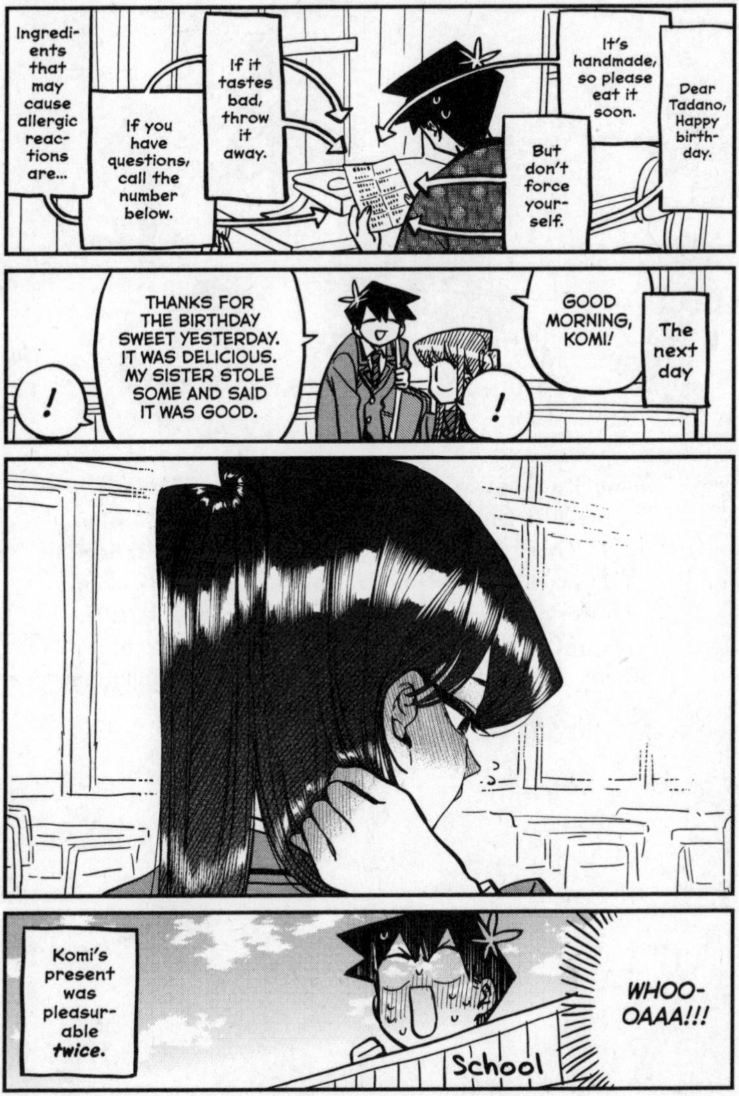
Dear Tadano, Happy birthday.
It's handmade, so please eat it soon.
But don't force yourself.
If it tastes bad, throw it away.
If you have questions, call the number below.
Ingredients that may cause allergic reactions are...
The next day
GOOD MORNING, KOMI!
!
THANKS FOR THE BIRTHDAY SWEET YESTERDAY. IT WAS DELICIOUS. MY SISTER STOLE SOME AND SAID IT WAS GOOD.
!
WHOO-OAAA!!!
School
Komi's present was pleasurable *twice*.

Tomohito Oda won the grand prize for *World Worst One* in the 70th Shogakukan New Comic Artist Awards in 2012. Oda's series *Digicon*, about a tough high school girl who finds herself in control of an alien with plans for world domination, ran from 2014 to 2015. In 2015, *Komi Can't Communicate* debuted as a one-shot in *Weekly Shonen Sunday* and was picked up as a full series by the same magazine in 2016.